Douglas T. Parrish

The Digital Enterprise

The Harvard Business Review Book Series

Designing and Managing Your Career, Edited by Harry Levinson

Ethics in Practice, Edited with an Introduction by Kenneth R. Andrews

Managing Projects and Programs, With a Preface by Norman R. Augustine

Manage People, Not Personnel, With a Preface by Victor H. Vroom

Strategy, Edited with an Introduction by Cynthia A. Montgomery and Michael E. Porter

Seeking Customers, Edited with an Introduction by Benson P. Shapiro and John J. Sviokla

Keeping Customers, Edited with an Introduction by John J. Sviokla and Benson P. Shapiro

The Learning Imperative, Edited with an Introduction by Robert Howard

The Articulate Executive, With a Preface by Fernando Bartolomé

Differences That Work, Edited with an Introduction by Mary C. Gentile

Reach for the Top, Edited with an Introduction by Nancy A. Nichols

Global Strategies, With a Preface by Percy Barnevik

Command Performance, With a Preface by John E. Martin

Manufacturing Renaissance, Edited with an Introduction by Gary P. Pisano and Robert H. Hayes

The Product Development Challenge, Edited with an Introduction by Kim B. Clark and Steven C. Wheelwright

The Evolving Global Economy, Edited with a Preface by Kenichi Ohmae

Managerial Excellence: McKinsey Award Winners from the *Harvard Business Review,* **1980–1994,** Foreword by Rajat Gupta, Preface by Nan Stone

Fast Forward, Edited with an Introduction and Epilogue by James Champy and Nitin Nohria

First Person, Edited with an Introduction by Thomas Teal

The Quest for Loyalty, Edited with an Introduction by Frederick F. Reichheld, Foreword by Scott D. Cook

Seeing Differently, Edited with an Introduction by John Seely Brown

Rosabeth Moss Kanter on the Frontiers of Management, by Rosabeth Moss Kanter

Ultimate Rewards, Edited with an Introduction by Stephen Kerr

Peter Drucker on the Profession of Management, by Peter F. Drucker

On Competition, by Michael E. Porter

The Work of Teams, Edited with an Introduction by Jon R. Katzenbach

Delivering Results, Edited with an Introduction by Dave Ulrich

John P. Kotter on What Leaders Really Do, by John P. Kotter

Creating Value in the Network Economy, Edited with an Introduction by Don Tapscott

Managing in the New Economy, Edited with an Introduction by Joan Magretta

World View: Global Strategies for the New Economy, Edited with an Introduction by Jeffrey E. Garten

Markets of One, Edited with an Introduction by James H. Gilmore and B. Joseph Pine II

The Digital Enterprise, Edited with an Introduction by Nicholas G. Carr

The Digital Enterprise

How to Reshape Your Business
for a Connected World

Edited with an Introduction by
Nicholas G. Carr

A Harvard Business Review Book

The *Harvard Business Review* articles in this collection are available as
individual reprints. Discounts apply to quantity purchases. For information
and ordering contact Customer Service, Harvard Business School Publishing,
Boston, MA 02163. Telephone: (617) 783-7500 or (800) 988-0886, 8 A.M.
to 6 P.M. Eastern Time, Monday through Friday. Fax: (617) 783-7555, 24
hours a day.

Library of Congress Cataloging-in-Publication Data
The digital enterprise : how to reshape your business for a connected
world / edited with an introduction by Nicholas G. Carr.
        p. cm. — (Harvard business review book)
    Includes index.
    ISBN 1-57851-558-0 (alk. paper)
    1. Management—Data processing. 2. Electronic commerce—
Management. 3. Information technology—Management. 4. Management
information systems. 5. Business enterprises—Communication systems—
Management. 6. Internet. I. Carr, Nicholas G., 1959– II. Harvard business
review book series
HD30.2 .D53 2001
658'.054678--dc21   00-069710

The paper used in this publication meets the requirements of the American
National Standard for Permanence of Paper for Publications and Documents
in Libraries and Archives Z39.48-1992.

Contents

Introduction: The New Business Code   vii
Nicholas G. Carr

Part I   Remodeling Business

1 Unbundling the Corporation   3
John Hagel III and Marc Singer

**2 Syndication: The Emerging Model for
  Business in the Internet Era**   21
Kevin Werbach

3 Where Value Lives in a Networked World   35
Mohanbir Sawhney and Deval Parikh

**4 Starting Up in High Gear: An Interview
  with Venture Capitalist Vinod Khosla**   51
David Champion and Nicholas G. Carr

**5 Transforming Life, Transforming Business:
  The Life-Science Revolution**   65
Juan Enriquez and Ray A. Goldberg

Part II   Remaking Markets

6 Getting Real About Virtual Commerce   83
Philip Evans and Thomas S. Wurster

7 **The Future of Commerce**   101
Adrian J. Slywotzky; Clayton M. Christensen and
Richard S. Tedlow; and Nicholas G. Carr

8 **Contextual Marketing: The Real Business
of the Internet**   119
David Kenny and John F. Marshall

9 **Beyond the Exchange: The Future of B2B**   131
Richard Wise and David Morrison

Part III   Reimagining Management

10 **Bringing Silicon Valley Inside**   151
Gary Hamel

11 **Meeting the Challenge of Disruptive Change**   175
Clayton M. Christensen and Michael Overdorf

12 **How We Went Digital Without a Strategy**   193
Ricardo Semler

13 **Managing for the Next Big Thing: An
Interview with EMC's Michael Ruettgers**   203
Paul Hemp

Executive Summaries   221

About the Contributors   231

Index   239

Introduction:
The New Business Code

Nicholas G. Carr

In late February 2000, just as the dot-com bubble was reaching the extreme of its tumescence, I flew across the country, from frigid Boston to balmy Silicon Valley, to interview the venture capitalist Vinod Khosla. Khosla, a cofounder of Sun Microsystems and a general partner with Kleiner Perkins Caufield & Byers, has thought as deeply as anyone about information technology's impact on business. On the afternoon we met in his firm's offices in Menlo Park, he was at once ebullient and wary. When asked his reaction to the flood of venture capital that was then pouring into Internet start-ups, he gave a mixed reply. On the one hand, he said, the easy money was encouraging a flurry of experimentation, allowing smart young entrepreneurs to test even their wildest ideas and thus speeding the adoption and refinement of the most powerful communication network the world has ever seen. On the other hand, investors' expectations had become irrational. Eager to make a killing, they were throwing cash at kids with untested technologies and half-baked business plans. Inevitably, said Khosla, there would be a counterreaction. He predicted that many of the high-flying start-ups would fall to earth, and a great deal of money would be lost. In response, fear would replace greed in investors' hearts, the deep pools of venture capital would dry up, and innovation would be hobbled.

As the year unfolded, Khosla's gloomy prognosis played out. One dot-com after another went bankrupt, the IPO market fell quiet, and venture capitalists tightened their purse strings. The business press, which had until then been the Internet economy's biggest booster, became its undertaker, publishing endless stories about failed start-ups and unemployed twenty-something ex-millionaires. By year's end, with the NASDAQ still vainly seeking a bottom, it was clear that the party was over and the hangover had begun.

No matter how painful, the market correction is a healthy event, for it serves not only to adjust investors' expectations but also to refocus the thinking of executives, entrepreneurs, and other members of the business community. The fads that have defined the Internet in the popular mind, from e-tailing to portals to business-to-business exchanges, are largely sideshows. The real impact of the Internet is taking place beneath the surface of commerce, where the basic economic forces that determine the behavior of companies and customers are shaped. An entirely new infrastructure for business is being put into place, and an entirely new kind of business—the digital enterprise—is coming into being. This book, which brings together many of the best writings about the Internet from the pages of the *Harvard Business Review*, illuminates the workings of the digital enterprise. It reveals that, whatever the vagaries of the stock market, new technologies are altering the economic trade-offs that determine the shape of business and rewriting the rules of competition.

Strategy Is Dead

As an editor, I'm paid to pay attention to words, and in the business world, that means paying attention to jargon as well. I've always been fascinated by the way jargon shapes, and at times distorts, the way we think about business. Perhaps the most striking change in the corporate lexicon over the past few years has been the supplanting of "business strategy" by "business model" as the term used to describe the way companies define and distinguish themselves. Today, everyone has something to say about business models, but not much is heard about strategy.

It's tempting to dismiss the change from "strategy" to "model" as mere semantics—the latest round in the eternal game of musical buzzwords played by consultants, academics, gurus, and journalists. But while it's true that "business model" is a uniquely squishy phrase, adaptable to almost any meaning, its adoption marks a fundamental change in business thinking. It underscores, in particular, the uncertain role of long-term planning in today's economy.

One could argue that the meaning of "strategy," as it applies to business today, was established in March 1979, when the *Harvard Business Review* published Michael Porter's seminal article "How Competitive Forces Shape Strategy." Porter argued that profitability in any industry is determined by five forces: the competition among existing players, the threat of new entrants, the power of suppliers, the power of customers, and the availability of substitute products. By rigorously analyzing these forces, the astute manager could determine the optimal positioning for his or her company, identifying and seizing control of the most lucrative combination of links in the value chain. In the Porterian universe, industries have fairly clear boundaries and fairly stable structures, and the success of a company is determined less by the quality of its products or the innovativeness of its people than by the logic of its strategy.

It's no coincidence that the ascendancy of such a highly codified form of business thinking came at the end of the Industrial Age. By the late 1970s, the industrial economy had been chugging along for almost a century, and, for the most part, its structure *was* fixed and competition *was* predictable. The professional manager had long since taken over from the entrepreneur.

The cult of strategy reached its logical, and absurd, conclusion in the 1980s, when managers spent all of their time "restructuring" their companies. Customers, products, and employees became unimportant. All that mattered was manipulating assets to earn higher financial returns. Strategy had become an end in itself.

Whenever a system becomes a parody of itself, it's a good bet that it's about to be replaced by a new one. That's exactly what has happened over the last ten or so years. The industrial era has given way to the information era. Structure and predictability have been replaced by formlessness and uncertainty.

In the early stages of any economic system, the rewards go to those who create the new, not those who conserve the old. Entrepreneurship, to paraphrase Gary Hamel, becomes more important than stewardship. Since the ultimate form of the new system remains unknowable, strategic planning, in its Porterian sense, has limited use. A new way of thinking about business is required.

That brings us back to the linguistic shift from business strategy to business model. But what exactly is a business model? Tom Malone, a business professor at the Massachusetts Institute of Technology who is developing an on-line catalog of business models, once offered me a simple definition: a business model is "what a company does and how it makes money doing it." I think that definition is as good as any, but I would boil it down even further. Whereas a business strategy is a theory—a line of reasoning that ends in a logical conclusion—a business model is a hypothesis. It's a tentative stab at the truth.

If we can build a smart, fast network at the edge of the Internet, companies will pay us to expedite the distribution of their on-line content and functions—that's Akamai's business model. If we can provide a forum where consumers share product reviews, we will become a tollgate for on-line commerce—that's Epinions's model. When business thinkers and practitioners use the term "business model," they are telling us that, in these early days of the digital economy, we aren't yet at the stage where we can prove theories. The best we can do is to test hypotheses.

Long Live Strategy

Ultimately, though, hypotheses are proven either true or false, and as we learn the outcomes of the myriad business experiments currently being conducted, our understanding of the fundamentals of the digital enterprise becomes clearer. We become better able to answer the core question—the *strategic* question—that has always and will always face business decision makers: Where will the profits reside in the economy, and who will capture them?

To understand the distribution of profits in any economy, you need to look at its underpinnings—the technological infrastructure that determines the way goods move, information is shared, and transactions are carried out. Once you get down to this fundamental level, you immediately see that the Internet economy is different from its industrial predecessor and that the distribution of profits will likely be different as well.

The core elements of the industrial infrastructure—physical things like highways, railroads, turbines, and telephone lines—were visible, easy to understand, and, most important, stable. Once put in place, they didn't change much. Because the infrastructure was hard to manipulate, the organizations that controlled it—such as transporters, telephone companies, and government agencies—came to have relatively little economic power. Caretakers of a fixed system, they had to content themselves with collecting only modest tolls. The real wealth and growth went to the users of the infrastructure—manufacturers, retailers, and financiers. They were the ones who had room to innovate.

The Internet infrastructure, in contrast, is constructed not of physical things but of information, in the form of digital code. Code is largely invisible, exceedingly difficult to understand, and highly unstable. Any software engineer has the potential to modify the code of the Internet and thus alter, in a small or a profound way, the entire infrastructure of business.

The malleability of digital infrastructure changes the rules of the game. It opens up opportunities for companies that neither create nor sell goods but simply manipulate the infrastructure to their own benefit. These intermediaries—the access providers, the search engines, the content cachers, the affiliate aggregators, the electronic market makers, and so on—become the innovators and the value creators. The users of the infrastructure, on the other hand, are often forced into a reactive posture, constantly adapting their business models to the changes in infrastructure. Economic power shifts from manufacturers and retailers to intermediaries, as we enter an age of what I've come to call "hypermediation."

Whether you're a modeler or a strategist, your success in business in the coming years will hinge on your ability to understand and anticipate the way digital code changes the business infrastructure and, in turn, the distribution of profits. Each of the pieces collected in this book explores the form and economics of the new digital infrastructure and considers its influence over the day-to-day decisions executives and entrepreneurs need to make. I have divided the writings into three sections. Part I, "Remodeling Business," provides new conceptual frameworks for thinking about the way business is conducted at the most fundamental level—how the value chain is constructed, how individual companies determine their positioning and scope, and how interactions between companies are carried out. Part II, "Remaking Markets," examines the many ways that the Internet is altering the buying process, both in consumer and in business-to-business markets. Finally, Part III, "Reimagining Management," looks at the operational implications of the Internet and offers practical advice on how to organize and motivate people.

Remodeling Business

The Internet and related information technologies are changing the very way we think about business, as this section makes clear. We begin with "Unbundling the Corporation," which won the McKinsey prize as the best article published in the *Harvard Business Review* in 1999. The authors, John Hagel and Marc Singer, explore how digitization is exposing fault lines that have long lay hidden beneath the surface of business organizations. No matter how monolithic companies may seem, the authors argue, most are really engaged in three kinds of businesses: one attracts and serves customers, another develops products, and the third manages operations. Although organizationally intertwined, these businesses have conflicting characteristics. It takes a big investment to find and develop a relationship with a customer, so profitability hinges on achieving economies of scope—gaining a large "share of wallet." But speed, not scope, drives the economics of product innovation. And the high fixed costs of capital-intensive infrastructure businesses require economies of scale. Scale, scope, and speed can't be optimized simultaneously, so trade-offs have to be made when the three types of businesses are bundled into one corporation.

Historically, these businesses have been bundled together because the transaction costs incurred in separating them (the "friction" inherent in business) were too high. But we are in the midst of a worldwide reduction in transaction costs, as electronic networks drive down the costs of communicating and of exchanging data. Activities that companies have always believed were central to their businesses are increasingly being offered by new, specialized competitors that don't have to make trade-offs. Ultimately, Hagel and Singer predict, traditional businesses will have no choice but to unbundle and then rebundle into large infrastructure and customer-relationship businesses and small, nimble product-innovation companies. Executives in many industries will be forced to ask the most basic question about their companies: What business are we really in? The answer will determine their fate in an increasingly frictionless economy.

In "Syndication: The Emerging Model for Business in the Internet Era," Kevin Werbach further explores the changing nature of business economics and its effect on how companies organize and operate. He argues that digitization, by permitting products, commerce, and corporations to be broken down into freely tradable modules, will force businesses into syndication networks. Syndication has long been a fundamental organizing principle in the entertainment world, but it's rare elsewhere in business. The fixed physical assets and slow-moving information that characterized the industrial economy made it difficult, if not impossible, to create the kind of fluid networks that are essential for syndication. Werbach writes that with the rise of the information economy, flexible business networks are not only becoming possible—they're becoming essential. As a result, syndication is moving from the periphery of business to its center.

Within a syndication network there are three roles that businesses can play. Originators create original content, encompassing everything from entertainment programming to products to business processes. Syndicators package that content, often integrating it with content from other originators. Distributors deliver the content to consumers. A company can play a single role, or two or three roles simultaneously. Syndication requires businesses to rethink their strategies and relationships in radical ways. Because a company's success hinges on its connections to other companies, it can no longer view its core capabilities as secrets to protect. Instead, it needs to see them as products to sell. FedEx, for example, is succeeding by distributing its sophisticated package-tracking capability to other companies operating on the Internet. As this new way of doing business takes hold, companies may look the same as they did before to their customers, but behind the scenes they will be in constant flux, melding with one another in ever-changing, self-organizing networks.

It used to be that companies shaped technology to fit their needs. Now, however, that relationship is being reversed: technology is shaping business. That phenomenon provides the backdrop to "Where Value Lives in a Networked World," by Mohanbir Sawhney and Deval Parikh. The authors assert that the seemingly endless upheavals of the digital age are actually more predictable than is commonly assumed. At the root of many of the changes lie two patterns in the migration of network intelligence. First, intelligence is "de-coupling"—that is, high-speed, digital communications technologies are pushing back-end processing intelligence and front-end customer-interface intelligence to opposite ends of the network. The processing intelligence is consolidating, on massive shared servers, for example, while the customer-interface intelligence is fragmenting among innumerable specialized devices. Second, network intelligence is becoming more fluid and modular. Small units of intelligence now float freely like molecules in the ether, coalescing into temporary bundles whenever and wherever necessary to create value. As Sawhney and Parikh show, these patterns aren't only determining the way the Internet works, they're influencing the structure of entire industries and individual companies. Today, they argue, the network *is* the economy.

The interview that my colleague David Champion and I conducted with Vinod Khosla comes next. Khosla provides the view of the entrepreneur, of the business creator. Understanding that particular view is essential to understanding the forces that are reshaping business. After all, it is the entrepreneur who is largely responsible for creating business's new, digital infrastructure. As Khosla explains, the explosion in business innovation is overturning many long-standing tenets of business. Because large companies are often at a disadvantage when it comes to moving quickly, they are seeing their economies of scale turn into diseconomies of scale. Similarly, highly formalized, highly efficient operating processes, long a fundamental advantage held by established companies, undermine an organization's ability to change at the pace required by today's markets. "Yesterday," says Khosla, "you optimized your business for cost and performance. Today, you have to optimize for flexibility and adaptability."

This section ends with a look ahead to a new technological revolution: the rise of life sciences. Not all information technologies are manmade; the greatest of them all—the genetic code—is a creation of nature, and it may end up having an impact on business that dwarfs even that of the Internet. In "Transforming Life, Transforming Business: The Life-Science Revolution," Juan Enriquez and Ray Goldberg explain how advances in genetics will not only have dramatic implications for people and society, they will also reshape vast sectors of the world economy. The boundaries between many once-distinct businesses, from agribusiness and chemicals to pharmaceuticals and health care to energy and computing, will blur and out of that convergence will emerge what promises to be the largest industry in the world: life science. As scientific advances continue to accelerate, more and more businesses will be drawn, by choice or by necessity, into the life-science industry.

Companies have realized that unlocking life's code opens up virtually unlimited commercial possibilities, but as the authors show, operating within this new industry presents a raft of wrenchingly difficult challenges as well. Companies must rethink their business, financial, and M&A strategies. They must make vast R&D investments with distant and uncertain payoffs. They must enter into complex partnerships and affiliations, sometimes with direct competitors. And perhaps most difficult, they must contend with a public that is uncomfortable with even the thought of genetic engineering. The optimal structure of the life-science industry—and of the companies that compose it—is as yet unknown. But the actions that executives take now will go a long way toward determining the ultimate role their companies play in the world's most important industry.

Remaking Markets

Part II of this book looks at the different ways the Internet is changing the marketplace, in both the consumer and business-to-business sectors. In "Getting Real About Virtual Commerce," Philip Evans and Thomas Wurster examine the key forces that are influencing the evolution of electronic markets. They argue that the first generation of e-commerce was simply a land-grab. Space on the Internet was claimed by whoever got there first with enough resources to create a credible business. It took speed, a willingness to experiment, and a lot of cyber-savvy. Companies that had performed brilliantly in traditional settings seemed hopelessly flat-footed, while the pure-play dot-coms, for all their agility, seemed clueless about how to turn a profit.

Now, Evans and Wurster contend, we are entering the second generation of e-commerce, and it will be shaped more by strategy than by experimentation. The key players—branded-goods suppliers, physical retailers, e-tailers, and pure navigators—will shift their attention from claiming territory to defending or capturing it. They will be forced to focus on strategy to achieve competitive advantage. Success will go to the businesses that get closest to consumers, the ones that help customers navigate the Web. Indeed, the authors argue, navigation is the battlefield on which competitive advantage will be won or lost. There are three dimensions of navigation: reach is about access and connection; affiliation is about whose interests the business represents; and richness is the depth of the information that a business gives to or collects about its customers. Pure navigators and e-tailers have the natural advantage in reach and affiliation, while branded-goods suppliers and physical retailers have the edge in richness. The authors offer practical advice to each player on competing in this latest generation of e-commerce.

"The Future of Commerce" offers three perspectives on the way markets will work in the coming years. Adrian Slywotzky argues that the Internet will overturn the inefficient push-model of supplier-customer interaction. He predicts that suppliers will no longer be able to force customers to choose from a limited set of preselected offerings. In all sorts of markets, customers will use choiceboards—interactive, on-line systems that let people design their own products by choosing from a menu of attributes, prices, and delivery options. He explores how the shifting role of the customer—from passive recipient to active designer—will change the way companies compete. Clayton Christensen and Richard Tedlow agree that e-commerce, on a broad level, will change the basis of competitive advantage in retailing. While the essential mission of retailing—getting the right product in the right place at the right price at the right time—is a constant, retailers have over the years fulfilled that mission in different ways, thanks to a series of disruptive technologies. The authors identify patterns in the way that previous retailing transformations have unfolded to shed light on how retailing may evolve in the Internet era. The third perspective is my own. I take issue with the widespread notion that the Internet will usher in an era of "disintermediation," in which producers of goods and services bypass wholesalers and retailers to connect directly with their customers. Instead, I argue that business is undergoing precisely the opposite phenomenon—hypermediation. Transactions over the Web routinely involve all sorts of intermediaries. It is these middlemen that are positioned to capture much of the profit.

While most of the attention given to the Internet has focused on the World Wide Web, the Web is not the only game in town. In fact, as David Kenny and John Marshall make clear in "Contextual Marketing: The Real Business of the Internet," the Web may not be the most important facet of the Internet. The painful truth, the authors write, is that the dominant model for Internet commerce thus far, the destination Web site, doesn't really suit the needs of businesses or their customers. Most consumer product companies don't provide enough value to induce customers to make the repeat visits—and disclose the detailed information—that make such sites profitable. Instead of trying to create destinations that people will come to, companies need to use the power and reach of the Internet to deliver tailored messages and information to customers. Companies have to become what the authors call "contextual marketers." Delivering the most relevant information possible to consumers in the most timely manner possible will become feasible, they say, as access to the Internet expands beyond the personal computer to shopping malls, retail stores, airports, bus stations, and even cars. The authors describe how the ubiquitous Internet will hasten the demise of the destination Web site—and open up attractive opportunities to reach customers through marketing "mobilemediaries": smart cards, e-wallets, bar code scanners, and so on.

Using the Internet to facilitate business-to-business, or B2B, commerce promises many benefits, such as dramatic cost reductions and greater access to buyers and sellers. Yet little is known about how B2B e-commerce will evolve. In "Beyond the Exchange: The Future of B2B," Richard Wise and David Morrison provide important clues. Drawing on the experience of the financial services industry, which has many of the same characteristics as the B2B industry, the authors argue that on-line exchanges will not be the primary source of value in B2B markets. Rather, value will tend to accumulate among a diverse group of specialists that focus on such tasks as packaging, standard setting, arbitrage, and information management. Originators will handle the origination and aggregation of complex transactions before sending them onto the exchanges for processing. E-speculators will jump in and out of high-volume markets, making profits by trading on the basis of sophisticated analyses of real-time market data. Independent "solution providers" will operate in niches, offering product sales as just one element in a suite of distinctive services. And sell-side asset exchanges will help groups of suppliers swap and resell orders among themselves. As for exchanges, they will get very big, but they are unlikely to ever be very profitable.

Reimagining Management

As markets change, so too must management. That's the subject of Part III of this book. In "Bringing Silicon Valley Inside," Gary Hamel sounds a call to arms, encouraging executives to emulate the entrepreneurs of Northern California. In Silicon Valley, he says, ideas, capital, and talent circulate freely, gathering into whatever combinations are most likely to generate innovation and wealth. Unlike most traditional companies—which spend their energy in resource allocation, a system designed to avoid failure—the Valley operates through resource attraction, a system that nurtures innovation. In a traditional company, people with innovative ideas must go hat in hand to the guardians of the old ideas for funding and staff. But in Silicon Valley, a slew of venture capitalists vie to attract the best new ideas, infusing relatively small amounts of capital into a portfolio of ventures. And talent is free to go to the companies offering the most exhilarating work and the greatest potential rewards. By setting up similar markets for capital, ideas, and talent inside their own walls, big companies can accelerate their own innovation and value creation.

In "Meeting the Challenge of Disruptive Change," Clayton Christensen and Michael Overdorf present a darker view of companies' ability to innovate. They argue that the reason large companies fail to capitalize on the opportunities brought about by major, disruptive changes in their markets lies in the very capabilities that define those companies. As any company grows, what it can and cannot do becomes more sharply defined in certain predictable ways. When the company is young, its resources—its people, equipment, technologies, cash, brands, suppliers, and the like—define what it can and cannot do. As the company matures, its abilities stem more from its processes—for example, product development, manufacturing, and budgeting. In the largest companies, values—particularly those that determine what are the companies' acceptable gross margins and how big an opportunity has to be before it is worth pursuing—define what the company can and cannot do. Because resources are more adaptable to change than processes or values, smaller companies tend to respond to major market shifts better than larger companies. The lesson that Christensen and Overdorf teach is a fatalistic one: more frequently than not, large companies cannot successfully transform themselves; they are what they are.

Ricardo Semler, in "How We Went Digital Without a Strategy," provides a more optimistic view of organizational change. Semler, the majority owner of Semco in São Paulo, Brazil, believes that real change cannot be dictated from above; it only happens when individual employees are given complete freedom to pursue their own interests. While many executives pay lip service to empowerment, Semler literally gives his employees complete control over what they do and how they do it. The company has no set work hours, no assigned offices, no policy manuals, no compensation standards; it doesn't even have an HR department. Semco's experience shows that such a radical approach can pay off in the digital economy. Until recently, the company earned the vast majority of its revenues from manufacturing.

But over the last few years it has moved successfully into services and from there into Web markets and other Internet initiatives. The company's ability to transform itself derives wholly from the freedom—and the funding—it gives its people.

We end with "Managing for the Next Big Thing," Paul Hemp's interview with Michael Ruettgers, the CEO of data-storage giant EMC, one of the most successful companies of the past ten years. Ruettgers speaks in detail about the managerial practices that have allowed EMC to anticipate and exploit technological advances and market opportunities ahead of its competitors. Emphasizing timing and speed has been critical to EMC's success. Rather than develop and introduce new products sequentially, the company simultaneously pursues multiple generations of new storage technologies, and it avoids excessive product refinements that can slow time to market. Through quarterly goal-setting and monthly forecasting meetings, the company imbues a sense of urgency in every one of its employees. Perhaps most important, it has many formal programs to bring the insights and opinions of customers into its own operations. EMC engineers, for example, frequently meet with customers in intensive working sessions to refine ideas to better meet market needs, and the company monitors customers' use of its products in real time. In many ways, EMC presents a model, or at least a prototype, of the digital enterprise—a company adapted to the new business infrastructure and new competitive pace of the digital age. EMC's story provides a positive note on which to close this book, for it reveals not only the challenges that lie ahead for all companies, but also the enormous rewards available to those companies that meet the challenges successfully.

PART

I

Remodeling Business

1
Unbundling the Corporation

John Hagel III and Marc Singer

In the late 1970s, the computer industry was dominated by huge, vertically integrated companies like IBM, Burroughs, and Digital Equipment. With their vast scale advantages and huge installed bases, they seemed unassailable. Yet just ten years later, the power in the industry had shifted. The behemoths were struggling to survive while an army of smaller, highly specialized companies was thriving. What happened? The industry's sea change can be traced back to 1978, when a then-tiny company, Apple Computer, launched the Apple II personal computer. The Apple II's open architecture unlocked the computer business, allowing the entry of many new companies that specialized in producing specific hardware and software components. Immediately, the advantages of the generalist—size, reputation, integration—began to wither. The new advantages—creativity, speed, flexibility—belonged to the specialist.

The story of the computer industry illustrates the crucial role that interaction costs play in shaping industries and companies. *Interaction costs* represent the money and time that are expended whenever people and companies exchange goods, services, or ideas.[1] The exchanges can occur within companies, among companies, or between companies and customers, and they can take many everyday forms, including management meetings, conferences, phone conversations, sales calls, reports, and memos. In a very real sense, interaction costs are the friction in the economy.

Taken together, interaction costs determine the way companies organize themselves and the way they form relationships with other parties. When the interaction costs of performing an activity internally are lower than the costs of performing it externally, a company will tend to incorporate that activity into its own organization rather than contract with an outside party to perform it. All else being equal, a company will organize in whatever way minimizes overall interaction costs.

The arrival of Apple's open architecture dramatically reduced interaction costs in the computer industry. By conforming to a set of well-documented standards, companies could, for the first time, easily work together to produce complementary products and services. As a result, tightly coordinated webs of specialized companies—with names like Apple, Intel, Microsoft, Sun, Adobe, and Novell—could form and ultimately compete effectively against the entrenched, vertically integrated giants. Many of the new companies grew very large very quickly, but they never lost their focus on carrying out specialized activities.

The moral of the story? Changes in interaction costs can cause entire industries to reorganize rapidly and dramatically. Today, that fact should give all managers pause, for we are on the verge of a broad, systemic reduction in interaction costs throughout the world economy. Electronic networks, combined with powerful personal computers, are enabling companies to communicate and exchange data far more quickly and cheaply than ever before. As more business interactions move onto electronic networks like the Internet, basic assumptions about corporate organization will be overturned. Activities that companies have always believed to be central to their business will suddenly be offered by new, specialized competitors that can do them better, faster, and more efficiently. Executives will be forced to ask the most basic and the most discomforting question about their companies: What business are we really in? Their answers will determine their fate in an increasingly frictionless economy.

One Company, Three Businesses

When you look beneath the surface of most companies, you find three kinds of businesses—a customer relationship business, a product innovation business, and an infrastructure business. Although organizationally intertwined, these businesses are actually very different. They each play a unique role; they each employ different types of people; and they each have different economic, competitive, and even cultural imperatives. (See Exhibit 1-1 "Rethinking the Traditional Organization.")

The role of a customer relationship business is to find customers and build relationships with them. If you're a bank or a retailer, for example, your marketing function focuses on drawing people into your branches or stores. Another set of employees—loan officers or store clerks, perhaps—assists the customers and tries to build personal relationships with them. Still other employees may be responsible for responding to questions and complaints, processing returns, or collecting customer information. Although these employees may belong to different organizational units, they have a common goal: to attract and hold on to customers.

The role of a product innovation business is to conceive of attractive new products and services and figure out how best to bring them to market. In a bank, for example, employees within various product units or in a centralized business-development function research new products like reverse mortgages and ensure that the bank is capable of bringing them to market successfully. In a retailer, buyers and merchandisers perform the product innovation role, constantly searching for interesting new products and effective ways to present them to shoppers.

The role of an infrastructure business is to build and manage facilities for high-volume, repetitive operational tasks such as logistics and storage, manufacturing, and communications. In a bank, the infrastructure business builds new branches, maintains data networks, and provides the back-office transactional services needed to process deposits and withdrawals and present statements to customers. In a retailer, the infrastructure business constructs new outlets, maintains existing outlets, and manages complex logistical networks to ensure that each store receives the right products at the lowest possible cost.

These three businesses—customer relationship management, product innovation, and infrastructure management—rarely map neatly to the organizational structure of a corporation. Product innovation, for example, typically extends beyond the boundaries of a product development unit to include such activities as conducting market research, qualifying component suppliers, training sales and support people, and designing marketing materials. Rather than representing discrete organizational units, the three businesses correspond to what are popularly called "core processes"—the cross-functional work flows that stretch from suppliers to customers and, in combination, define a company's identity.

Exhibit 1-1   Rethinking the Traditional Organization

As interaction costs fall, companies will come under pressure to unbundle their core processes, each of which has very different economic, cultural, and competitive imperatives.

	Product Innovation	Customer Relationship Management	Infrastructure Management
Economics			
	Early market entry allows for a premium price and large market share; speed is key	High cost of customer acquisition makes it imperative to gain large shares of wallet; economies of scope are key	High fixed costs make large volumes essential to achieving low unit costs; economies of scale are key
Culture			
	Employee centered; coddling the creative "stars"	Highly service oriented; "customer comes first"	Cost focused; stress on standardization, pre-dictability, efficiency
Competition			
	Battle for talent; low barriers to entry; many small players thrive	Battle for scope; rapid consolidation; a few big players dominate	Battle for scale; rapid consolidation; a few big players dominate

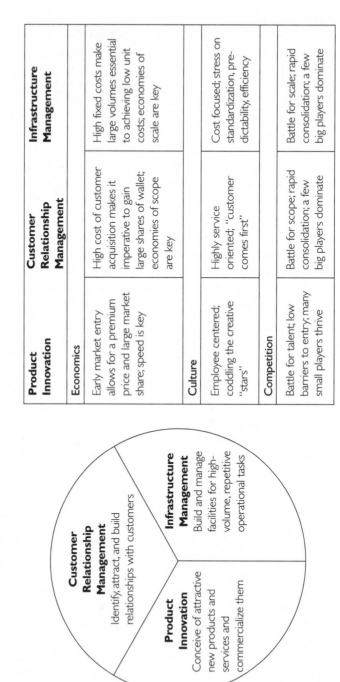

Customer Relationship Management
Identify, attract, and build relationships with customers

Infrastructure Management
Build and manage facilities for high-volume, repetitive operational tasks

Product Innovation
Conceive of attractive new products and services and commercialize them

Managers talk about their key activities as "processes" rather than as "businesses" because, with rare exceptions, they assume that the activities ought to coexist. Nearly a century of economic theory underpins the conventional wisdom that the management of customers, innovation, and infrastructure must be combined within a single company. If those activities were disbursed to separate companies, the thinking goes, the interaction costs required to coordinate them would be too great. It's cheaper to do them yourself.

Working from that assumption, large companies have in recent years expended a lot of energy and resources reengineering and redesigning their core processes. They've used the latest information technology to eliminate handoffs, cut waiting time, and reduce errors. For many companies, streamlining core processes has yielded impressive gains, saving substantial amounts of money and time, and providing customers with more valuable products and services.

But as managers have found, there are limits to such gains. Sooner or later, companies come up against a cold fact: the economics governing the three core processes conflict. Bundling them into a single corporation inevitably forces management to compromise the performance of each process in ways that no amount of reengineering can overcome.

Take customer relationship management. Finding and developing a relationship with a customer usually requires a big investment. Profitability hinges on achieving economies of scope—extending the relationship for as long as possible and generating as much revenue as possible from it. Only by gaining a large share of a customer's wallet and retaining that share over time can a company earn enough to offset the big up-front investment.

Because of the need to achieve economies of scope, customer relationship businesses naturally seek to offer a customer as many products and services as possible. It is often in their interests to create highly customized offerings to maximize sales. Their economic imperatives lead to an intently service-oriented culture. When a customer calls, people in these businesses seek to respond to the customer's needs above all else. They spend a lot of time interacting with customers, and they develop a sophisticated feel for customers' requirements and preferences, even at the individual level.

Contrast that kind of business with a product innovation business. Speed, not scope, drives the economics of product innovation. Once a product innovation business invests the resources necessary to develop a product or service, the faster it moves from the development shop to the market, the more money the business makes. Early entry into the market increases the likelihood of capturing a premium price and establishing a strong market share.

Culturally, product innovation businesses focus on serving employees, not customers. They do whatever they can to attract and retain the talent needed to come up with the latest and best product or service. They reward innovation, and they seek to minimize the administrative distractions that might frustrate or slow down their creative "stars." Not surprisingly, small organizations tend to be better suited than large bureaucracies to nurturing the creativity and fleetness required for product innovation.

If scope drives relationship management businesses and speed drives innovation businesses, scale is what drives infrastructure businesses. Such businesses generally require capital-intensive facilities, which entail high fixed costs. Since unit costs fall as scale increases, pumping large amounts of product or work through the facilities is essential for profitability.

The culture of infrastructure businesses is characterized by a one-size-fits-all mentality that abhors all kinds of customization and special treatment. To keep costs as low as possible, they are motivated to make their activities and outputs as routine and predictable as possible. They account for every penny and frown on anything that does not directly contribute to efficient operations, viewing it as a needless extravagance. Where customer relationship businesses focus on customers and innovation businesses focus on employees, infrastructure businesses are impersonal—they focus on the operation.

When the three businesses are bundled into a single corporation, their divergent economic and cultural imperatives inevitably conflict. Scope, speed, and scale cannot be optimized simultaneously. Trade-offs have to be made. To protect its manufacturing scale, for example, a company may prohibit its salespeople from selling another company's products, thus limiting their ability to achieve economies of scope. Or a company may institute standardized pay scales that, while rational for the vast majority of its people, alienate its most talented product designers. Or to protect customer relationships, a company may require a degree of customization that slows product introductions and creates inefficiencies in the production infrastructure.

The Regional Bell Operating Companies—the local telephone carriers in the United States—provide a good example of how these tensions can play out. The retail telephone operation within an RBOC is a customer relationship business; it focuses on acquiring customers and keeping them happy. The wholesale telephone operation is, by contrast, an infrastructure management business; it maintains the RBOC's physical communications facilities and furnishes specialized support services like network management. To maximize their scale economies, the RBOCs could lease their wholesale facilities to specialized telephone-service resellers, which focus on the customer relationship business. But the phone companies are wary of entering into such relationships because they fear that the resellers will drain customers away from their own retail phone business.

The RBOCs have, in other words, deliberately limited the growth and profitability of their infrastructure businesses to protect their customer relationship businesses. Their decision has encouraged specialized infrastructure businesses, operating their own fiber-optic networks, to enter the competitive fray in metropolitan areas, creating a further threat to the RBOCs.

Most senior managers make such compromises because they believe, or assume, that they have no other option. How, after all, can a core process be removed from a company without somehow undermining its identity or destroying its essence? Such a mind-set, although historically justified, is now becoming increasingly dangerous. While traditional companies strive to keep their core processes bundled together, highly specialized competitors are emerging that can optimize the particular activity they perform. Because they don't have to make compromises, these specialists have enormous advantages over integrated companies. (See Exhibit 1-2 "The Unbundling of the Corporation.")

Organizational Fault Lines

Under the pressures of deregulation, global competition, and advancing technology, a number of industries are already fracturing along the fault lines of customer relationship management, product innovation, and infrastructure management. Look at the newspaper industry, for example. Not so long ago, all three core processes were tightly integrated in most newspapers. A paper took on full responsibility for attracting its customers—both readers and advertisers. It developed most of its product—the news stories presented in its pages. And it

Exhibit 1-2   The Unbundling of the Corporation

The unbundling of the corporation into its three component businesses—customer relationship management, product innovation, and infrastructure management—is only the first step in the reshaping of organizations. The customer relationship and infrastructure businesses can be expected to consolidate as companies pursue economies of scope and scale. The product business will likely remain fragmented, with many small, nimble companies competing on the basis of speed and creativity.

Todays
integrated
corporations . . .

. . . will
undergo a
process of
unbundling . . .

. . . before
restructuring
into new
forms.

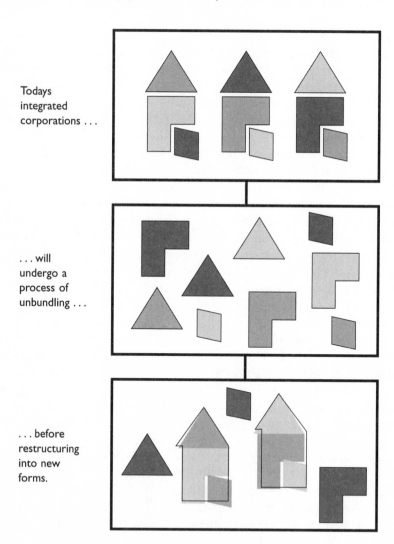

managed an extensive infrastructure, printing its editions on its own presses and distributing them with a fleet of its own trucks.

Today the industry is beginning to look very different. Much of the typical newspaper's product is outsourced to specialized news services; the average metropolitan newspaper depends heavily on wire services, syndicated columnists, and publishers of specialty magazine inserts for the words and images that fill its pages. In addition, many newspapers aspire to shed their scale-intensive printing facilities and rely instead on specialized printers to produce the paper each day. As they move away from product innovation and infrastructure management, the newspapers are able to concentrate on the customer relationship portion of the business—helping to connect readers and advertisers. Papers like the *Los Angeles Times*, for example, are creating special sections geared to particular regions or interests, which enable advertisers to better target specific sets of readers. The unbundling is making the newspaper business much less capital intensive, allowing more resources to be devoted to building customer relationships.

A similar unbundling is taking place in many areas of the banking industry. Credit cards, for example, began as a product offered by traditional banks, which operated their credit card businesses as a tightly integrated bundle of activities. Each bank designed and introduced its own credit cards, acquired and maintained its own customer relationships, and handled all the back-office processing for every credit card transaction (while relying on MasterCard and VISA to establish general protocols for those transactions). Over the past decade, however, the credit card business has rapidly unraveled as specialized players have focused on each of the three activities. Affinity groups—from the AARP to American Airlines—have assumed responsibility for finding customers and maintaining relationships with them. Specialized credit-card companies like CapitalOne and Providian Financial are focusing on product innovation, creating new features and pricing programs. And a range of infrastructure companies are processing transactions, managing call centers, and performing other scale-intensive tasks. In fact, infrastructure specialists like First Data now process more than half the credit card transactions in the United States.

An influx of specialized companies has also begun to reshape the pharmaceutical industry. Some product innovators in biotechnology, like Genentech, Amgen, and Myriad Genetics, are focusing on specific techniques such as gene mapping. Others, like Medicis Pharmaceutical and Bausch & Lomb, are concentrating on specific disciplines like dermatology. Rather than invest in their own product development in all these areas, larger drug companies are taking equity stakes in or allying with these niche players. Roche Holding, for example, has purchased over two-thirds of Genentech, and Merck has entered into a collaborative research and licensing agreement with Aurora Biosciences. On the infrastructure side of the business, the big drug companies have begun to outsource the planning and execution of large-scale pharmaceutical trials to contract-research organizations like Quantum. And big distribution specialists like McKesson and Cardinal now warehouse and deliver most drugs.

As the newspaper, credit card, and pharmaceutical industries went through the unbundling process, established companies faced a series of hard choices. They had to rethink their traditional roles and identities, challenge their organizational assumptions, and in many cases fundamentally change the way they operated. Now, as electronic commerce reduces interaction costs throughout the economy, more and more companies will face equally tough, if not tougher, decisions.

Organization and the Internet

To see into the future of business organization, you need only look at how Internet companies are organizing today. Portal businesses like Yahoo! are focusing increasingly on customer relationship management while relying on other companies to provide innovative Web-based products and services on the one hand and infrastructure management on the other. Many people still think of Yahoo! as a search engine, but in fact its searching product is provided by another company, Inktomi, an innovator whose expertise in parallel computing enables its engine to search millions of Web pages almost instantly. And Yahoo! has forged relationships with big Internet-access providers like AT&T, which manage a large portion of the Internet's infrastructure. Yahoo! is thus freed to concentrate on attracting customers, gathering data on them, and connecting them with both advertisers and merchants. It is positioned to become what we call an *infomediary*—a company whose rich store of customer information enables it to control the flow of commerce on the Web.[2]

Because electronic commerce has such low interaction costs, it is natural for Web-based businesses to concentrate on a single core activity—whether it be just customer relationship management, just product innovation, or just infrastructure management. That's not to say that all current Internet companies are pure players. Excite, for example, is principally a customer relationship business, but it has acquired several product-innovation companies, including Jango and Classifieds2000, in order to offer new on-line services to customers quickly. Similarly, America Online has incubated a number of product businesses internally to ensure a steady supply of content for its customers. We would argue, though, that such hybrid models are transitional, necessitated by the infancy of electronic commerce. As the Internet industry matures, mixed models will become less attractive and less sustainable. (See "Whither Amazon.com?")

Whither Amazon.com?

Amazon.com, the on-line book and media retailer, has emerged as one of the most powerful players in electronic commerce. Thus far in its brief history, Amazon has pursued a hybrid strategy, focusing on both customer relationship management and infrastructure management. Its user-friendly site, its vast selection, and its low prices have earned the company the trust and the business of thousands of on-line shoppers. In return, Amazon has been able to assemble a great store of information on the buying habits of each of its customers. It recommends books and CDs to customers on the basis of their previous purchases, and through its 1-Click program, it streamlines the buying process by storing detailed customer information, including credit card numbers.

At the same time, Amazon has built a powerful infrastructure for processing and delivering on-line orders. By working closely with big book distributors—who are themselves in the infrastructure business—Amazon is able to ship books, CDs, DVDs, and other products rapidly without maintaining huge inventories. In effect, Amazon acts as a sophisticated transshipper. Once a customer places an order for a book that is not in Amazon's stock, the order is immediately passed on to one of the distributors (or directly to a publisher), which includes the book in its next daily shipment to Amazon's facility. When the book arrives, Amazon quickly repackages it, together with other products that the customer has ordered, and ships it to the customer.

Amazon has so far been successful in building both of its businesses. But to become truly profitable over the longer term, it may have to choose which of the two businesses to focus on, or it may have to unbundle itself into two separate organizations. Already, some tensions in Amazon's business model are beginning to appear.

The company is, for example, aggressively building up an affiliate network—a set of Web sites that sell Amazon's books in return for a cut of the revenues. So far, the company has signed up tens of thousands of affiliates, ranging from tiny, personal home pages to huge portals like America Online, Yahoo!, and Excite.

Because these affiliates increase Amazon's sales, they're great for the company's scale-intensive infrastructure business. But they raise problematic issues for its customer relationship business. Many of these affiliates, after all, are themselves in the customer relationship business and are thus actively competing with Amazon for customer information and loyalty. If it turns out that Amazon's customer relationship business is more lucrative than its infrastructure business, the company's aggressive affiliate program may prove to have been a big mistake.

As electronic commerce spreads out into other, more traditional industries, they too will begin to fracture. Take the automotive business, for example. Small entrepreneurial companies like Auto-by-Tel and Autoweb.com have recently emerged on the Web and are already beginning to gain control over customer relationships. These companies' sites provide car buyers with a broad range of information about current models and pricing. The sites then collect detailed data about the customers and their preferences and use that information to refer customers to appropriate automobile dealers. In 1997, Web site referrals accounted for about 2% of all nonfleet new-car sales. Although 2% is a small percentage, it represents 300,000 cars, or $6 billion in revenue—and those numbers are growing explosively. J.D. Power & Associates predicts that one-third of all new-car buyers will buy cars using the Web by the year 2000.

As the infomediaries gain more control over customer purchases and, even more important, over customer information, car companies will have to rethink the role of the traditional automobile dealer. Dealers may give up their customer relationship business entirely and focus narrowly on the infrastructure business—managing showrooms, for example. The independent, on-line infomediaries would take over the role of acquiring and managing customer relationships. As they develop a deeper understanding of each customer, the infomediaries could play an ever more central role in determining which make and model a customer buys. In fact, they could come to fulfill virtually all of a customer's car-related needs:

- selecting the auto loan with the best terms
- selecting the insurance package with the best rate and the most cost-effective trade-off between premiums and deductibles
- providing a list of qualified repair and maintenance shops and towing companies
- recommending car phone companies and phone service packages
- providing reminders of required servicing and then recording maintenance information for the customer's records.

Auto manufacturers would love to access all this valuable information, but they could never collect it as efficiently or effectively as the infomediaries. A carmaker might be able to gather data on the people who bought its own models, but it would be hard-pressed to assemble information on people who bought competitors' models. Instead, car manufacturers may decide—or be forced—to unbundle their businesses, outsourcing the customer-relationship-management role to the infomediary and focusing on product innovation. Who knows? Automobile manufacturers already outsource a significant portion of subassembly manufacturing—perhaps some day, they might outsource all their manufacturing operations to infrastructure management businesses.

In financial services, similar forces are at work. Companies like Microsoft, Intuit, and E*Trade are using the Internet to build customer relationship businesses, drawing control of customers' purchases away from traditional banks and brokerages. Building on the popularity of its Quicken personal-financial-management software, for example, Intuit has attracted hundreds of thousands of customers to its Web site, where it offers easy access to products and services from a broad range of financial service providers. Customers can identify the best deals on CDs, mortgages, and checking and savings accounts. They can get tips on tax planning, financial planning, and retirement planning. And they can access brokers like E*Trade and Charles Schwab to trade on-line.

As Intuit and other infomediaries gather greater stores of information about customers and their buying behavior, they will be able to extend their control over the relationship business. They will know individual customers' circumstances and preferences, anticipate their needs, and identify appropriate products and providers. The infomediary might, for example, notify a customer that mortgage rates have dropped enough to make refinancing worthwhile, or, based on the way a customer uses his credit card, it might recommend a card with a higher annual fee but a lower interest rate as a better alternative. Or knowing the customer has a new baby, it might recommend a particular life-insurance package or a mutual fund for college savings.

As infomediaries build these customer relationships, traditional banks will find themselves in a tight spot. They might try to turn into infomediaries, but that's unlikely. Most banks have proven reluctant to resell other institutions' products (except when those institutions don't sell competing products). And even if banks did offer other companies' products, customers might question their objectivity as information suppliers. Even more fundamental, most banks are still struggling to integrate their computer systems so that they can merge all their information about a customer—a prerequisite for an effective customer-relationship business.

Given these constraints, many banks might have to concede the role of customer relationship manager to the new infomediaries. Some might choose to focus on developing attractive product and service portfolios that could be marketed through the infomediaries. Others might choose to concentrate on back-office processing operations, providing transactional support for products like credit cards, loans, and investment accounts. Each of the three businesses will likely provide attractive opportunities, but it's unlikely that one company will be able to do them all and still continue to increase its profits over the long haul.

A Road Map for Unbundling

As more and more industries fracture, many traditional companies will find themselves cut off from their customers. Just to reach their markets, they will have to compete or cooperate with an increasingly powerful group of infomediaries. To survive, they may have no choice but to unbundle themselves and make a definitive decision about which business to focus on: customer relationship management, product innovation, or infrastructure management.

As we've seen, the economics driving each of these businesses are different, and those economics will determine their ultimate structures. Although industries will fracture, they will not necessarily break into lots of small pieces. In fact, the structure of only one of the three businesses—product innovation—is likely to be characterized by large numbers of small businesses competing on a level playing field where barriers to entry are low. The product innovator's need to provide a fertile environment for creativity tends to favor smaller organizations, as does its need for speed and agility in bringing products to market.

The other two businesses will probably consolidate quickly, as a small number of large companies assume dominance. Since economies of scope are necessary in the customer relationship business, it's likely that only a few big infomediaries will survive. America Online's decision to acquire Netscape, with its popular Netcenter Web portal, provides strong evidence that the consolidation of this business is already well under way. Similarly, in the infrastructure business, economies of scale create irresistible pressures toward the formation of large, focused enterprises.

Once a company decides where it wants to direct its energies, it will probably need to divest itself of its other businesses. That will be a big challenge. Few senior managers of large companies have ever attempted a systematic divestiture program. The divestitures that have occurred have usually been spin-offs of recent acquisitions whose expected synergies never materialized. Even AT&T's highly publicized divestiture of its computer and telecommunications-equipment businesses, NCR and Lucent, falls largely into this category. For most companies, the closest analogue to the kind of divestiture we're talking about is the establishment of outsourcing relationships in which infrastructure management activities like logistics, manufacturing, or data processing are contracted to outside providers.

Divestiture is, of course, a radical step. It's fair to say that in most cases executives will need to perceive a significant and immediate threat before they will consider such aggressive surgery. For that reason, the first divestiture programs will probably be launched by companies whose markets are in the midst of major technological or regulatory change, such as the computer, telecommunications, media, and banking industries. Companies in other industries will be able to learn from their successes—and their mistakes.

If a company has chosen to compete in customer relationship management or infrastructure management, where size matters, divestiture won't be enough. It will also need to build scope or scale through mergers and acquisitions. It is likely that each acquired company will have to go through a similar process of unbundling, shedding unneeded businesses to help fund the next wave of acquisitions and integrating the remaining businesses into the existing operation. The secret to success in fractured industries is not just to unbundle, but to unbundle and rebundle, creating a new organization with the capabilities and size required to win.

Rebundling will be a very different process from the vertical integration that has often characterized traditional acquisition programs. Because companies will be focusing on a single activity—relationship management or infrastructure management—their acquisitions will be aimed at achieving horizontal integration. They will be seeking to build scope or scale first within their own industry and then, to further leverage their capabilities, across related industries.

Senior managers will face many painful decisions as they make the wrenching changes that are needed to realign their businesses. Difficult as the choices may be, it is likely that there won't be much time in which to make them. Once interaction costs begin to fall, the ensuing reorganization of an industry can happen remarkably quickly—as we saw with the computer industry. Sources of strength can turn into sources of weakness almost overnight, and even the most successful company can quickly find itself in a position that has become untenable.

Notes

1. We believe that the term *interaction costs* is more accurate than the common term *transaction costs*. Transaction costs, as economists have defined them, include the costs related to the formal exchange of goods and services between companies or between companies and customers. Interaction costs include not only those costs but also the costs for exchanging ideas and information. They thus cover the full range of costs involved in economic interactions. For more about the implications of falling interaction costs see Patrick Butler *et al.*, "A Revolution in Interaction," *The McKinsey Quarterly*, 1997, No. 1.

2. While big portal companies like Yahoo! and Excite have the potential to evolve into infomediaries, they are not there yet. To play a true infomediary role, they will need to deepen their ability to create detailed customer profiles and, even more important, they will need to build a greater degree of trust with their customers. Many portals are renting large portions of their Web space to vendors, not just for ad-

vertisements but also as part of exclusive sales partnerships. Such arrangements generate near-term revenues, but they may undermine customers' trust over the longer run. For further reading on infomediaries, see "The Coming Battle for Customer Information" by John Hagel III and Jeffrey F. Rayport (*HBR*, January–February 1997).

2
Syndication: The Emerging Model for Business in the Internet Era

Kevin Werbach

Business executives have a lot to learn from talk show host Jerry Springer—not about resolving conflicts through chair-throwing brawls but about syndication, the ideal way to conduct business in a networked, information-intensive economy.

Syndication involves the sale of the same good to many customers, who then integrate it with other offerings and redistribute it. The practice is routine in the world of entertainment. Production studios syndicate TV programs, such as the *Jerry Springer Show*, to broadcast networks and local stations. Cartoonists syndicate comic strips to newspapers and magazines. Columnists syndicate articles to various print and on-line outlets. Consumers of entertainment—the people watching the TV shows or reading the newspapers—are generally unaware of the complex, ever-shifting business relationships that play out behind the scenes. But without syndication, the American mass media as we know it would not exist.

Elsewhere in the business world, syndication has been rare. The fixed physical assets and slow-moving information of the industrial economy made it difficult, if not impossible, to create the kind of fluid networks that are essential to syndication. But with the rise of the information economy, that's changing. Flexible business networks are not only becoming possible, they're becoming essential. As a result, syndication is moving from the periphery of business to its center. It is emerging as the fundamental organizing principle for e-business. (See "Why Syndication Suits the Web.")

Why Syndication Suits the Web

Syndication has traditionally been rare in the business world for three reasons. First, syndication works only with information goods. Because information is never "consumed," infinite numbers of people can use the same information. That's not the case with physical products. If I sell you a car or a watch, I can't turn around and sell those same items to someone else. As long as most of the business world was engaged in the production, transport, and sale of physical goods, syndication could exist only on the margins of the economy.

Second, syndication requires modularity. While a syndicated good can have considerable value in and of itself, it does not normally constitute an entire product; it's a piece of a greater whole. Howard Stern's radio show attracts a sizable audience, but it needs to be combined with many other shows to create a station's programming. Dave Barry's columns have lots of dedicated readers, but they need to be combined with many other pieces of content to make a newspaper. In the old, physical economy, modularity was rare. The boundaries between products, supply chains, and companies tended to be clearly demarcated and impermeable.

Third, syndication requires many independent distribution points. There's little to be gained by creating different combinations and configurations of content if there's only one distributor, or if every distributor is controlled by a content creator. Think of Hollywood in its early days. Major movie studios such as MGM and Warner Brothers not only produced films but also owned the theaters that showed the films. Since a theater owned by Warner Brothers played only Warner Brothers movies, there was little room for syndicators. But when the U.S. government broke up those arrangements in 1948 on antitrust grounds, studios and distributors became independent from theaters. Syndication of entertainment content began to flourish. In most industries, however, there still tend to be limited numbers of distribution outlets, and they often have tight relationships with the companies that create the goods they sell.

With the Internet, information goods, modularity, and fragmented distribution become not only possible but essential. Everything that moves on the Internet takes the form of information. The hyperlinked architecture of the Web is modular by nature. And because anyone can start a Web site, there are literally millions of different distribution points for users. In such an environment, syndication becomes inescapable.

Although few of the leading Internet companies use the term "syndication" to describe what they do, it often lies at the heart of their business models. Look at E*Trade. Like other on-line brokerages, E*Trade offers its customers a rich array of information, including financial news, stock quotes, charts, and research. It could develop all this content on its own, but that would be prohibitively expensive and would distract E*Trade from its core business: acquiring and building relationships with on-line customers. Instead, the company purchases most of its content from outside providers—Reuters and TheStreet .com for news, Bridge Information Systems for quotes, BigCharts.com for charts, and so on. These content providers also sell, or syndicate, the same information to many other brokerages. E*Trade distinguishes itself from its competitors not through the information it provides but through the way it packages and prices that information. Just like a television station, it is in the business of aggregating and distributing syndicated content as well as providing other in-house services such as trade execution.

On the Web, unlike in the physical world, syndication is not limited to the distribution of content. Commerce can also be syndicated. One company can, for example, syndicate a shopping-cart ordering and payment system to many e-tailers. Another company can syndicate a logistics platform. Another can syndicate fraud detection and credit-scoring algorithms. Another can syndicate human resource processes. Businesses themselves, in other words, can be created out of syndicated components. The much-discussed "virtual company" can become a reality.

Syndication is a radically different way of structuring business than anything that's come before. It requires entrepreneurs and executives to rethink their strategies and reshape their organizations, to change the way they interact with customers and partner with other entities, and to pioneer new models for collecting revenues and earning profits. Those that best understand the dynamics of syndication—that are able to position themselves in the most lucrative nodes of syndication networks—will be the ones that thrive in the Internet era.

The Three Syndication Roles

Traditionally, companies have connected with one another in simple, linear chains, running from raw-material producers to manufacturers to distributors to retailers. In syndication, the connections between companies proliferate. The network replaces the chain as the organizing model for business relationships. Within a syndication network,

Table 2-1   The Structure of Syndication

Players	Originators	Syndicators	Distributors	Consumers
Role	Create original content	Package content and manage relationships between originators and distributors	Deliver content to consumer	View or use content; create revenue through fees, purchases, or viewing ads
Traditional Examples	Dreamworks Charles Schulz Oprah Winfrey	King World United Features	New York Times CBS CNN	
Web Examples	Inktomi Quote.com Motley Fool	iSyndicate LinkShare Motley Fool	Women.com Yahoo! Motley Fool	

there are three roles that businesses can play. *Originators* create original content. *Syndicators* package that content for distribution, often integrating it with content from other originators. *Distributors* deliver the content to customers. A company can play one role in a syndication network, or it can play two or three roles simultaneously. It can also shift from one role to another over time. (See Table 2-1 "The Structure of Syndication.")

Here's a simple example of a syndication network from the media business. Scott Adams, an originator, draws the popular *Dilbert* cartoon strip. He licenses it to a syndicator, United Features, which packages it with other comic strips and sells them to a variety of print publications. A newspaper, such as the *Washington Post,* acts as a distributor by printing the syndicated cartoons, together with articles, photographs, television listings, advertisements, and many other pieces of content, and delivering the entire package to the doorsteps of readers.

Now, lets look at how the syndication roles are emerging on the Internet:

Originators. The Internet broadens the originator category in two ways. It expands the scope of original content that can be syndicated, and it makes it easier for any company or individual to disseminate that content globally. Anything that can exist as information—from products and services to business processes to corporate brands—can be syndicated.

A good example of an Internet originator is Inktomi, a start-up that created a powerful Internet search engine using its proprietary technologies for connecting many inexpensive computers to act as a virtual supercomputer. By the time Inktomi was ready to enter the market, other companies such as Yahoo! and Excite already had well-established search engine brands. Inktomi's executives knew that it would be difficult for a new competitor to take them on directly. But the executives also saw that many other large Web sites wanted to offer search engine functionality but didn't have the technology. Rather than sell itself to any one of these companies, Inktomi decided to syndicate its application to all of them. Web sites are able to customize the Inktomi service for their users, offer it under their own brands, and combine it with other functions and content that they develop on their own or purchase from other originators.

Inktomi generates revenues through per-query charges and by sharing the dollars its customers generate from selling banner advertisements on their search pages. The company has applied the same business model and core technologies to other services such as content caching and comparison shopping. In the first quarter of 2000, it answered 3.4 billion search queries, its quarterly revenues hit $36 million, and its market capitalization surpassed $10 billion.

Syndicators. By bringing together content from a variety of sources and making it available through standard formats and contracts, syndicators free distributors from having to find and negotiate with dozens or hundreds of different originators to gather the content they want. In other words, syndicators are a form of infomediary, collecting and packaging digital information in a way that adds value to it. In the physical world, stand-alone syndicators are rare outside the entertainment field, but this business model is becoming increasingly prominent on the Net.

Screaming Media is a leading content syndicator. It collects articles in electronic form from some 400 originators and, using a combination of automated filtering software and human editors, categorizes each article as it flows through its servers. It then delivers to its customers—currently, more than 500 different sites—only the content relevant to their target audience. A site catering to auto-racing enthusiasts, for example, would receive a steady stream of up-to-date racing news and features. The site could license content directly from originators such as the Associated Press, but the vast majority of that content would be irrelevant to its audience. Screaming Media charges monthly fees based on the volume of filtered content its customers desire. It pays some of that money back to the content originators as royalties, allowing everyone involved to benefit from the transaction.

LinkShare is another on-line syndicator, but unlike Screaming Media, it syndicates commerce rather than traditional content. More than 400 on-line retailers have contracted with LinkShare to administer their affiliate programs—programs that enable other sites to provide links to the e-tailers in return for a small cut of any sales those links generate. LinkShare aggregates all the programs on its own site, providing an easy, one-stop marketplace for affiliate sites. In this network, the e-tailers act as the originators, LinkShare is the syndicator, and the content sites are the distributors. LinkShare also provides the technical infrastructure for monitoring transactions and tracking and paying affiliate commissions, and it offers ancillary services such as reporting for both affiliates and retailers. The e-tailers pay LinkShare a combination of up-front fees and per-sale commissions.

Distributors. Distributors are the customer-facing businesses. They use syndication to lower their costs for acquiring content and to expand the value they provide to consumers. E*Trade is one example of a distributor. Another is Women.com, an on-line destination for women. Women.com's staff creates its own content, which it integrates with syndicated information from partners such as ABC News and *Good Housekeeping* magazine. Women.com also offers a range of syndicated services, including free Web-based e-mail accounts from WhoWhere, a subsidiary of Lycos, and weather forecasts from AccuWeather. As a distributor, Women.com's role is to organize all this material into a compelling, targeted offering that attracts visitors.

At the same time, Women.com also distributes shopping services syndicated from a variety of partners, including eToys, Neiman-Marcus.com, RedEnvelope, and FogDog. Much like a traditional department store, Women.com organizes these on-line retailers' merchandise into relevant categories, such as gifts, clothing, cosmetics, and electronics, and it promotes featured products with pictures and descriptions. There are two important differences from the physical world, however. First, when a customer makes a purchase, she does so through a special hyperlinked connection to the partner site rather than through Women.com. Women.com need not hold inventory, process transactions, or manage fulfillment, but it receives a percentage of each sale for bringing in the customer. Second, distributors have far more flexibility on the Web. If PlanetRx offers Women.com a better commission on cosmetics than Eve.com, or if one set of products sells better than another, Women.com can quickly swap the products it promotes to maximize its revenues. It never has to worry about unsold inventory or a time lag in reconfiguring its supply chain.

From Scarcity to Abundance

Internet syndication opens up endless opportunities for entrepreneurs, and it provides enormous freedom to all companies. It enables businesses to choose where they wish to concentrate their efforts and to piggyback a myriad of other businesses that can handle the remaining elements of a complete end-to-end service. Unlike outsourcing, it does not restrict flexibility. Syndication relationships can change rapidly—by the second, in fact—and companies can quickly shift between different roles. (See "Beyond Outsourcing.") But because syndication networks are so complex, they also present a host of challenges.

Beyond Outsourcing

On the surface, syndication looks a lot like outsourcing. They both involve the use of outsiders to supply a business asset or function. But syndication holds two large advantages over traditional outsourcing. First, because syndication deals with information rather than physical resources, a company can syndicate the same goods or services to an almost infinite number of partners without incurring much additional cost. A physical call-center outsourcer, for example, must hire more people, lease more office space, and buy more equipment as it adds customers. But a content or e-commerce originator doesn't have to invest in more people, space, or machinery when it adds another distributor. Software practically scales for free.

The second advantage is that on-line syndication can be automated and standardized in a way that physical outsourcing can't. An important feature of syndication relationships is that business rules, such as usage rights and payment terms, can be passed between companies along with the syndicated asset or service—both take the form of digital code. Moreover, because the Internet is an open system, the rules can be coded in standard formats that can be shared by any company. That allows syndication networks to be cre-

\

ated, expanded, and optimized far more quickly than is possible in the physical world.

Syndication provides choices far beyond those that companies had with outsourcing, but the existence of those choices makes a coherent strategy all the more important. Companies should look for relationships that offer the greatest speed and flexibility, but they should also carefully identify the business terms they consider most important. Should you pay an up-front fee for a syndicated search service for your site, or would it make more sense to receive the service for free but let the provider run a banner ad? Should you use a syndicated procurement application from a company that sells the aggregated purchasing data it collects, or should you pay more for an application from a company that won't use your data? The flexibility of the Internet architecture—and the limitless creativity of Internet entrepreneurs—means that every company will face a multitude of complex choices in structuring relationships. Be prepared.

For a sense of what business is like in a syndication network, consider the Motley Fool, a popular on-line company that provides financial information to investors. The Motley Fool plays all three syndication roles simultaneously. It originates content, which it uses on its own Web site and on its America Online site, and which it also offers through syndicators like iSyndicate. It acts as a syndicator itself, providing stock-market commentary in various formats to sites such as Yahoo! and the *San Jose Mercury News*'s SiliconValley.com, as well as to 150 print newspapers and 100 radio stations. And it distributes syndicated business stories from news wires such as Reuters and syndicated financial applications from FinanCenter's CalcBuilder.com.

At an operational level, the Motley Fool's business is extremely complicated. The various elements of content that flow between it and its partners are updated according to different schedules and are subject to different business rules governing how material can be used and how payments are distributed. In some cases, the Motley Fool makes money through up-front licensing fees; in other cases, it receives a share of advertising revenue on other sites that run its content; and in still other cases, it takes a share of transaction revenues. Fortunately, however, the content flows, the business rules, and the revenue streams can largely be managed by software. As long as you get the code right, the business runs smoothly.

The bigger challenge lies at the strategic level. Given the unpredictable and ever-changing flows of revenues, profits, and competition on

Table 2-2   *Everything Changes*

Business in a syndicated world bears little resemblance to its industrial predecessor. To succeed, executives need to change the way they think about nearly every aspect of strategy and management.

	Traditional Business	Syndication
Structure of Relationships	Linear supply-and-demand chains	Loose, weblike networks
Corporate Roles	Fixed	Continually shifting
Value Added	Dominated by physical distribution	Dominated by information manipulation
Strategic Focus	Control scarce resources	Leverage abundance
Role of Corporate Capabilities	Sources of advantage to protect	Products to sell
Role of Outsourcing	Gain efficiency	Assemble virtual corporations

the Web, companies need to choose their place in a syndication network with care, and they need to be adept at reconfiguring their roles and relationships at a moment's notice. The syndicated world of the Web is radically different from the traditional business world, where assets tended to be fixed and roles and relationships stable. To thrive in a syndication network, executives first have to shed many of their old assumptions about business strategy. (For more on these differences, see Table 2-2 "Everything Changes.")

In setting strategy, companies have always sought to organize their markets so as to place themselves in the sweet spot of the value chain—the place where most of the profits reside. Traditionally, the way to do that has been to seize upon or create scarcities. Control over a scarce resource is always more valuable than control over a commodity. Procter & Gamble cranks out a constant stream of new products and product extensions because it wants to maximize its control over supermarkets' limited shelf space. Home Depot seeks to crush local hardware stores with broad selection and low prices because it wants to be the only place in town to buy saws and bathroom fixtures. Other companies seek to dominate a source of supply, to patent a product, or to establish control over some other scarce resource.

The Internet, however, replaces scarcity with abundance. Information can be replicated an unlimited number of times. It can be reassembled and recombined in infinite combinations. And it can be distributed everywhere all the time. There are no limits on shelf space on the Net, every store is accessible to every shopper, the lanes of supply and distribution are wide open, and even the tiniest new company can achieve enormous scale in almost no time. Because the constraints of physical inventory and location don't apply, creating and maintaining scarcities isn't an option.

Instead, successful strategies must be designed to benefit from abundance. Companies need, in other words, to seek out and occupy the most valuable niches in syndication networks—which turn out to be those that maximize the number and strength of the company's connections to other companies and to customers. And because those connections are always changing, even the most successful businesses will rarely be able to stay put for long.

Amazon's Syndication Strategy

The maneuverings of Amazon.com can best be understood through the lens of syndication strategy. Jeff Bezos, Amazon's founder and CEO, quickly established his fledgling company as the leading on-line distributor of books and information about books by capitalizing on the abundance of the Web: his site could offer a dramatically larger selection than any physical bookstore. But since the Web's abundance is open to all comers, that early advantage could not be sustained for long. Other on-line booksellers soon matched Amazon's selection, and consumers began to use shopping bots to compare many merchants' prices instantly. Though Amazon is the largest retailer on the Web, thousands of competitors are always just a click away. If Bezos had simply tried to maintain Amazon's role as a distributor, he would have doomed his company to endless price wars and vanishing margins, no matter how many different products it distributed.

But Amazon hasn't stood still. It has constantly repositioned itself to play different syndication roles. In 1996, for example, it launched an aggressive affiliate program called Amazon.com Associates. Instead of relying solely on attracting customers to its site, Amazon can use this program to take its site to where customers already are. The more than 400,000 sites that have signed up to be affiliates each provide their own visitors with hyperlinks that enable them to make purchases through Amazon. In effect, Amazon is syndicating its store to other locations. While Amazon loses some control over merchandising and has to pay out 5% to 15% commissions on revenues generated by affiliates, the benefits far exceed the costs. Amazon puts itself in front of more potential customers than it could attract directly, especially in niche categories where affiliates provide specialized content and organize product listings for a specific audience. And it turns hundreds of thousands of nonemployees into a virtual sales force, which never gets paid until a sale is realized.

More recently, Amazon has taken on a new syndication role. Through its zShops program, it now hosts hundreds of small e-commerce providers on its own site. These shops gain access to Amazon's 13 million customers as well as its sophisticated tools for smoothing the on-line ordering process. In return, they pay Amazon a listing fee for each item, plus a 1.25% to 5% commission on each sale. zShops turns Amazon into a distributor—not of books or other products but of on-line shops. In addition to the revenue boost, Amazon gets additional traffic from customers interested in the niche zShops offerings. Amazon has also started signing distribution deals with larger e-tailers such as Drugstore.com and Living.com, which offer products complementary to its own. Amazon receives substantial payments and equity from these partners in exchange for placement on its site, and it also gives customers fewer reasons to shop elsewhere.

By acting as a syndicator and a distributor of e-commerce, Amazon is turning the absence of scarcity on the Web from a threat to an advantage. The multitude of other sites that users visit are no longer alternatives to Amazon; they are opportunities for Amazon to expand its presence—and its earnings.

Rethinking Core Capabilities

Amazon's experience holds a very important lesson for all companies. In a syndicated world, core capabilities are no longer secrets to protect—they are assets to buy and sell. One of Amazon's most distinctive capabilities is its ordering system. Instead of keeping that system to itself—as traditional strategists might have counseled—Amazon uses syndication to sell the capability to both stores and content sites throughout the Web. Amazon draws the line at direct competitors such as Barnesandnoble.com, which it is suing for infringing on a patent of its ordering system, though even this distinction may ultimately give way as the benefits of syndication multiply. In an economy of scarcity, core capabilities are sources of proprietary advantage. In an economy of abundance, they're your best product. If you try to sequester them, you may gain a short-term competitive edge, but your competitors will soon catch up. If you syndicate them, you can turn those competitors into customers.

In some cases, the syndicated assets themselves may be valuable enough to generate big revenues. But even if they aren't, the other benefits of syndication can be significant. Like Amazon, companies can use syndication to broaden their distribution in an efficient manner. Syndication can also bring companies data about customer usage patterns. And it can generate leads and reinforce brands. All of these are benefits that companies have traditionally sought to derive by dominating their markets and by exercising exclusive control over information. But with competitive advantages increasingly difficult to lock in—thanks to the leveling power of the information economy—syndication provides a superior route to the same benefits.

Think about what Federal Express has done with its package-tracking system. FedEx invested a great deal of money to develop unique technologies and an infrastructure for monitoring the location of every package it handles. This capability gave it an edge on competitors. Now, however, FedEx is syndicating its tracking system in several ways. The company allows customers to access the system through its Web site to check the status of their packages. It provides software tools to its corporate customers that enable them to automate shipping and track packages using their own computer systems. And it allows on-line companies to customize its tracking system, integrate it with their own offerings, and distribute it through their own sites.

Someone who orders flowers through Proflowers.com, for example, can check the delivery status directly on the Proflowers site. Behind the scenes, it's the FedEx application querying the FedEx database, but whereas FedEx just tracks the package, Proflowers also provides information from its own records about what's inside the box and what the sender wrote on the accompanying card. FedEx doesn't charge Proflowers for using its technology; it is, in a very real sense, giving away one of its core capabilities. What does it get in return? Plenty. By integrating its technology with the Proflowers ordering system, it makes it much harder for the customer to switch to a different delivery company. By enabling Proflowers to serve its customers better, it ensures that more packages of flowers will be shipped in FedEx planes and trucks. And by incorporating its brand name on the Proflowers site, it publicizes its services and promotes its brand.

As more and more business turns into e-business, smart managers in every company will find ways to use syndication to do what FedEx has done.

The New Shape of Business

Beyond its impact on individual companies' strategies and relationships, syndication promises to change the nature of business. As organizations begin to be constructed out of components syndicated from many other organizations, the result will be a mesh of relationships with no beginning, end, or center. Companies may look the same as before to their customers, but behind the scenes they will be in constant flux, melding with one another in ever-changing networks. The shift won't happen overnight, and of course there will always be functions and goods that don't lend themselves to syndication. But in those areas where syndication takes hold, companies will become less important than the networks that contain them.

Indeed, individual companies will routinely originate, syndicate, or distribute information without even being aware of all the others participating in the network. A particular originator may, for example, have a relationship with only one syndicator, but through that relationship it will be able to benefit from the contributions of hundreds or even thousands of other companies. While every participant will retain some measure of control—choosing which syndication partners to have direct relationships with and deciding which business rules to incorporate into its syndicated transactions—no participant will control the overall network. Like any highly complex, highly adaptive system, a well-functioning syndication network will be self-organizing, constantly optimizing its behavior in response to an unending stream of information about the transactions taking place among its members.

Syndication may not be a new model, but it takes on a new life thanks to the Internet. Virtually any organization can benefit from syndication, often in several different ways if it's willing to view itself as part of a larger, interconnected world rather than seeking exclusive control at every turn. The tools and intermediaries that facilitate syndication relationships will become more sophisticated over time. Already, though, there are many syndication networks in place and many examples of successful syndication strategies. As the Internet economy continues to grow in importance, syndication will grow along with it as the underlying structure of business.

3
Where Value Lives in a Networked World

Mohanbir Sawhney and Deval Parikh

In recent years, it seems as though the only constant in business has been upheaval. Changes have occurred at every level, from the way entire industries are structured, to the way companies interact with customers, to the way basic tasks are carried out in individual organizations. In response, many managers and management thinkers have thrown up their hands, proclaiming an era of radical uncertainty. Business has become so complex, they say, that trying to predict what lies ahead is futile. Plotting strategy is a fool's game. The best you can do is become as flexible as possible and hope you'll be able to ride out the waves of disruption.

There's some truth in that view. The business world has become much more complicated, and the ability to adapt and respond is now as important as the ability to anticipate and act. But we take issue with the assumption that the changes we've been seeing are random, disconnected events and thus unpredictable. We have studied the myriad upheavals taking place in business, and we've concluded that many of them have a common root, which lies in the nature of intelligence in networks. Put simply, the digitization of information, combined with advances in computing and communications, has fundamentally changed how all networks operate, human as well as technological, and that change is having profound consequences for the way work is done and value is created throughout the economy. Network intelligence is the Rosetta stone that can enable executives and entrepreneurs to decipher many of the phenomena shaping the future of business.

The evolution in network intelligence may sound like an awfully abstract topic, but it has immediate and very concrete implications. The future of many technology companies, from Dell to AT&T to hordes of Internet start-ups, hinges on their ability to recognize and adapt to shifts in network intelligence. And even if your company is not directly involved in the communications or computing business, it will not be immune to the impact of shifts in network intelligence. In a highly connected world, the location and mobility of network intelligence directly influences the way companies organize their people, market products, manage information, and work with partners. "The network is the computer," Sun Microsystems has famously proclaimed. We would go even further: the network is the economy.

Intelligence in the Network

Let's start with some basic definitions. A network is a conduit for information; it can be as simple as two tin cans tied together with a string or as complicated as the Internet. The intelligence of a network is its functionality—its ability to distribute, store, assemble, or modify information. A simple analog network, like the two tin cans, is considered "dumb"; it's just a pipe that transports information without enhancing it. A complex digital network, like the Internet, is "smart"; it can improve the utility of information in multiple ways. That's crucially important for one simple reason: in an information economy, improving the utility of information is synonymous with creating economic value. Where intelligence resides, so too does value.

As networking technologies have advanced in recent years, both the location and the mobility of network intelligence have changed dramatically. (See Exhibit 3-1 "The Two Patterns in Intelligence Migration.") By understanding the patterns underlying those changes, you can gain valuable insight into the way economic value is shifting across industries and among companies. And that knowledge can help you to act while others merely react.

THE DECOUPLING OF INTELLIGENCE

In the absence of a network, intelligence is static; it can be applied only where it lives. If different kinds of intelligence are needed to perform a task, they must all be bundled together in the same place. For

Exhibit 3-1   The Two Patterns in Intelligence Migration

As network technologies have advanced in recent years, both the location and the mobility of network intelligence have changed dramatically. As for location, back-end intelligence becomes embedded in a shared infrastructure at the network's core, while front-end intelligence fragments into many different forms at the network's periphery, where the users are. As for mobility, large units of intelligence that were once disconnected become small units of free-floating intelligence that coalesce into temporary bundles whenever and wherever necessary to solve problems.

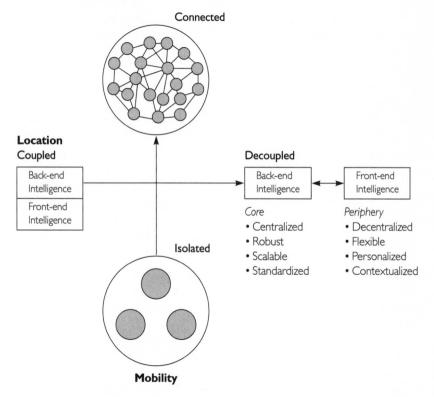

instance, a personal computer not connected to a network has to contain all the intelligence needed to process, store, and display information for a wide variety of user tasks. But the nature of the front-end intelligence needed to interact with users is very different from the nature of the back-end intelligence needed to process and store information. The user wants a computer that is easy to use, portable, flexible, and personalizable. But under the hood, the machine needs to be powerful, reliable, and easy to maintain. The bundling of these two types of intelligence necessitates compromises in design. For a laptop computer to be light and portable, for instance, it cannot have the most powerful microprocessor, a motherboard capable of additional slots, or a very large hard disk for storage.

When a PC is networked, however, it is no longer necessary for the different types of intelligence to be combined. Front-end intelligence can be separated from back-end intelligence. Instead of being replicated on every individual PC, the back-end intelligence can be consolidated onto powerful, efficient, and reliable network servers. And the front-end intelligence, freed from basic processing functions, can be much more customized to particular people and tasks. The PC can morph from a single jack-of-all-trades-master-of-none machine into an array of small, specialized electronic tools.

In more general terms, modern high-speed networks push back-end intelligence and front-end intelligence in two different directions, toward opposite ends of the network. Back-end intelligence becomes embedded into a shared infrastructure at the core of the network, while front-end intelligence fragments into many different forms at the periphery of the network, where the users are. And since value follows intelligence, the two ends of the network become the major sources of potential profits. The middle of the network gets hollowed out; it becomes a dumb conduit, with little potential for value creation. Moreover, as value diverges, so do companies and competition. Organizations that once incorporated diverse units focused on both back-end processing and front-end customer management split into separate infrastructure and customer-relationship management businesses, with very different capabilities and strategies.[1] (See "Value Trends in the Network Age.")

Value Trends in the Network Age

In a networked world, where everyone and everything is connected, economic value behaves very differently than it does in the traditional, bounded world. Here are four high-level value trends that all companies should be conscious of as they position themselves in the digital economy.

Value at the Ends
Most economic value will be created at the ends of networks. At the core— the end most distant from users—generic, scale-intensive functions will con-

solidate. At the periphery—the end closest to users—highly customized connections with customers will be made. This trend pertains not only to technological networks like the Internet but to networks of companies engaged in shared tasks and even to the human networks that exist within companies.

Value in Common Infrastructure

Elements of infrastructure that were once distributed among different machines, organizational units, and companies will be brought together and operated as utilities. Shared infrastructure will take the form not only of basic computing and data-storage functions but also of common business functions, such as order processing, warehousing and distribution, and even manufacturing and customer service.

Value in Modularity

Devices, software, organizational capabilities, and business processes will increasingly be restructured as well-defined, self-contained modules that can be quickly and seamlessly connected with other modules. Value will lie in creating modules that can be plugged in to as many different value chains as possible. Companies and individuals will want to distribute their capabilities as broadly as possible rather than protect them as proprietary assets.

Value in Orchestration

As modularization takes hold, the ability to coordinate among the modules will become the most valuable business skill. Much of the competition in the business world will center on gaining and maintaining the orchestration role for a value chain or an industry.

THE MOBILIZATION OF INTELLIGENCE

In a connected world, intelligence becomes fluid and modular. Small units of intelligence float freely like molecules in the ether, coalescing into temporary bundles whenever and wherever necessary to solve problems. Consider SETI@home, a project launched by the University of California at Berkeley to search for extraterrestrial life. Radio signals received by the world's biggest telescope dish—the 1,000-foot Arecibo Observatory in Puerto Rico—are carved into 330-kilobyte "work units" and distributed over the Internet to PCs around the world. Individual computer owners donate their spare computing cycles—their processing intelligence—to the project by allowing their computers to analyze data in the background or when idle. Within a year of its launch in May 1999, more than 2 million people in 226 countries had provided about 280,000 years of computer time to the effort. SETI@home has a total computing power of roughly 12 teraflops, making it four times as powerful as the world's fastest supercomputer. The network makes it possible to pool the intelligence residing in millions of computers across the globe into an ad hoc system with massive computing capability.

The mobilization of intelligence has profound organizational implications. Connected by networks, different companies can easily combine their capabilities and resources into temporary and flexible alliances to capitalize on particular market opportunities. As these "plug-and-play" enterprises become common, value shifts from entities that own intelligence to those that orchestrate the flow and combination of intelligence. In other words, more money can be made in managing interactions than in performing actions. That explains why companies like Cisco and Hewlett-Packard are evolving into intelligent hubs that coordinate the interactions among a network of channel partners, suppliers, and customers. By connecting the business processes of manufacturing service providers like Solectron and Flextronics to the business processes of channel partners and customers, Cisco and HP are able to coordinate the intelligent flow of information in their business networks. As a consequence, they are able to extract the bulk of the value created by the network, much as the conductor of a symphony orchestra garners the lion's share of the audience's applause.

Just as the decoupling of intelligence requires a reliable high-speed network, the mobilization of intelligence requires a common language. Without the existence of universal protocols for information exchange, individual pieces of intelligence cannot communicate and collaborate. For instance, the mobilization of intelligence among devices requires device-to-device communication protocols like Bluetooth and Jini. The mobilization of intelligence from the Internet to wireless devices requires protocols like the Wireless Applications Protocol (WAP). And the organization of plug-and-play business networks requires the widespread adoption of protocols for describing products and processes like Extensible Markup Language (XML). The development of these and other network standards will play a large role in determining the future shape of business.

Reshaping Industries

The decoupling and mobilization of intelligence are changing the competitive landscapes of many large industries. The most dramatic effects, not surprisingly, are being felt in network-based businesses like telecommunications. When traditional telephone companies built their analog systems, they had to bundle many different kinds of intelligence—for processing, transport, and user functionality—into the middle of their networks. The wires needed to be smart because the user device was dumb—a simple rotary phone. But the emergence of digital networks based on the Internet Protocol (IP) has turned the old networks into huge, expensive albatrosses around the phone companies' necks. Because intelligence can now be embedded in servers, software, and intelligent devices located at the core as well as at the periphery of the network, the middle of the network can and should be dumb. All that's needed is a fast and reliable pipe, with a little bit of routing intelligence.

This shift poses a grave threat to service providers like AT&T, which rely on voice and data transport for the bulk of their revenues. As transport becomes a commodity, rates for long-distance telephony are plummeting. Start-ups like Dialpad and Go2Call are even offering free PC-to-phone long-distance service over the Internet. The real value in telecommunications is shifting to the ends of the network. At the core, infrastructure providers like Sun, Cisco, Nortel, and Lucent are earning big profits. And at the periphery, companies like Yahoo!, InfoSpace, America Online, and Phone.com are extracting value by controlling the user interface and managing customer relationships. Even in the emerging broadband and wireless arenas, service providers will find it difficult to make money just by selling access to the Internet. They will have to provide value-added infrastructure services—like hosting, systems integration, and network maintenance—or find a way to earn commissions on the transactions that flow through their pipes.

The computing business is going through a similar transformation. The functionality that was once built into computers or sold as software packages can now be delivered over the Internet, much as utility companies deliver electricity through power lines. Just as corporations and consumers no longer need to own their own generators, they'll soon be freed from having to own their own computing hardware and applications. Already, consumers can use Yahoo!'s servers to store their e-mail messages, calendars, address books, digital photographs, digital wallets, faxes, and data files. And businesses can now purchase, on an as-needed basis, the computer applications required for customer service, human resource management, accounting, and payroll from outside service providers.

Obviously, this trend has profound implications for traditional hardware and software companies. To go where the value is, they'll have to transform themselves from product companies to service providers, or they'll have to shift their focus from selling primarily to end users to selling to the big infrastructure providers like Yahoo! and Exodus. Dell Computer, in a major effort to reinvent itself, is taking both paths. In February 2000, Dell announced a series of initiatives called "Dell E Works" aimed at broadening its revenue base beyond traditional hardware. It now offers its enterprise systems and storage products over the Internet through its Dell Hosting Service, and it is expanding into services like e-consulting and Web hosting. It is also enlarging its customer base to include Internet service providers (ISPs) and hosting companies that provide computing as a utility. As part of this effort, it is moving beyond its reliance on the Windows operating system by embracing Linux, an OS better suited to running the robust servers owned by the computing utilities. The new initiatives are already paying off. In the quarter that ended July 28, 2000, Dell's "beyond the box" revenues increased 40% from the previous year, accounting for 16% of the company's net revenues.

Reshaping Companies

The impact of intelligence migration is being felt within companies as well as across industries. The shrinking of middle management in many organizations, for example, is another manifestation of the hollowing of the middle, as intelligence gets pushed to the core (in this case, top management) and the periphery (frontline employees). Before robust digital networks and easy-to-use collaboration tools like e-mail, groupware, and intranets existed, it was difficult to communicate information through a large organization. So a lot of middle managers were needed to package and distribute information between top management and frontline employees. But now that people are connected electronically, information and intelligence can be transported more seamlessly. As a result, the information-transport function of middle managers has become superfluous. Just as the telecom network can have dumb pipes with intelligent ends, the organization can have a dumb information network that allows senior managers to communicate directly with frontline employees. Leadership and strategy get centralized at the top management level, while the ability to act and make decisions is pushed to the periphery of the organization. The challenge for the remaining middle managers is to redefine their roles as coordinators, facilitators, organizers, and mentors—to provide new kinds of organizational intelligence.

The mobilization of intelligence is having other organizational effects as well. Rather than being centralized in discrete units, a company's capabilities are becoming more distributed and more modular. The Internet lets geographically dispersed individuals and teams connect to solve customer problems or respond quickly to market opportunities. A company can, for example, locate its R&D capabilities in Silicon Valley, its engineering capabilities in India, its manufacturing capabilities in China, and its customer-support capabilities in Ireland. The interaction of the far-flung units is mediated, moment by moment, by the network, not by a large, expensive, and slow-moving managerial staff. In fact, it may now make more sense to talk about a company's "distributed capabilities" instead of its "core capabilities." (See "Network Intelligence in the Public Sector.")

Network Intelligence in the Public Sector

The migration of network intelligence affects more than business. It also affects public sector activities, such as government, national security, and education. Governments, for example, will be challenged to use electronic networks in general and the Internet in particular to deliver information and services to citizens in much more diverse and personalized ways. The monolithic government bureaucracy will shatter, and new forms of distributed government will emerge. Interestingly, some of the most creative governmental applications of the Internet are found in developing nations. One example is the Indian state of Andhra Pradesh, with a population of 70 million. Under the leadership of its cybersavvy chief minister N. Chandrababu Naidu, it is rolling out an "e-government" system that will let citizens pay taxes and fees, apply for licenses and permits, and participate in municipal meetings through their home computers or public Internet kiosks.

The defense establishment will also need to radically reshape itself to adapt to the digital world, where threats to national security tend to be distributed among far-flung terrorist activity "modules" rather than centralized in power-ful states. Centralized intelligence will need to be decentralized and dispersed. (Perhaps the CIA will be replaced by the DIA—the Distributed Intelligence Agency.) And the military will need to be reorganized to emphasize relatively small autonomous units at the edges connected through a network to a central core of coordination and command.

Some of the most radical changes will take place in education. Students will no longer need to come together in centralized institutions to take general courses. Using the intelligence of the Internet, they will able to remotely access modules of education and training content, assembling courses of instruction that respond to their immediate and particular needs. Universities will need to shift from providing generalized just-in-case knowledge to providing customizable just-in-time knowledge.

The same kind of flexible collaboration is also changing business-to-business interactions. We see it in the sharing of Internet-based business infrastructures. Direct competitors are, for example, coming together to share supply chain platforms by forming consortia like Covisint (in the automobile industry), Envera (in the chemicals industry), and Transora (in the packaged-goods industry). We see it as well in the packaging of corporate capabilities, such as FedEx's order tracking functionality and General Electric's consumable supplies ordering, as modules that other companies can purchase and plug in to their own operations. More profoundly, the ability to creatively combine capabilities distributed among many different companies is enabling complex virtual enterprises to be formed on the fly. A whole new class of software, created by companies like Bowstreet, G5 Technologies, and Hewlett-Packard, is emerging that will form the glue for such plug-and-play organizations. By coding business processes in common protocols, such as XML, this software enables different companies' processes to be easily connected or disconnected to suit their business needs.

Companies that really understand how intelligence migration is reshaping business are often able to better exploit the power of the Internet. Avon is a good case in point. Its first response to the Internet back in 1997 was to launch a site for selling cosmetics directly to customers. The site failed to generate much business—it accounted for only 2% of the company's sales in 1999—and, more important, it felt like a real threat to the company's most valuable asset: its half-million-member independent sales force.

Now, Avon is rethinking its Internet strategy. It is planning to create a site that provides "personal portals" for each of its sales representatives. The reps will use the site to place and track orders, get current information on products, and analyze the buying patterns of their customers—it will, in effect, become the shared "back office" for their individual businesses. Here, again, we see infrastructure intelligence migrating to the core (to Avon) and customer intelligence being pushed to where it can be applied with the highest degree of customization (to the periphery, with the reps). Consolidating the infrastructure provides an important benefit to Avon. One of the company's biggest problems is high turnover among its sales representatives. The reps, who often work part-time, tend to drift in and out of the work force, and when they leave, they take their customer relationships with them. Now, for the first time, Avon will have centralized information about all its end customers. This information will outlive the tenures of the individual representatives and can easily be transferred to new reps.

So what will Avon do with its existing e-commerce site? It will limit its sales to fewer than 500 of the company's 6,000 products. Customers who want any of the other products will be referred to their local Avon rep, who will call on them in person. The site will now support rather than threaten the reps.

Profiting from Intelligence Migration

In addition to changing the way existing businesses operate, the decoupling and mobilization of network intelligence are opening attractive new business opportunities. Forward-thinking companies are beginning to use four strategies to capitalize on the migration patterns (see Table 3-1 "Four Strategies for Profiting from Intelligence Migration"):

Arbitrage. Because intelligence can be located anywhere on a network, there are often opportunities for moving particular types of intelligence to new regions or countries where the cost of maintaining the intelligence is lower. Such an arbitrage strategy is particularly useful for people-intensive services that can be delivered over a network, because labor costs tend to vary dramatically across geographies. PeopleSupport, for example, operates a large center in Manila

Table 3-1   Four Strategies for Profiting from Intelligence Migration

Arbitrage	Move intelligence to new regions or countries where the cost of maintaining it is lower.
Aggregation	Combine formerly isolated pieces of dedicated infrastructure intelligence into a large pool of shared infrastructure that can be provided over a network.
Rewiring	Connect islands of intelligence by creating a common information backbone.
Reassembly	Reorganize pieces of intelligence from diverse sources into coherent, personalized packages for customers.

that provides live on-line help services to customers of U.S. companies. By transporting the intelligence of a long-distance support staff over the Internet, the company is able to exploit the difference in labor costs between the Philippines and the United States. The arbitrage strategy can also be used for other people-intensive services like medical transcription, market research, transaction processing, and back office support. Countries in the Indian subcontinent, Eastern Europe, and Latin America provide rich pools of low-cost human resources that can be accessed over a network. Additionally, countries like India with a significant English-speaking population and skilled engineering talent can provide specialty engineering services for software development, engineering design, architectural design, and statistical analysis.

Aggregation. As intelligence decouples, companies have the opportunity to combine formerly isolated pools of dedicated infrastructure intelligence into a large pool of shared infrastructure that can be provided over a network. Loudcloud, based in Sunnyvale, California, is an example of an emerging new breed of utility that employs the aggregation strategy. Loudcloud offers "instant" infrastructure to e-businesses by converting the various aspects of intelligence required to operate a Web site into a suite of services called Smart Cloud. Each aspect of intelligence is offered as a distinct service, including a Database Cloud (storage), an Application Server Cloud (processing), a Mail Cloud (dispatch), a Staging Cloud (testing), and an eServices Cloud (applications). The Smart Cloud services are coordinated by Opsware —an operating environment that automates tasks such as capacity scaling, configuration, service provisioning, and software updating.

Nike used Loudcloud's services to accommodate a dramatic traffic surge on its site during the recent Olympic Games in Australia. Opsware enabled Nike to scale up its computing needs on a temporary, just-in-time basis, allowing it to avoid the complexity and expense of expanding its capacity permanently. As Nike's traffic increased, the site received more server and storage capacity, and when the traffic died down after the Games, Opsware decommissioned the added computers. Loudcloud billed Nike just like a utility does, on the amount of services actually used.

Rewiring. The mobilization of intelligence allows organizations to more tightly coordinate processes with many participants. In essence, this strategy involves creating an information network that all participants connect to and establishing an information exchange standard that allows them to communicate. Consider how the start-up e-Trak is rewiring the information chain for the towing of illegally parked vehicles. The towing process involves a complex sequence of interactions among the police officer at the towing site, the dispatcher in the police station, the towing company, and the towing company's drivers. Traditionally, the police officer radios the dispatcher in the police station, who then calls various tow companies. The tow companies in turn radio their drivers to find a suitable truck in the area. Once a truck is located, confirmation is passed from the towing company to the dispatcher and back to the officer. This inefficient process takes a lot of time, during which the officer is forced to remain near the vehicle.

E-Trak sets up an information network that connects law enforcement agencies to towing companies. Police officers initiate a tow request through a radio link or a mobile display terminal connected to a network. The tow information is sent to the e-Trak system, which uses a database to automatically select the best towing company based on availability and proximity. The towing company receives the tow information through an e-Trak terminal in its office, and it communicates with the driver via radio, computer, or pager. The e-Trak system has allowed law enforcement agencies to cut response times from 30 minutes to ten minutes, letting them handle twice as many tows without increasing staff.

Reassembly. Another new kind of intermediary creates value by aggregating, reorganizing, and configuring disparate pieces of intelligence into coherent, personalized packages for customers. One example of such a reassembler is Yodlee, a start-up that has developed technology to consolidate and summarize information from multiple on-line sources on one Web site. Users get one-click access to a diverse set of personal information, including bank balances, travel reservations, investments, e-mail, shopping, bills, and calendars, and they can access it from a PC, handheld device, or Web-enabled phone. The Yodlee platform also allows the different pieces of intelligence to communicate with one another by securely and intelligently transmitting personal information across multiple accounts, services, platforms, and devices. For example, severe weather data transmitted to a Web-enabled phone could initiate an automatic call to inquire about potential flight delays for a travel reservation.

What Managers Need to Do

The migration of intelligence raises different sorts of challenges for different companies. To prepare your company, start by undertaking a straightforward analysis. First, define what intelligence is in your business. List the various types of intelligence that exist in your organization, using Table 3-2, "Aspects of Intelligence in Networks," as a guide. Think about intelligence that resides in objects, such as software applications, databases, and computer systems, as well as in the skills and knowledge of your people. Next, ask yourself where intelligence lives in your organization. Is it organized by geography, by line of business, or by customer type? Then, ask yourself where intelligence should live—assuming you could connect all your customers, employees, business processes, and trading partners in a seamless network with infinite bandwidth. Is the current location of your company's intelligence the best location?

Think about the decoupling pattern. Are you making compromises by bundling intelligence that is best centralized with intelligence that is best decentralized? Conceptualize your organization as a network with a core (the back end) and a periphery (the front end). At the back end, can you centralize processes that are shared across different business units to create an internal "utility company"? Can you convert dedicated infrastructure into shared infrastructure by pushing

Table 3-2   Aspects of Intelligence in Networks

The intelligence of a network is functionality—its ability to distribute, store, assemble, or modify information. Here we break down intelligence into some of its most common forms.

Activity	Definition	Physical Analog
Configuring	arranging information in a way that responds to a need	configurator software
Dispatching	moving information from its source to its appropriate destination	router
Storing	collecting information so that it can be accessed quickly and easily	database
Processing	converting raw information into useful outcomes	microprocessor
Interacting	facilitating the exchange of information	keyboard
Coordinating	harmonizing activities performed by multiple entities toward a common goal	operating system
Learning	using experience to improve the ability to act	expert system
Sensing	detecting and interpreting signals in the environment	antenna

some business processes beyond the walls of the organization to external utility companies? At the front end, can you get closer to your customers and partners by pushing intelligence nearer to them? Can you allow your customers, your sales force, and your channel partners to access and process intelligence directly, so that they have the ability to configure and personalize it themselves?

Think about the mobilization pattern. Are there opportunities to connect, combine, and configure isolated pools of intelligence in creative ways? Reconceptualize your business in terms of the sequences of activities that your customers are trying to accomplish. Think about gaps in the information flows needed to support the sequences. Are you currently doing things in time-consuming, manual ways that could easily be automated if the right information were available? Think about opportunities to rewire your information chains by creating a single network for all your partners. And think about how you might aggregate and reassemble pieces of intelligence from different sources in ways that will save your customers time and effort.

By understanding the implications of intelligence migration for your own company, you will be better able to chart a clear-headed strategy in a time of apparent turmoil. Strategy has always been about finding the right position in a chain of value-creating activities—a position that gives you rather than your competitors control over the flow of profits. That hasn't changed. What has changed is the nature of the value chain itself. Increasingly, it takes the form of a network.

Notes

1. See chapter 1, "Unbundling the Corporation," by John Hagel III and Marc Singer.

4
Starting Up in High Gear: An Interview with Venture Capitalist Vinod Khosla

David Champion and Nicholas G. Carr

The Internet has opened unparalleled opportunities for entrepreneurs. But the mad rush to cash in is raising hard questions about the way new ventures are funded and brought to market—as well as about their long-term prospects. Vinod Khosla is in an ideal position to discuss both the opportunities and the challenges facing entrepreneurs and their backers today. He's an accomplished entrepreneur himself, having cofounded Sun Microsystems in the early 1980s. And since joining venture capitalists Kleiner Perkins Caufield & Byers in 1986, he has helped steer companies like Amazon.com, Excite, Juniper Networks, and Cerent to success.

In a wide-ranging interview conducted in February at the Kleiner Perkins offices in the heart of Silicon Valley, Khosla shared his thoughts on the Internet's impact on business and the economy, the state of new venture creation and financing, the secrets of entrepreneurial success, and the way Kleiner Perkins capitalizes on new business ideas. He also offered some cautionary words to established companies looking to shift their businesses onto the Internet.

Have the keys to success for entrepreneurs changed much since you started Sun 20 years ago?

Yes and no. It has always taken a certain combination of fearlessness and naiveté to be a successful entrepreneur, and that hasn't changed. A few years back, when I was learning how to hang glide, I watched an instructional movie that ended with a dedication like this: "To those who dare to dream the dreams, and then are foolish enough to try to make those dreams come true." That's a perfect description of an entrepreneur. You have to have the big idea, but you also have to be foolish enough to believe you can pull it off. When we started Sun, if we had had any idea how hard it is to build a computer company, we never would have tried. We were in our twenties, and we had no clue about the challenges we were facing. We just plowed ahead. Each obstacle became something new to conquer. All entrepreneurs are like that, I think.

What has changed, though, is the landscape in which entrepreneurs operate. Everything moves much faster now, which means there's a lot less room for error. In the early 1980s, it didn't matter to IBM what we were doing at Sun—we were just a sneaky little start-up. Even when our revenues had reached $100 million, we were nothing next to IBM's billions, and they couldn't be bothered to pay attention to us. Back then, you had miles of runway before you showed up on the radar screens of large companies. That's not the case today. Amazon may have flown under Barnes & Noble's radar, but even Amazon had a much shorter free ride than we did at Sun. Now you have almost no time before you're under attack. Every corporation in America has its eyes focused squarely on start-ups. Webvan was in Safeway's sights as soon as it launched.

The notion that entrepreneurs have to spend a lot of time creating business plans has always seemed silly to me, but now in most cases it's completely absurd. In the past, you might have been able to write a business plan that could last a year or two before you had to change it. Now you have to change course all the time—you have to adapt, not plan. The best you can do, I think, is have a sense of direction—an intuition about where the big opportunities are. Sure, I want to know that the management team and the entrepreneurs are capable of coming up with a strategy—but I now view that process as a discovery process, a way to hone ideas, rather than as a planning process.

The last few years have been a great time to be an entrepreneur. The Internet has created seemingly unlimited opportunities for new businesses. How long can it go on?

We're just a few minutes past the big bang. We've probably got ten more years of strong economic growth ahead of us, powered in large part by the expansion of communications bandwidth and the economic transformation enabled by the Internet. The first growth wave of the new economy was set off by the dramatic reduction in the cost of computing power. A lot of us at Kleiner Perkins believe we're now going to see the same thing in bandwidth: as optics and other new networking technologies roll out, bandwidth will become so plentiful that it will be essentially free. That will accelerate the shift of commerce, particularly business-to-business commerce, onto the Internet, and it will open up even greater opportunities for entrepreneurs. Just as oil fueled the old industrial economy, bandwidth will fuel the new knowledge economy. (See "The Next B2B Boom.")

The Next B2B Boom

Business-to-business commerce has been an area of tremendous entrepreneurial activity over the past year. According to Vinod Khosla, remote services may be one of the next hot opportunities. Here are his remarks on the topic.

Pretty much everyone now acknowledges that business is being completely reinvented. Because transaction costs are much lower on the Internet than in traditional channels, companies are rapidly shifting their business functions and supplier relationships onto the Web. United Technologies, for example, is saving up to 40% on supplies by purchasing them through Web auctions hosted by FreeMarkets. Using the Internet saves Cisco more than $700 million annually in customer support—it has 80% fewer customer support employees per billion dollars of revenue than competitors like Lucent and Nortel.

But the Internet doesn't just make traditional transactions more efficient, it changes the very nature of the buy-or-make decision. It lets companies outsource many functions that they once had to handle themselves. I'll give you an example. I was scheduled to make an early-morning presentation recently, and I didn't have time to even think about it until the afternoon before. I patched a bunch of slides together from older presentations, but it was a jumble of different formats and fonts. I needed to have it professionally designed, and it had to be done that night. I posted the job at a site run by eLance.com, a company Kleiner Perkins has invested in, and in a half hour I had bids from ten freelancers. I picked one who offered a good price and showed an impressive portfolio, and in a couple of hours I had a first draft. I made some changes and shot it back, and by midnight I had the final copy. I have no idea who did the work—it was probably someone on the other side of the world.

There is no reason to suppose that in the future, customer support, bill processing, accounting, or any of the traditional functions of corporations will need to be done within a particular corporation or geographical area. Even critical functions like engineering design, architectural design, and manufacturing are being virtualized. They will be offered as remote services, and you will be able to purchase them when needed, just as you would buy a drink or place a phone call. Thanks to the Internet, it will be possible to perform all these services in the most efficient place, be it Fargo, North Dakota, or New Delhi, India. The remote-service marketplace will be worth trillions of dollars and, more important, it will be truly global.

As we get more and cheaper bandwidth, we'll see a proliferation of such remote services, and they will fundamentally change the way we work.

To put it in perspective, compare the Internet industry to the personal computer industry. In its first ten years, the PC industry created $100 billion of new wealth in new companies—that's not counting the wealth created in established companies like IBM and Hewlett-Packard. The Internet crossed the $100 billion mark in just four years. Ultimately, I'd say we'll see four or five trillion dollars of new wealth created or reassigned. That's an incredible amount of money, and much of it will end up in the hands of companies that didn't even exist just a couple of years ago.

A lot of people look at the traditional measures for the economy and start scratching their heads about this long period of growth we're enjoying. That's because the traditional measures are industrial measures; they miss what's really going on. The old econometric models take into account the cost of oil, but they totally ignore the cost of bandwidth. The old yardsticks don't make sense anymore because what's going on today is a fundamental change in the structure of our economy. It's a repeat of the last major economic upheaval, when manufacturing displaced agriculture. A hundred years back, agriculture accounted for more than half of all jobs in the United States. Today, it accounts for only about 3%. Twenty years ago, manufacturing was the biggest employer—accounting for half of all jobs. In 30 years, manufacturing will probably account for less than 10%. The knowledge economy will be the new employer.

To create the kind of new wealth you're talking about, we're going to have to see massive investments in information technology. Where's the money going to come from?

It's going to come out of corporate budgets. Companies invest wherever they're going to get the biggest returns, and right now that's IT.

Exbibit 4-1   The Explosion in Technology Spending

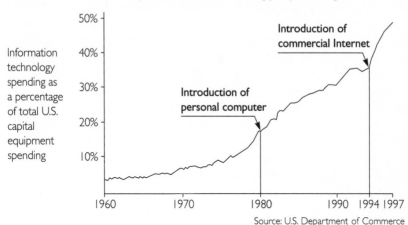

Information technology spending as a percentage of total U.S. capital equipment spending

Introduction of commercial Internet

Introduction of personal computer

Source: U.S. Department of Commerce

Look at the trend in capital expenditures. Twenty years ago, information technology accounted for about 10% of capital expenditures in the United States. Today, it's 45%, and it's still going up. The payback time on Internet investments is measured in months, which is far, far shorter than the two to five years that have been the historic norm. As long as you have such quick paybacks, you're going to see more and more money pour into IT. And remember, much of the rest of the world hasn't even begun to make those investments. There'll be plenty of money. (See Exhibit 4-1 "The Explosion in Technology Spending.")

The rush to capitalize on Internet opportunities has set off a flood of venture financing. According to one study, more than $14 billion in venture capital was invested in the fourth quarter of 1999—a fourfold increase over the year before. Do you have any concern that there's too much money out there?

A bit. What's positive about it is that every conceivable economic experiment is being tried. All that cash is driving enormous innovation everywhere in business, and that's one of the fundamental strengths of the U.S. economy right now. About 40% of our GDP growth is coming out of the tech sector, and most of that can be traced to the vibrancy of entrepreneurial initiatives. If you take tech growth out of the equation, the U.S. economy looks a lot like the European economy and not much better than the Japanese.

That's the good news. The dark side is that we're very much in a greed cycle. As we make this transition to a new economy, we're going to alternate between greed and fear, and greed holds sway right now. On a macro level, we can see the greed in the stock market. Over the long run, people who invest in the tech sector will earn great returns because the winners will be big winners. But at the moment I'd say about 90% of the public companies in the sector are overvalued. We'll see a great deal of volatility in stock valuations for some time. The danger is that when the price corrections happen, we'll overreact on the fear side. Investment will dry up and the pace of experimentation will severely slow, putting the health of the overall economy at risk.

What concerns me even more, though, is the effect of the current greed cycle on entrepreneurs and their infant businesses. Today, if you have a plan for a new business, you circulate it in the venture community and you get funded in a week. What you don't get is an honest, painstaking critique. What are the downsides in your plan? What are the shortcomings? What are the weak links? The strengths of your idea get a lot of attention, but the weaknesses get ignored—and ultimately it's the weaknesses of your plan that will kill you. A start-up is only as strong as its weakest link.

So I think the venture community is doing a disservice to entrepreneurs by funding them without forcing them to undergo a tough, critical examination. In the long run, it cripples new businesses. Take the issue of talent, which is the most critical issue any start-up faces. Usually an entrepreneurial team has only one real skill set—they're great technologists or they're great marketers. When the venture process works well, the VCs help the entrepreneurs build the complete team. Without the full team, you can have early success—you can start having strong traffic growth on your site, you can get to $50 million in revenue, you can have a hot IPO—but after that, things start to break down. The lack of managerial skills, for instance, starts to foreclose further growth—and you can't add those skills later because the top talent isn't going to want to join your company once it's gone public. As a result, great ideas never reach their full potential.

Frankly, the velocity of money is so high now, it's getting ugly. Too many people have too mercenary an attitude. When companies like

Intel and Oracle and Apple and Sun got started, it wasn't about money. It was about passion, vision, and a desire to create something new that would have a lasting impact on people and the economy. The financial rewards flowed from that bigger vision. There are still entrepreneurs who are driven by passion, but I fear that many of them—and many of their backers—are more focused on the deal, on the big payoff. It's distasteful to see this sort of money grab.

The lure of riches is pulling many new players into the venture arena. We're seeing management consulting firms setting up incubators for start-ups and big companies launching internal VC efforts. Are those kinds of efforts helping or hurting entrepreneurs?

At their core, a lot of them aren't even about the entrepreneurs. The McKinseys, the Bains, and the BCGs of the world have a big problem right now: they're losing their best people, especially the people who are really action-oriented, to start-ups. So a lot of these incubator initiatives are employee retention programs more than anything else. They're a way to give employees a taste of—and hopefully some of the economic rewards of—a start-up within the safety of an established firm. It's a way to provide equity compensation in an economy that, in technology at least, is more and more an equity economy, not a cash-compensation economy.

The problem is, most of the organizations rushing in to help entrepreneurs aren't qualified to do so. Just because you raise venture capital doesn't make you a venture capitalist. Just because you call yourself an incubator doesn't mean you have the skills to bring a business idea to fruition. Entrepreneurs need to ask themselves: Have these people ever really helped build a small company into something big? Have they dealt with our area of technology at a level detailed enough to provide valuable assistance? It's not enough to have just one piece of expertise—a strategy piece or a systems integration piece or whatever. You need to see the big picture as well as all the little pieces, and that kind of ability only comes out of direct experience. Unless you have built a company yourself, you're not qualified to advise entrepreneurs.

As for big companies incubating start-ups, that's very hard to do. It has been done—companies like Charles Schwab have done a wonderful job—but by and large it fails. Again, it's a matter of talent. Big, established companies neither attract nor nurture the kind of people who know how to create new businesses. These companies have little or no experience with entrepreneurship.

That's not to say that new forms of venture assistance aren't needed. As the amount of investment pouring into the venture arena has increased, many traditional VC firms have had to shift their focus to bigger deals, and that's created a need for new players to advise early-stage start-ups. But if I were an entrepreneur looking for such advice, I don't think I'd go to an institution that has no experience creating new businesses. I'd probably turn to angel investors who have succeeded as entrepreneurs—people like Jim Barksdale and Tom Jermoluk.

Given the current "velocity of money," it must be tempting to rush through the development process. How do you give ideas the critical attention they need, and how do you get entrepreneurs to focus on building companies that will endure?

We're blessed with a pretty good brand, and that encourages people to come work with us, especially second-time entrepreneurs who know they need a lot of things besides money. We also do far fewer investments per partner than most other firms, so we can be more selective and spend more time with each of the companies we back. And we try to stay focused on the long term. In evaluating each other, we look back ten years and say, "How have your investments done?" That's the metric we've always used—you're judged according to how well your companies have performed over the long haul. The assumption is that you can never sell a stock once you've bought it.

We also genuinely challenge the entrepreneurs who come to us. The most common failing in entrepreneurs is that they underestimate the scale they should aim for. Getting to $1 million in revenues seems such a big challenge to them that it blinds them to all else. As a result, they may miss out on opportunities that will get them to $1 billion in revenues. I'll give you an example. I'm on the board of a start-up called FireDrop, which just launched its product—an e-mail-based communication platform called Zaplets. FireDrop started last September with just two people. Now it has about 60 employees. The founders had no idea how high to aim—they were talking in terms of 10,000 page views a day. But I told them, "It's not material until you get to a hundred million." I try to get people to think in terms of miles, not inches.

Our other focus is on getting the right mix of people. A company's gene pool gets established early and determines the company's direction and performance for years to come. So we try to make sure from the start that the people in the company have a wide range of skills, operational biases, and strategic beliefs. The companies that can manage conflicts between different points of view are the ones that will break new ground.

In the final analysis, though, our single biggest advantage may be the fact that we've screwed up in more ways than anybody else on the planet when it comes to bringing new technologies to market. That's a big institutional asset. Our hope is that we're smart enough not to repeat the old mistakes, just make new ones. There's no shortcut to good judgment—you can only earn it the hard way.

Kleiner Perkins is known for its pioneering investments in companies exploiting the biggest new technologies, from the Internet to fiber optic networks. What's your secret?

The first challenge, of course, is to uncover the new ideas, and to do that, you have to do a lot of digging. I spend a lot of time visiting new companies, for example, and in the course of those visits I'll often hear about an interesting new technology. Then I'll start talking to experts in the technology, and I'll go to the right conferences and do some background reading. I'll discuss the opportunities with some of the other partners here, and if the basic economics look attractive enough —if there's a large potential market—the firm will launch a formal initiative.

That's what we did in 1994 with the Internet. We laid the groundwork by following the bulletin boards and early chat rooms, because back then those were the only places to really learn about the Internet. That turned into a formal initiative, which led to a series of investments and ultimately to the launches of Amazon, Netscape, and Excite—all at roughly the same time. More recently, we've gone through a similar process with optical networking.

We're also very, very fortunate in that we have the best and brightest minds coming to us. Every single day, people walk into our offices and educate us in a new area—the technology, the market, the economics. It's through discussions with these people that we start to develop our own ideas. Then we go back to the same people and they critique our thinking from many different points of view. It was people like Dave Huber at Corvis, Jim Foster at Cisco, and Pradeep Sindhu at Juniper who helped me develop my thinking on optics, for example. Foster originally got me thinking about how much a big leap in bandwidth would change the way we build networks and the components we use to build them, and that led to a lot of ideas about big business opportunities. To be honest, I feel decidedly dumb next to those people—I think of them as my teachers.

When you look back at all the companies you've had a hand in launching, which one would you point to as the best example of a venture-building process?

It's hard to point to just one. The smoothest, best-executed deal was probably Juniper Networks, which we helped develop from day one. Pradeep Sindhu, Juniper's founder, had come up with a technological breakthrough in the way enterprise routers work. But he had never worked in the router business, and he didn't recognize the full commercial possibilities of his ideas. He didn't see that enterprise routers could also serve as Internet routers. So the first thing we did was help him define the market for Internet routers. Then we gave him a crash course in building a business. I had him take an office for three weeks next to Milo Medin, who was then at @Home. As Milo's shadow, he absorbed what it meant to run a public Internet-protocol network—what the big issues and problems were. It was a fast way to bring him up the learning curve.

When he got back, we started having weekly staff meetings, just Pradeep and I. The first thing we focused on was getting the right set of people for the company—the right gene pool. We started out on the technical end. Pradeep had helped architect the Ultrasparc processor at Sun, so he had strong skills in building technical architectures and could apply those skills to routers. But he needed somebody with experience in building and operating an IP network, and he needed somebody who'd done operating systems software for routers and somebody who'd done protocols for routers. So we drew out a map that said, "Here are the ten different areas of expertise we need." Then we made a list of the companies doing the best work in each area, and we listed the five people in each company who would make good targets. We went after those people, and piece by piece we assembled a multidisciplinary team that could make Juniper a leader.

On top of the technical layer, we put together a management layer, recruiting Scott Kriens, who'd founded StrataCom, as the CEO. We needed the technical layer in place first, because without it we couldn't have attracted the top management talent. At that point, the company was off and running, and I basically just got out of the way. There wasn't much else I needed to do. So from my point of view, it was the most bang for the least buck—the buck being my time. It was the perfect incubation. Our starting investment was $200,000, and now the company's worth many billions.

Juniper is an example of a process where from the start, everything goes right. But the real test in venture capital is what you do when things go wrong. I'm equally proud of my work with a company like the chip maker NexGen, which endured a lot of hardships as it grew. NexGen had very good technology, but it was competing against the Intel monopoly, and in the early 1990s it just ran out of cash. Even though we were originally a small investor, our firm was the only one to help when things got tough. We helped shuffle management and recruit a broader engineering team, including a new VP for engineering. We helped redefine the company's strategy and got additional financing in place. Most important, we mentored the management team on dealing with day-to-day issues.

The effort was intense, but it has paid huge dividends. In 1996, AMD bought NexGen for almost $1 billion. More important than the money, though, is the fact that the NexGen chips—the AMD-K6 and, more recently, the Athlon—became the first true challenge to Intel. NexGen broke Intel's monopoly and made an important economic contribution. From a personal standpoint, working with struggling companies like NexGen is rewarding precisely because it entails such a difficult journey.

Let's shift from start-ups to incumbents. Why has it been so hard for many established companies to adapt to the Internet?

There are a number of reasons. One of the most important is that their top executives still tend to think of technology as a tool. Back when I was in business school, we were taught that first you develop your strategy and then you pick your tools—and technology was just one among many. But now technology is a driver of business strategy.

The answers to questions like "What business model makes sense?" and "What strategy makes sense?" are now a function of your assumptions about where technology is headed. And inside your company, your technology architecture determines how you procure supplies, how you provide customer support, how you configure your products, how you manage your sales channel—everything. It's naive to think of a Web site as an "Internet strategy." The Internet is causing a complete overhaul of all aspects of business. It means new business models and new sources of competitive advantage. It demands new assets and different strategies.

An obvious consequence is that the CIO has suddenly become the second most important executive in a company. For a long time, the number two strategic person tended to be the top marketing executive; now it's the technologist. A visionary CIO—not the old model of the CIO—is the key to a company's success. Some big companies understand that—I'm thinking of Cisco, Schwab, Wells Fargo, Federal Express, Wal-Mart—but most don't.

As the speed of business picks up, we're seeing other basic assumptions about strategy being overturned as well. Think about the concept of scale, for instance. It used to be that the bigger you got, the lower your costs were and the better you did. Economies of scale were everything. Of course, being big also meant you were less able to adapt to change, but that didn't matter much because the rate of change was fairly low. You could get McKinsey to give you a new strategy every five years. Being big and slow was better than being small and nimble. That's turning around. The rate of change has become so high that the drawbacks of scale are outweighing the benefits. We're seeing diseconomies of scale.

A similar thing is happening with business processes. It used to be that the best companies had well-documented, state-of-the-art processes that all their employees knew and followed. Everything they did was carefully planned. But now, with decision-making time shrinking rapidly, the slowness of highly planned processes is a big disadvantage. I'll give you an example from the late 1980s. IBM had a great product-planning process, and they applied it to the first few laptops they developed. Following the process, they methodically researched every element of those machines. The laptops were beautifully designed. Unfortunately, they never got to market. By the time IBM finished the development process, the products were out-of-date. We're seeing this problem all over the place today: great processes that are completely unsuited to the new pace of business.

Yesterday, you optimized your business for cost and performance. Today, you have to optimize for flexibility and adaptability. Change is continuous now; it's not a discrete event anymore.

That's a pretty scary thought if you're a big company that has spent all its time building up scale advantages and optimizing its processes.

It's a very scary thought if you're unwilling or unable to change. Large traditional companies are unsuited to the new environment for a host of reasons. First, they tend to be risk-averse, which is a big liability. There's so much experimentation going on right now that avoiding risk is the biggest risk you can take. If you're not experimenting, you can be sure you'll be shut out.

Second, they're too hierarchical in the way they communicate. Information moves slowly, and they just don't have the free flow of ideas that you need to succeed. Some hierarchy is necessary in decision making, but it should not extend to the flow of information.

Third, they don't have the right talent. When you can no longer depend on process and planning, instinct becomes very important. But big companies have never rewarded people for making gut calls, so over time they've bred the instinct out of their organizations. And it's very hard to teach instinct. Process can be taught—anybody can learn to follow a process—but to get good instinct you really have to bring in new people, create a new gene pool. One CEO recently said to me, "I hope 30% of my senior managers are not here at this time next year." That's a harsh thought, but it's a necessary thought. This isn't "be nice" time—it's shake-up time. If you don't make the hard decisions now, the best talent will continue to flow to start-ups.

In the end, though, it's not the big things that are going to kill you, it's the accumulation of little things. Most companies always do the top three or four critical things right. They start a Web site, they do the stuff that Bain and BCG tell them to. The problem is, everybody gets those things right. It's the microdecisions—the thousands of little decisions that a company makes every day—that are hard to get right. What ad agency do you pick? Which engineer do you hire? The little things separate the dot-coms from the incumbents. A new company has no baggage. It can rethink everything from scratch and tune every decision to the new realities of communications and computing. But in a big company, the whole infrastructure and culture acts like gravity, pulling you back to where you started from. You can never reach escape velocity.

When I have some young entrepreneurs stepping up to bat against Wal-Mart or Ford or AT&T, I tell them, "Guys, you're gonna go up to the plate with two strikes against you. There are a lot of things you don't have—like brand, like distribution, like scale, like staying power. So you can't make too many mistakes. But you've got one huge advantage: your competition has minor-league pitchers." It's not that the big guys' assets aren't valuable. They are. If they could apply the instincts of an entrepreneur to those assets, the big guys would be unbeatable. But that almost never happens because big companies, whatever they might say, aren't open to change.

5

Transforming Life, Transforming Business: The Life-Science Revolution

Juan Enriquez and Ray A. Goldberg

A Note from the Editors at the *Harvard Business Review*

The speed with which the Internet transformed business during the last decade took many people by surprise. In this decade, the first of the twenty-first century, we may see an equally dramatic transformation, driven not by computers and communications but by genetic engineering.

To date, the news on genetic engineering has been dominated by the controversy surrounding genetically modified foods. Much less attention has been given to the even more profound changes that lie ahead—for people, for society, and, not least, for business. In this important article, Juan Enriquez and Ray A. Goldberg describe how the ability to manipulate the genetic codes of living things will set off an unprecedented industrial convergence: farmers, doctors, drugmakers, chemical processors, computer and communications companies, energy companies, and many other commercial enterprises will be drawn into the business of life science.

This transformation promises to be every bit as wrenching as the one set off by the Internet. The challenges are as great as the opportunities. We hope this article alerts people to the far-reaching implications of genetic engineering for business and starts a broad and much-needed discussion of the many issues that will need to be resolved as the pace of scientific advance quickens.

In 1990, the U.S. government launched the largest and most ambitious biology project ever conceived: the mapping of the human genome. Led by the Department of Energy and the National Institutes of Health, the project had a budget of $2 billion and soon came to involve more than 350 laboratories around the world. The goal was to complete the map by 2005.

Progress came slowly, however. At its halfway point in 1997, the initiative had gone through 90% of its money but had accurately sequenced only 2.68% of the genome. Then, in May 1998, one of the project's leading scientists, Craig Venter, dropped a bombshell. Believing the mapping could be done much more quickly and efficiently, Venter announced that he was partnering with the Perkin-Elmer Corporation to establish a company, Celera Genomics, that would map the genome by the year 2000—with no public funds whatsoever. A *New York Times Magazine* cover story summed up the audacity of Venter's plan: "It was as if private industry had announced it would land a man on the moon before NASA could get there. As if an upstart company intended to build the first atom bomb."

By shifting the mapping of the human genome from the world of science to the world of commerce, Venter underscored a fact that should reverberate with everyone involved in business today: advances in genetic engineering will not only have dramatic implications for people and society, they will reshape vast sectors of the world economy. The boundaries between many once-distinct businesses, from agribusiness and chemicals to health care and pharmaceuticals to energy and computing, will blur, and out of their convergence will emerge what promises to be the largest industry in the world: the life-science industry.

A number of companies, from global giants like Monsanto and DuPont to start-ups like Geron and Advanced Cell Technology, have already bet their futures on life science. They realize that unlocking life's code opens up virtually unlimited commercial possibilities. But they are also finding that operating within this new industry presents a raft of wrenchingly difficult challenges. They must rethink their business, financial, and M&A strategies, often from scratch. They must make vast R&D investments with distant and uncertain payoffs. They must enter into complex partnerships and affiliations, sometimes with direct competitors. And perhaps most difficult of all, they must contend with a public that is uncomfortable with even the thought of genetic engineering, much less its practice.

As scientific advances accelerate, more and more companies will be drawn, by choice or by necessity, into the life-science business. They, too, will confront challenges unlike any they've faced before. And the way they meet those challenges will not just determine their commercial success; it will also have a direct influence over the future of life on our planet.

Accelerating Breakthroughs

Man's effort to transform life is hardly new. For centuries, farmers have been selectively breeding plants and animals to increase their yield of food and their resistance to disease. But it wasn't until the mid-1800s, when the Austrian botanist Gregor Mendel began his studies of heredity, that breeding was transformed from a craft into a science. By the early twentieth century, the laws governing heredity were well understood. The underlying mechanism remained obscure, however, until the 1950s, when James Watson and Francis Crick discovered the molecular structure of DNA.

Watson and Crick's breakthrough opened the door to genetic engineering. But the early efforts to decipher DNA sequences were frustrated by the sheer complexity of the challenge. Through the 1980s, researchers struggled to map the codes of individual genes—never mind the entire genome. Over the past decade, however, the pace of discovery has accelerated dramatically. A series of technological advances in disciplines as varied as spectroscopy, robotics, and computing has given scientists a powerful new set of tools for discovering, mapping, and modifying genetic information. In 1995, the first full genome of a living organism, the bacterium that causes meningitis, was sequenced, and a dozen other gene maps soon followed. In 2000, if the current schedule holds, we will see the completion of the first map of the entire human genome. (See "Mapping a Genome.")

Mapping a Genome

The code of all life forms is written in deoxyribonucleic acid, or DNA. DNA takes the form of a double helix that resembles a long spiral staircase. The rungs linking the two sides of the staircase are composed of pairs of nucleotides—either adenine and thymine or cytosine and guanine. These base pairs contain the instructions for the various biological processes required for an organism to live and reproduce. The complete set of instructions for an organism is known as its genome.

Because the human genome contains more than 3 billion base pairs, mapping it is extraordinarily difficult. Today researchers are using two different methods to complete the map. The publicly funded project overseen by the National Institutes of Health is carefully dividing DNA into segments, which are then cloned and distributed to hundreds of labs for sequencing. The results are deposited in a public database and then gradually integrated until the whole genome is revealed. It is akin to having several teams laying bricks until various walls come together in a coherent structure.

The private company Celera Genomics, by contrast, is trying to complete the whole sequencing process within a single lab. It uses powerful computers to identify overlaps in the base pairs of DNA segments. In a sense, it is like using a computer to assemble a 70-million-piece 3-D jigsaw puzzle.

As our knowledge of the science of life has progressed, the commercial possibilities have multiplied, attracting a large and increasingly varied set of companies. To understand just how broad life science's business impact promises to be, it's useful to draw an analogy to information technology. The development of binary computer code enabled all kinds of information, from text to sound to video, to be communicated digitally. Previously disparate industries such as publishing, television, movies, radio, telecommunications, and computing suddenly found themselves using a common language—the language of zeros and ones. And once you share a common language, they soon found, you often share a common business. In the last few years, we've seen all these industries rapidly converge as digital communications have become ubiquitous.

A similar dynamic will play out in life science. Genetic code, after all, is a type of language. Rather than zeros and ones, it is made up of four letters—A, T, C, and G—which represent the four nucleotides that form DNA: adenine, thymine, cytosine, and guanine. Just as alterations in computer code change the shape of information, alterations in genetic code change the shape of life. All industries that deal with living things or with organic compounds will thus have a common language and, in turn, a common business. They will converge. Moreover, since genetic code is itself a form of information and thus subject to digital manipulation, computer and other information technology companies will also play central roles in the life-science industry.

The Great Convergence

To see how advances in genetics erase the boundaries between industries, you need only look at what's happened to the agricultural seed business over the past decade. Seeds have gone from little-noticed commodities to hot products, and the valuations of companies that distribute them have multiplied as agricultural, chemical, and pharmaceutical conglomerates have vied to acquire them. Pioneer Hi-Bred, a large seed company based in Iowa, had a market value of $544 million and a price/earnings ratio of 9.5 in 1980. In 1997, DuPont bought 20% of the company for $1.7 billion, giving it a market value of $7.05 billion and a P/E ratio of 23.8. In 1999, DuPont acquired the remaining 80% of Pioneer for $7.7 billion, making its market value close to $10 billion and its P/E ratio 31.5.

Why did seeds suddenly become so valuable? Because seeds are the best means for selling genetically engineered plants to farmers. A company can modify a plant's genetic makeup, breed the new plant, encapsulate the genetic information in seeds, and then distribute huge volumes of those seeds to farms. Control over the seeds, moreover, provides control over the intellectual capital they contain, which is essential to recouping the enormous investments required for genetic engineering.

Of course, genetically modified seeds were of immediate interest to agricultural conglomerates. Newly designed crops promised to be easier to grow, process, and ship. The seeds were also of keen interest to chemical companies, which saw them as direct threats to their pesticide and herbicide businesses. By planting crops engineered to be resistant to common pests, farmers would be able to reduce their dependence on costly chemicals and mitigate the damage their farming does to the environment. Many large chemical companies read the writing on the wall and dove into the seed business as part of a more general shift toward biotechnology. In one of the most remarkable business transformations in history, Monsanto spun off its commodity chemical businesses into a new company, Solutia, in September 1997 and invested $8 billion in various biotech and seed companies. DuPont acquired interests in Pioneer and other seed companies and announced that life science would be its focus for the twenty-first century. Dow Chemical invested in seed and other agribusiness companies through its Agro-Sciences unit.

Pharmaceutical companies like Novartis, Zeneca, and Schering-Plough also joined in the bidding war for seed companies. They, too, saw genetically engineered seeds as a threat to their traditional business. Just as crops can be designed to have higher nutritional value, they can also be designed to have higher medicinal value. Broccoli, for instance, is known to switch on the body's defenses against cancer. Some agribusiness labs are trying to take the characteristics of a wild Italian broccoli, which appears to be 100 times more effective in building up cancer defenses, and engineer them into commercial varieties. Other companies are trying to create bioengineered corn that will target and poison cancer cells, fight osteoporosis, and reduce heart disease. Still others are reprogramming the genes of some fruits and vegetables to turn them into vaccines against diarrhea, tetanus, diphtheria, hepatitis B, and cholera. To be vaccinated in the future, you may not need to get a shot. You may just have to eat an apple.

As distinctions between food and medicine fade, we will see a proliferation of crop-based drugs, or "agriceuticals." The blurring of agriculture and pharmaceuticals is not limited to seeds and plants, either. Animals are also being turned into drug-manufacturing facilities. Genzyme Transgenics has engineered goats to give milk containing antibodies that can serve as human medicines. Drug companies like BASF and Bristol-Myers Squibb and leading cancer specialists like Dr. Judah Folkman are working with Genzyme to have the goats produce large volumes of proteins for cancer treatment. A single herd of goats may soon replace a $150 million drug factory. Several companies are even trying to produce antigens in mosquitoes' saliva, turning the insects into living vaccines for various diseases. Someday people may go out of their way to have mosquitoes bite them.

There's another reason that pharmaceutical companies are encroaching on the turf of their chemical and agricultural counterparts. They realize that more and more discoveries with important implications for human health will come out of agricultural and chemical research labs. As organisms evolve, they usually retain many of their old genes, which means most life forms share similar genetic structures. Almost every mouse gene, for example, has a counterpart within the human genome, and humans and chimpanzees share almost 99% of all the genes known to influence their biological processes. As a result of the consistency in genetic makeup, breakthroughs in the genetic treatment of diseases for animals often hold the keys to treating human diseases. If you can cure a type of cancer in a mouse, you can sometimes use similar therapies to treat related cancers in humans. The big drug companies have no choice but to play in this game.

Ripple Effects

The convergence of the agricultural, chemical, and pharmaceutical industries is only the beginning. As our knowledge of genetic code and how to manipulate it grows, ripple effects will be felt across many industries. (See Table 5-1 "Diving into the Gene Pool.") Take health care, for example. The ability to understand what diseases individuals might be predisposed to, how they might react to specific medicines, and what they might do to prevent future illness will change the practice of medicine. Already, companies like Affymetrix are building silicon chips embedded with hybrid bits of DNA that can test for 6,000 genetic conditions in any given individual. Chips the size of quarters will soon be able to test for as many as 400,000 conditions, and once the human genome is available, they may be able to screen for almost all known genetic diseases and defects. Such powerful diagnostic tools will lead to highly personalized medical treatments and, at the same time, they will refocus much of medical practice on prevention rather than intervention. William Haseltine, the CEO of Human Genome Sciences, a leading pharmaceutical company, believes that we will see a huge shift in the ratio of doctor bills to pharmaceutical costs. The current ratio is approximately 9 to 1. He predicts that it could become 1 to 1 in the next 25 years.

Table 5-1   Diving into the Gene Pool

The life-science industry, which already encompasses some of the world's largest businesses, will expand to involve many more types of companies.

Already involved	Becoming involved	Soon to be involved
chemicals	environmental	robotics
pharmaceuticals	mining	household appliances
agriculture	energy	Internet communications
food processing	cosmetics	information services
mutual funds	supermarkets	media
law firms	pharmacies	
	military	
	computer hardware and software	

Delivery vehicles for medicines will also proliferate. Everyday products like soaps, cosmetics, foods, and beverages may dispense daily preventative medical prescriptions. It would not be surprising to see consumer goods companies like Procter & Gamble and cosmetics companies like L'Oréal building alliances or merging with genomics, agribusiness, and pharmaceutical firms. New distribution channels are also likely to emerge. In addition to being distributed through traditional dispensaries like HMOs and pharmacies, genetically engineered products could be delivered through outlets like supermarkets and even health clubs.

Because genetic research involves the processing of vast amounts of data, computer hardware and software companies are increasingly being drawn into the life-science sector as well. Indeed, the focus of medical research, which during the past century shifted from the in vivo study of live organisms to in vitro experiments inside labs, is now shifting toward "in silico" research using computer databases. Compaq has already built one of the world's most powerful computers to help Celera sequence the human genome. IBM has launched DiscoveryLink, an attempt to unify pharmaceutical, biotechnology, and agriscience databases, and it recently announced the start of a five-year, $100 million effort to build a new supercomputer, dubbed "Blue Gene," that will be used for genetic research. In addition to the big computer companies, a slew of high-tech start-ups like Pangea, Gene Logic, Sequana, Incyte, and Compugen are pioneering "bioinformatics"—the use of software to facilitate drug discovery.[1]

Genetic breakthroughs will have applications beyond food, health, and medicine. Consider the energy business. It's long been possible to convert the energy stored in plants into ethanol—a substitute for gasoline—but energy prices have never been high enough to make the procedure cost-effective; it has therefore required huge government subsidies. However, if plant genomes were engineered in a way that enabled their starches to be transformed into alcohol at higher volumes, oil companies could produce economically attractive gasoline substitutes. The power for automobiles may in the future come from renewable plant sources, not from wells. Genetically modified plants could also be the source for complex petrochemical derivatives like man-made textiles. DuPont has already developed a bacterium that turns sugar into polyester; other plastics and artificial fibers are sure to follow. Even mining and environmental service companies are moving into life science. Radioactivity-resistant bacteria are now being used to clean up contaminated soils and mine low-grade uranium.

In the not-too-distant future, it seems clear that the language of genetic code will be shared by innumerable companies that once had little to do with one another. We will likely see an industrial convergence of even greater magnitude than the one set off by the development of digital computer code.

A Difficult Transition

The convergence will not be easy, however. The vast opportunities opened by life science are matched by the vast challenges involved in capitalizing on them. Many of the industry's early pioneers are struggling to create successful businesses. Monsanto is a case in point. Its highly publicized decision to abandon its traditional chemicals business and remake itself as a life-science company was met with great enthusiasm. Investors, seeing an initial upswing in the company's profitability and realizing that margins and market valuations in the pharmaceuticals sector are far higher than in chemicals or agriculture, bid up Monsanto's stock, pushing the company's P/E ratio from an average of 10 in 1990 to a whopping 114 in 1998.

But the global agricultural industry fell into a depression at the end of the decade. Monsanto's big investments in seed and other agribusiness concerns began to weigh on the company, and its profits eroded. In addition, as other agrichemical businesses began to consolidate, the company saw its once-leading share of the crop-protection market shrink to only 12%, putting it at a scale disadvantage. When Monsanto's proposed merger with American Home Products was called off in October 1998, it began running out of the cash required to fund its aggressive R&D programs. Under siege, the founder and leader of the life-science industry began to look for a friendly suitor. Last December, it announced it would merge with the drugmaker Pharmacia & Upjohn, and the two companies indicated they would sell off part of Monsanto's agrichemical business in a public offering.

Dow Chemical has faced similar frustrations. A relative latecomer to life sciences, it found itself having to play catch-up with DuPont and Monsanto. But that was no easy task. Many of the most attractive market niches were already occupied, and seed and pharmaceutical companies were carrying huge price tags. Instead of spending its cash trying to build a broad life-science capability, Dow ultimately decided to retrench. In August 1999, it bought Union Carbide, signaling its intention to focus on traditional chemicals.

If the challenges are great for chemical companies, they're even greater for drug companies. After all, when drug companies expand into agriculture they are moving into a business with lower profitability than their traditional business. The experience of Novartis, the Swiss drug giant, reveals the difficulties in such a move. When Novartis was formed in 1996 through the merger of Sandoz and Ciba, its then-chairman, Alex Krauer, announced his intention to maintain "a worldwide leadership position in life sciences." Having spun off its specialty-chemicals and construction-chemicals units, the company continued to bolster its life-science capabilities by investing in seed companies and other agribusiness assets. In 1998, the company had the world's largest crop-protection operation, the third largest seed business, and a major animal-health unit.

But agribusiness has very different business characteristics from pharmaceuticals. Not only are its margins lower, but it is far more cyclical. As demand for agricultural products softened in the late 1990s, Novartis suffered. In the first half of 1999, the sales of its agribusiness units dropped 10% from the previous year; their operating income fell 41%. At the same time, Europe's growing public backlash against genetically modified foods threatened to turn into a PR nightmare for the company. Its own baby-food division, Gerber, stopped using foods produced with Novartis's genetically modified seeds.

In December 1999, Novartis announced that it was getting out of agribusiness to focus its energies on health care. It would merge its agribusiness assets with those of AstraZeneca, another European drugmaker struggling with the transition to life sciences, and spin them off into a new company called Sygenta. "After a thorough review of its business portfolio strategy," Novartis stated in a press release, "the benefits of concentrating on the health care businesses outweigh the modest synergies between the health care and agribusiness activities."

The problems that Monsanto, Dow, Novartis, and other life-science pioneers face are daunting. But it would be a mistake to interpret them as a sign that an integrated life-science industry will never come into being. Rather, they are the inevitable birthing pains that accompany the formation of any large new industry. The optimal structure of the life-science industry—and of the companies that compose it—is as yet unknown. We are in a period of trial and error in which companies are experimenting with different operating and financial structures. The price of such experimentation is very high, particularly when many companies are bidding for the same assets, and missteps and failures will undoubtedly occur. Magnifying the challenge is the confusion felt by stock analysts and investors when they see industries with very different financial characteristics begin to meld. They have no rules of thumb for gauging the value of the new entities, and they lack patience with any experiments that weaken the bottom line. A whole new set of financial assumptions needs to be developed, and that, too, takes time.

Convergence and consolidation will happen, however. The massive costs involved in producing life-science products make it essential for companies to develop huge scale in their R&D efforts. The pharmaceutical industry has always spent heavily on research. To bring a single new drug to market, a company typically sifts through thousands of compounds, tests a few hundred, and carries out very expensive trials on as many as ten. The process can take more than a decade and cost half a billion dollars. But with gene-based drugs, the discovery process becomes even more complex and costly. Powerful computers can design millions of compounds that may warrant study, and it even becomes possible to customize treatments to individual patients. The life cycles of drugs will in some cases collapse from decades to months. The traditional drug pipeline, designed to enable companies to introduce one or two drugs a year, will need to be replaced by a much faster, much more flexible model. (See "Patenting Life.")

Patenting Life

The rush to commercialize genetic information has led to a flood of patents and patent applications. The U.S. Patent and Trademark Office awarded the first patent on a living organism to Ananda Chakrabarty and Scott Kellogg for research done in 1972. The award created considerable controversy and was challenged in court, leading to a landmark Supreme Court ruling in 1980 that upheld the patent on a five to four vote. In 1991, the Patent Office received 4,000 applications for genetic patents, and in 1996, the number hit an astonishing 500,000. Overwhelmed, the Patent Office put restrictions on applications in October of that year.

A single company, Human Genome Sciences, has already received patents on 106 complete human genes, including some that may be crucial to treating osteoporosis and arthritis, and it has patents pending on more than 7,500 genes. It is not only genes that are being patented; whole animals, like the Harvard mouse, are now under patent. Through March 1998, patents had been granted on 85 animals, and 90 more were under consideration.

The patent activity underscores the need for companies to act quickly—or face getting shut out of key areas of the life-science business. In particular, companies need to create networks of partnerships and affiliations that will give them access to, and some ownership of, the valuable intellectual capital currently being developed. These networks should cross old industry borders. With thousands of new compounds and procedures being discovered yearly, a company in one industry may uncover—and patent—a solution to a problem that a company in a very different industry has been working on for decades.

At the same time, the rush to patent genes raises profound ethical and social questions. Will scientific studies and breakthroughs continue to be shared with the broad scientific community? Will advances that could improve the quality of life for all people be restricted to only a few? Will poor nations be able to tap into the benefits of bioengineering? The agribusiness industry is already struggling with such questions. In the past, seed companies routinely shared new technologies with public and nonprofit institutions, ensuring that developing countries had access to new and improved crops. But given the high costs of developing genetically modified crops, it is now feared that the agribusiness and agrichemical conglomerates that dominate the seed business will be less willing to share their proprietary technologies. Indeed, last December, five U.S. farmers and one French farmer filed an antitrust lawsuit against Monsanto accusing the company of conspiring to control markets for corn and soybean seeds. Novartis, DuPont, and seven other companies were named as coconspirators. Although some of the largest farm organizations have criticized the suit, its existence underscores the level of mistrust that currently prevails.

While strong protections for intellectual property are essential for promoting continued investment, life-science companies cannot turn their backs on poor countries and poor consumers. For life science to be a sustainable, thriving industry over the long term, companies will need to share the benefits they create.

The required R&D expenditures are staggering. Even in the face of soft demand in many of its markets, Monsanto raised its R&D expenditures 35% during 1998 to more than $1.2 billion, while also spending more than $4 billion to acquire seed companies. DuPont, which spent less than 3% of its revenues on R&D in 1980, spent 11% in 1998. The ongoing merger discussions among Pfizer, Warner-Lambert, American Home Products, SmithKline Beecham, Glaxo, and other pharmaceutical giants are all spurred by the need to build R&D scale (as well as to gain efficiencies in marketing and distribution). One of the great challenges facing life-science companies is plotting an M&A strategy that provides the necessary R&D scale without leaving them financially crippled. And then, of course, they have to integrate the companies they purchase, which is always a complex and dangerous undertaking.

Even successful megamergers will not be sufficient. Companies will also need to partner with other players, large and small, to ensure they have access to the latest advances in science and data processing—and to spread the huge economic risks inherent in drug development. Drug companies will outsource approximately 20% of their R&D this year, up from only 4% in 1994—and that percentage promises to continue to rise. Managing ever more complex networks of alliances will pose another great test for the managers of life-science companies.

Managing the Public's Fear

While the financial, organizational, and operational challenges facing life-science companies are great, the biggest challenge of all may be the public's misgivings about genetic engineering. Ever since Dr. Frankenstein created his much-misunderstood monster, any attempt to modify life has been met with fear and often, outright panic. People's instinct when confronted with the possibility of genetic engineering is to concentrate not on the potential benefits—cures for diseases, healthier and longer lives, more nutritious foods, less pollution—but on the potential for accidents and abuse.

That instinct has been reinforced by the way the life-science business has evolved so far. To date, most of the products of genetic engineering have taken the form of genetically modified crops. Although many of them have made food production and distribution more efficient, they have not provided consumers with food that is significantly cheaper, safer, or tastier. Since the benefits are unclear, people naturally focus on the risks. When they hear about genetically modified sweet corn, they don't rush out to buy it. Instead, they worry whether they might suffer long-term health problems by eating it or whether its introduction might upset nature's balance. As the public's worries have grown, government agencies have launched efforts to examine how genetically modified products might be better regulated and labeled, and these efforts have made people even more wary. Once in motion, the cycle of fear becomes difficult to counter.

Public fears are particularly acute in Europe, where a series of food scares, ranging from mad cow disease to contaminated Coke, have undermined people's trust in regulatory authorities. While 90% of Americans believe the U.S. Department of Agriculture's statements on biotechnology, only 12% of Europeans trust their national regulators. Within the United Kingdom, the percentage of people who strongly oppose genetically modified foods reached nearly 40% in 1998, an 11% jump from two years earlier. Demonstrations against genetic engineering have become common in European capitals. Rather than trying to allay the public's fears, many European companies are playing to them. Nestlé, Carrefour, Danone, Marks & Spencer, and Unilever are all aggressively marketing products guaranteed to be free from genetic alterations.

Compared with Europeans, Americans have been fairly placid about genetic engineering. But, despite the wishful thinking of many industry executives, that tranquility may not last. As noted risk analyst Peter Sandman has pointed out, many of the factors that lead to widespread outrage are present in the battle over genetically modified products: high stakes, strong emotions, global impact, wide differences in opinion, and powerful antagonists, among others. In this environment, isolated events can easily snowball, as we saw on two occasions during 1999. Early in the year, a study indicating that pollen from genetically modified corn plants was killing the caterpillars of monarch butterflies received widespread media attention, raising the public's fears and leading to outcries for tougher regulation. And late in the year, the death of a young man undergoing experimental gene therapy—the first such death in thousands of trials—led many to demand that such treatments be scaled back or halted altogether.

Escalating public opposition poses the greatest single threat to the successful growth of the life-science business. Left unchecked, it will force companies to spend ever greater amounts of time and money calming the public and clearing regulatory hurdles. And it will undermine the demand for and the prices of genetically modified foods and even medicines. We are already seeing this dynamic play out in many commodity food markets. "All-natural" soybeans, for example, sell for a significant premium over soybeans that have had genetic modifications. If genetically altered products end up being sold at a discount, companies will have little incentive to make the big investments required to produce them. In a telling submission to the Securities and Exchange Commission late last year, Monsanto warned that the growing public backlash against genetic research could do substantial harm to its financial results.

Life-science companies themselves bear much of the blame for the current situation. All too often, they have either ignored or derided their critics, insisting that the technologies they are pioneering are perfectly safe and that concerns about them are baseless. They've done little to teach the public about genetic engineering and its benefits, and they haven't clearly explained the intensive testing regimens and safeguards built into the process of developing genetically modified organisms. The combination of silence and defensiveness has simply increased the general public's mistrust and inflamed the passions of opponents.

Fortunately, life-science companies are beginning to engage in public dialogue. Monsanto, DuPont, Pioneer Hi-Bred, and others are dedicating large portions of their Web sites to information on genetic research and its benefits, and their executives are speaking publicly about the issues. Some are even holding conversations with fierce adversaries. Last October, for example, Monsanto CEO Robert Shapiro discussed biotechnology at a Greenpeace conference in London. Such conversations can be painful—emotions run high on all sides—but they are necessary. Any company with an interest in life science that is not involved in educational and communication efforts is putting its future at risk.[2]

The Road Ahead

As the impact of genetic engineering shifts from the farm to the home, its attractions will become much more apparent to people. The benefits of fungus-resistant corn may seem remote to the average consumer, but the benefits of gene therapies that help children fight debilitating diseases like cystic fibrosis or of agriceuticals that increase life expectancy will be very real. Consumers' aversion to genetically modified products and genetic therapies will give way to a desire to purchase them, and lack of supply may become a far larger problem than lack of demand. A recent survey shows that more than 60% of Americans would like to be genetically profiled to identify their predisposition to diseases, and an equal number would be willing to pay more for genetically customized drugs. Eventually, the tide of public opinion seems certain to change, and the products of genetic engineering will sell at a premium.

But we're still far from that point. This year—the first of a new millennium—promises to be a watershed in the emergence of life science as an industry. The completion of the sequencing of the human genetic code will set the stage for dramatic advances in medicine while focusing the attention of the public on biotechnology as never before. Mergers, divestitures, and partnerships will continue to alter the structure of the young industry—and put millions, even billions, of dollars at risk. The actions that executives take now—both in shaping their businesses and in shaping public opinion—will go a long way toward determining the ultimate role their companies play in the world's largest and most important industry.

Notes

1. Monsanto's CEO put it well when he said in an HBR interview that "biotechnology is really a subset of information technology because it is about DNA-encoded information." See Joan Magretta, "Growth Through Global Sustainability: An Interview with Monsanto's CEO, Robert B. Shapiro" (*HBR* January—February 1997).
2. For a model of effective and forthright communication about life science, we recommend a speech given by DuPont CEO Chad Holliday before the Chief Executives Club of Boston on September 22, 1999. The text of the speech can be found at www.dupont.com/corp/whats-new/speeches/chad/biotech.html.

PART

II

Remaking Markets

6
Getting Real About Virtual Commerce

Philip Evans and Thomas S. Wurster

In its first generation, electronic commerce has been a landgrab. Retail space on the Internet was claimed by whoever got there first with enough resources to create a credible business. It took speed, a willingness to experiment, and a lot of cyber-savvy. Companies that had performed brilliantly in traditional settings seemed totally lost. Indeed, there isn't a major e-retail category in which a bricks-and-mortar retailer has leading market share. Even Wal-Mart, that master of information technology, has so far proven hopelessly flat-footed on the Web.

Achieving profits during this landgrab—or even being on a trajectory toward profits—was deemed unnecessary by cheering investors. The stock market has voted a higher valuation for Amazon.com than for the entire traditional book retailing and publishing industries combined, even though Amazon has yet to turn a profit. In private, some e-commerce entrepreneurs confess perplexity as to how they ever will make a profit. They have, of necessity, focused far more on growth. Strategy is subordinated to tactics, which are subordinated to experimentation. The Great White Hope is an acquirer: let somebody else solve the problem. Meanwhile, keep growing at 200% a year.

But that phase is ending: the obvious land has been grabbed, the traditional incumbents are getting serious, and the Internet stock bubble is losing some buoyancy. We are entering the second generation of electronic commerce. The key players—branded-goods suppliers, physical retailers, electronic retailers, and pure navigators—will shift their attention from claiming territory to defending or capturing it.

They will be forced to focus on competitive advantage and on strategies to achieve it. Virtual commerce has to get real.

Navigation as a Separate Business

In the familiar world of physical commerce, shoppers have it tough. If you want to buy a shirt, for instance, you have a million different choices and, to make comparisons among them, you have to hop in your car and drive to malls and downtown department stores. A broad search is time-consuming, difficult, and, inevitably, incomplete. Nobody does it. Instead, consumers rely on product suppliers and retailers to help them navigate among their choices. Those businesses, in turn, exploit the consumers' search costs to build competitive advantage. They create navigational tools—everything from branding and advertising to relationship building and merchandising—to help consumers short-circuit the complexities of a comprehensive search and find products they're willing to buy. Sellers, in other words, exercise some control over the navigation function because it is comparatively difficult and expensive for the consumer to navigate this web of information unaided. Indeed, in most consumer businesses, far more profitability derives from influencing navigation—by means of a strong brand identity, say—than from manufacturing or distributing the physical product itself.

On the Internet, by contrast, millions of people exchange massive amounts of information directly, quickly, and for free. Consumers can search much more comprehensively and at negligible cost. Navigation and selection occur independently of physical warehousing and distribution. Physical shopkeepers, who used to exert enormous influence over consumer choice, no longer enjoy special advantages. Product suppliers can sell directly to customers. Electronic retailers can focus on navigation and outsource fulfillment. And "pure" navigators, like the Yahoo! search engine and Quicken software, can organize information, helping people make sense of it without being party to the transaction at all.

The importance of this shift—wherein navigation can be a separate business, unbundled from production, marketing, and distribution—cannot be overemphasized. Navigation is the battlefield on which competitive advantage will be won or lost. At stake is much of the profit potential of most consumer-products suppliers and retailing businesses. For navigation is a business with enormous potential scope. The services navigators provide will correspond only coincidentally to any physically defined business or industry. Many people continue to view Amazon.com, for example, as an on-line bookseller, but its true business is navigation. It has rapidly broadened its offerings from books and CDs to movies to drugs to toys. Precisely because it is not clear what limits the domain for which Amazon is the preferred navigator, Amazon is worth more than the entire publishing industry put together.

Navigation has three dimensions. *Reach* is about access and connection. It means simply how many customers a business can access or how many products it can offer. *Affiliation* is about whose interests the business represents. *Richness* is the depth and detail of the information that the business gives the customer or collects about the customer. It is along these dimensions that the struggle for competitive advantage will take place. (See "The Three Dimensions of Navigational Advantage.") And different players start with very different advantages.

The Three Dimensions of Navigational Advantage

Reach is about access and connection. It means, simply, how many customers a business can connect with and how many products it can offer to those customers. (Reach has come to mean "eyeballs" on the Web, but we're broadening the definition here to include upstream reach to a variety of products and suppliers as well.) Reach is the most visible difference between electronic and physical businesses, and it has been the primary competitive differentiator for e-businesses thus far.

Richness is the depth and detail of information that the business can give the customer, as well as the depth and detail of information it collects about the customer. Electronic businesses haven't yet learned to compete seriously on the richness dimension. (They've made far more progress on reach.) But richness holds enormous potential for building close relationships with customers in a future dominated by e-commerce.

Traditional businesses have always had to make a trade-off between richness and reach. Doing both—getting highly detailed, customized information to and from a massive audience—was prohibitively expensive. E-commerce businesses can exploit the dramatic displacement of the trade-off permitted by electronic connectivity and information standards. For very little money, an e-business can provide a wide base of customers (reach) with access to a broad range of products (also reach) and detailed, complete information about each product (richness). It can also collect huge amounts of information about each customer (richness again) and use it to sell more products and services.

The same technological forces that blow up the trade-off between richness and reach also open a third competitive dimension—*affiliation,* or whose interests the business represents. Until now, affiliation hasn't been a serious competitive factor in physical commerce because, in general, no company ever devised a way to make money by taking the consumers' side. However, it's a natural progression for pure navigators to affiliate with customers; they aren't selling anything except, possibly, information—and therein could lie a huge competitive advantage. E-retailers with navigational functions are also shifting their affiliation toward customers. Traditional manufacturers and retailers must find ways to fight, co-opt, or imitate their e-commerce competitors' affiliation strategies.

Competing on Reach

Before the advent of e-commerce, category killers and retail superstores competed brilliantly on reach by offering convenient locations and broad selection. But theirs is a format constrained by the economics of things. The largest physical Barnes & Noble bookstore in the United States still carries only 200,000 titles. Amazon.com offers 4.5 million volumes and is "located" on some 25 million computer screens. This orders-of-magnitude jump in reach is possible precisely because the navigation function (catalog) is separated from the physical function (inventory). The average music superstore carries 50,000 titles; EveryCD was so confident of its reach that it offered prizes to customers who found a title missing from its catalog. Careerpath.com links potential employers with job seekers in a classifieds market already more than 50 times larger than that of any physical newspaper. Unconstrained by physical limitations, reach explodes. That explosion extends beyond conventionally defined industry boundaries. If consumers value comprehensive search capabilities, then the smart navigator will span across the search domain that consumers prefer. The first navigator to do so will capture an advantage. This has barely happened so far—e-retailers still largely mimic physical antecedents—but it will. Dell sells more than computers. Amazon has rapidly moved beyond books.

For insurgents—for e-retailers in particular—this raises the terrifying prospect of unstable business boundaries. CDNow carved out a dominant, reach-based position in the CD sales category, only to lose it in just a few months to Amazon. CDs (we see after the fact) are not a domain within which consumers meaningfully define reach. The idea of "CD retailing" as a discrete business is a mental throwback to the world of physical retailing. The same may be true for toys, banking, groceries, and other categories. The erosion of category boundaries will continue, as electronic retailers encroach on one another's territories and probe the true boundaries of consumer search domains.

The explosion of reach on the Internet also raises an acute dilemma for product suppliers. At first blush, it looks like a godsend—a chance to break free from the stranglehold of the retailer and build direct relationships with the final consumer. But any attempt to do so is by definition a navigational vehicle offering the consumer limited product reach. This might be offset by other factors, but if product suppliers offer navigation to only their own offerings, they put themselves at an inherent disadvantage. Stuck in a mind-set that confuses navigation with marketing, they may forgo competing in the emerging navigation business.

For many supplier businesses, that is just fine: they do not wish to be in the navigation business, and they welcome an explosion of information channels by which consumers can find their products and services. Small wine makers, which frequently are constrained by limited distribution channels, welcome the success of Virtual Vineyards and view the prospects of intensified retailer competition with equanimity. Small publishers consider Amazon to be a blessing. But for many large suppliers, the navigation function (variously called sales, marketing, advertising, branding, and promotion) is precisely where their differentiation and competitive advantage lay. To lose control of navigation would be to lose ownership of a primary source of competitive differentiation. But how can they keep it?

The knee-jerk reaction of product suppliers is to try to keep the new navigators from achieving critical mass. Consumer-product suppliers, after all, are the ultimate source of information on product features, price, and availability. If sellers don't let Yahoo! or Quicken parse their product lists and compare them with those of their competitors, then Yahoo! and Quicken will be confined to their current roles of glorified phone directory and checkbook.

There are two problems with that defensive strategy. The first is that technically it is difficult to stop a navigator from parsing information that's available electronically. If customers can go to the Web site, so can navigators. It doesn't have to be a personal visit: technologies enable a navigator to visit dozens of Web sites, query them, return the responses, and then sort the answers—all within a few seconds.

Obviously, the seller can stop this game, if only by refusing to operate a Web site. But therein lies the second and more fundamental issue: it is not obvious that it is in any single seller's interest to do so. A navigator is still a source of incremental business to a seller. Unless the selling business is highly concentrated, it is unlikely that the navigator's ability to achieve critical mass will depend on the availability of data from any one source. Therefore, while denying data to the navigators may be in the interest of all sellers *collectively*, it is not in the interest of any one seller *individually*. The banking industry collectively committed to common strategies to fend off the threat from new navigators such as Quicken and Microsoft Money. But one by one, individual banks found that they had more to gain from participating in the common information standard that these navigators were creating. The collective defense collapsed.

So if critical mass cannot ultimately be denied, then the old players have to match the reach of the new. Product suppliers that want to communicate with the consumer directly must do whatever it takes to achieve the reach that buyers value. That may mean entering into joint ventures with competitors to achieve critical mass. It may mean navigating to other companies' products and services. Universal and BMG, two of the world's largest music companies, have done both, creating an electronic joint venture, GetMusic.com, that offers a full selection of albums drawn from their own as well as other companies' rosters. Solo efforts would be hopelessly outmatched by the reach of CDNow and Amazon. Whenever the domain of search extends beyond the supplier's own offering, the supplier will be disadvantaged, perhaps fatally. (See "The Doomsday Scenario.") Therefore alliances are essential. Even with—especially with—competing suppliers.

The Doomsday Scenario

It's possible to imagine circumstances under which the new navigational businesses, exploiting richness and reach, will capture all the value in an industry. First, navigation becomes a business in its own right. Pure navigators compete against one another. Since they are operating a network business, reaching buyers and sellers is critical to their competitive advantage. Struggling for reach, navigators push for market share. Over time, they merge and concentrate. In parallel, but driven by the same logic, the e-retailers like Amazon.com broaden their business definitions beyond physical industry categories.

As their reach extends, the affiliation loosens between navigators or e-retailers and their suppliers. The largest ones start bargaining on the consumer's behalf. Consumers enjoy their new leverage, and they reward it with their patronage. Affiliation becomes a further basis for competitive differentiation. A positive feedback loop develops. The navigators that perform best cross a threshold of critical mass. Consumers prefer them because they offer greater product reach, and manufacturers concede them advantageous terms because they offer greater consumer reach. Reach builds on itself. These navigators then march toward positions of monopoly in their respective domains. Physical retailers are demoted to the role of distributor. Product suppliers see their business commoditized, or at least forced to compete on product-specific characteristics such as cost, technology, and features. Much of the value potential of the business is drained. Amazon and Yahoo! rule. That is exactly what Wal-Mart did to parts of the apparel business.

It has already happened in electronic commerce. SABRE, originally conceived as a marketing arm for American Airlines, is now an independent navigation company that is valued at nearly twice as much as American Airlines. Priceline.com, an Internet auction site for deep-discount travel bookings, was valued in its April 1999 public offering at $10 billion—higher than the values of United, Northwest, and Continental airlines combined. These navigators create more shareholder value than the suppliers to which they navigate. And by exploiting reach and by affiliating with the ticket purchaser, they make air travel even more of a commodity.

Farfetched for your business? Maybe. But it is a logic: a set of forces that shape the strategy calculations for everyone. If a supplier or retailer is to avoid these forces, it needs a countervailing strategy. If an electronic retailer or pure navigator wants to exploit these forces, it must understand how incumbents will try to forestall it.

Physical retailers may have to take a similar approach. Most treat their Web presence as a means of driving traffic to their physical locations: a store window dressed up in HTML. Treating electronic retailing as a serious business in its own right—indeed as both the greatest threat and opportunity that they face—forces them to act quite differently. They have to define their product mix as the e-retailers do, not as the physical constraints of their bricks-and-mortar stores forced them to. This may necessitate acquisitions and joint ventures. They need to fulfill orders in whatever way is most efficient for the electronic business—separating, if necessary, from their traditional warehousing infrastructure. They have to exploit synergies with the physical retail business, but only where that helps the electronic business to compete. Above all, they have to think of e-commerce as a business in its own right and not compromise its success in an effort to protect the traditional physical model. They must *expect* the new business to cannibalize the old.

Of all the incumbent retailers, catalog companies are best positioned to make the shift. Their lines of business are already defined around brand identities and search domains that make intuitive sense to consumers. They revise their offerings continuously through sophisticated data-mining techniques. Their fulfillment systems are designed for remote delivery. It is not surprising that the pre-Internet retailers that have most successfully managed the transition to electronic commerce are Lands' End and Victoria's Secret.

But other incumbents will find managing the transition to the Web much more difficult. Product suppliers and physical retailers still see the Internet as an arena for marketing and promotion: a new channel for doing old things. If they persist in that view, they will handicap themselves against new competitors—whether e-retailers or pure navigators—that see e-commerce as a business in its own right and pursue reach single-mindedly.

Competing on Affiliation

E-commerce businesses are already tilting their affiliation away from suppliers toward the consumer—Net-savvy consumers are forcing them to. Book publishers, for example, have long paid physical booksellers to promote books by giving them special placement in the store. But when Amazon did the electronic equivalent—letting publishers pay for superior Web page placement—consumer indignation at the conflict of interest and the betrayal of trust forced it to publish such arrangements on Amazon's home page. Affiliation is shifting, in ways that even the electronic retailers cannot control.

This change in affiliation is partially a manifestation of Internet culture and the greater transparency under which everyone operates.

But it is also a consequence of the blowup of the trade-off between richness and reach. When a sales agent sells only one product line (such as life insurance), he will push that as aggressively as he can: he has little choice but to serve as an agent for the product supplier. Give that salesperson the whole universe of alternative products to offer, and he is much more likely to present them neutrally. Go further and equip the consumer with all the information she needs to compare sales agents, and the odds are that the salesperson will try harder to please the consumer than he will to please any single product supplier.

Microsoft CarPoint provides car buyers with the data and software to compare alternative models along 80 objective specifications. Physical dealers never offer that kind of information. Nor (quite rationally) do the car makers on their proprietary Web sites. Microsoft can do this because Internet technology enables such rich information to be assembled from wide-reaching sources at negligible cost. Microsoft chooses to do this because it thereby establishes an advantage against its competitors in the navigation business.

Microsoft needn't be paid by the consumer for this tilt in affiliation to occur. Its income can still come from advertising, hyperlinks, and the sale of associated products or services. But if the consumer *is* willing to pay, that only strengthens the argument. Conventional wisdom says that the consumer will never pay for navigation, but that may prove incorrect. (It was once widely believed that consumers would never pay for television programs, but they now pay regularly for cable, satellite, pay-per-view, and rented videos, because they deem the quality worth the price.) The paucity of paid navigation today may reflect the willingness of companies to give it away more than the unwillingness of consumers to pay. Paid navigators, serving the most sophisticated consumers in their largest and most complex purchases, are quite likely to emerge. Where they do, the tilt in affiliation will be intensified.

The pure navigator is poised to exploit the affiliation dimension. Lipper and the Motley Fool are in a better position for navigating to mutual fund investments than Fidelity precisely because they are *not* in the business of selling funds. Pure navigators can serve as "meta-navigators," using technologies that compare multiple electronic retailers.

Consumer-affiliated navigators are most useful when the selection criteria are simple and well defined. When the choice requires qualitative weightings of nonstandard factors, pure navigators may be at a disadvantage to suppliers because they lack the necessary product-information richness. Consumers are unlikely to delegate the task of selecting a new car to a human or electronic agent because it is too complex and subjective a task. However, after they have selected a model, their choice of dealer (if dealers still exist) may be purely a matter of price and availability, and a consumer-affiliated navigator could handle that job easily. Within one purchase, there may be different steps where consumer affiliation has varying importance.

The player in the worst position to exploit affiliation is the product supplier because by definition the supplier has an interest in the transaction that is different from the consumer's. In many businesses this does not matter: with sports cars and high fashion, customers welcome blatantly nonobjective product hype as part of the consumption experience. But when consumer affiliation matters (and the pure navigators have every reason to propagate the idea that it always matters), the product supplier has a problem.

One response is to exploit the way that navigational businesses evolve beyond product categories. Offer a navigation service that solves consumer problems instead of merely pushing products. Add in objective data and decision-support software about content unrelated to your own business. Provide objective information about products and services in the consumer's search domain that you do *not* sell. Perhaps provide comprehensive but not necessarily comparable data on your own products and those of direct competitors, but slightly bias the presentation through the ordering and emphasis of alternatives. American Airlines did all this long ago with SABRE. Dell is currently embedding its extraordinarily successful Internet sales presence within a much broader configuration and retailing service. By so doing, it matches the reach of current computer retailers, provides comprehensive and genuinely unbiased navigation to the products it does not make, and preserves the option to promote its own products. The overall navigational proposition favors consumer affiliation, yet seller affiliation is preserved where it matters to Dell. It is the best defense in computer retailing against the threat of a cyber-Wal-Mart—be it Amazon, Microsoft, or for that matter, Wal-Mart itself.

Dell's strategy illustrates another way affiliation tilts toward the consumer, without the consumer paying for the privilege. To preserve a subtly biased presentation of its computers, Dell might offer a rigorously comprehensive and objective guide to peripherals. Wonderful for Dell if it works, but cold comfort to the manufacturers of peripherals, whose wares are now subjected to rigorous evaluation. The obvious response would be for the manufacturers of a group of (noncompeting) peripherals to get together and offer a flattering representation of their own products attached to a rigorously comprehensive and objective guide to computers. If the two navigators then split the browsing and buying populations for computer-related products equally, the result would be that half the electronic sales volume for computers and for peripherals would be driven by unbiased navigators—more than half, as consumers learn to cherry-pick. Acting to preserve their own business from commoditization, sellers happily commoditize one another's.

Of course, the fundamental reason this happens in the virtual world but not in the physical one is that the consumer's preferred search domain does not correspond to any physical industry. Therefore supplier industries have the greatest difficulty keeping control of navigation. Precisely because they lose control of reach, they can also lose control of affiliation.

Competing on Richness

When competing on reach and affiliation, traditional players have to struggle to keep abreast of electronic retailers and pure navigators. But they have natural advantages when it comes to richness. Traditional retailers can exploit their detailed information about customers. Suppliers can use extensive product information to their advantage. Doing so will most certainly involve revisiting how they think about branding.

RICH CUSTOMER INFORMATION

Retailers have always been well positioned to collect and use information about their customers, but the Internet greatly enhances their ability to do so. 1-800-FLOWERS, for example, now uses the Internet as its primary communications channel with customers because it lets the company offer many more customized services at a minimal incremental cost. The company maintains a customer information file with anniversary and birthday information, as well as a record of gifts sent to specific recipients. It can thus alert customers when a birthday or anniversary is approaching and suggest presents. These gifts are no longer just flowers; the business has evolved beyond its physical origins into an electronic concierge service.

The Web offers an unparalleled opportunity for this kind of cheap and infinitely discriminating customization of offers, products, and advertisements. Data-mining techniques can be applied to browsing behavior as well as to purchasing history and demographics. And the data are largely unexploited: until recently, Excite! collected 40 gigabytes of customer data *each day* and did nothing with it; Amazon has been affectionately nicknamed "Spamazon" by recipients of its undifferentiated bulk e-mails. All that will change as technologies developed by Firefly, MatchLogic, Aptex, and others trace patterns in the terabytes.

Some e-retailers are already becoming sophisticated. CDNow, for example, solicits information about which recording artists its customers like the most. The company relates that information to the individual's actual music purchases and then applies a statistical matching technology, created by Net Perceptions, to identify a universe of people with similar tastes. It can then recommend music that the larger group has purchased. Reach is largely irrelevant, and the motivation is obviously to sell recordings, but many customers love the service and have become loyal to CDNow as a result. Rich consumer information becomes a basis for building relationships.

The great advantage of the physical retailers is the rich data that they collect from *other* sources. Web-derived information, even when thoroughly mined, is actually a surprisingly thin database compared with those developed by grocery stores and credit card companies. However, by putting the two kinds of information together and using the Web as a means of customizing on the fly, businesses have the potential to build powerful relationships and strong competitive advantage.

Two factors limit strategies based on rich consumer information. The first is privacy constraints, which require that consumers be informed of, and agree to, any exchanges of data. Increasingly, this is simply a condition of doing good business. The second factor is consumers' option to search and organize information for themselves. Consumers using Quicken, for example, can customize their own statement of net worth: they do not need to give all their financial data (still less all their assets) to a financial institution. More insidiously, if the customer data file has real value, the consumer could collect the same information as the navigator and sell it.

These two factors do limit the power of rich customer information but, within those limits, electronic and physical retailers have an effective weapon. No single player is likely to have the ideal database, and digital information can be bought and sold, so alliances and markets for swapping information will probably begin to form. The originators and primary aggregators of such information, whether they are grocery stores, portals, credit agencies, or the consumers themselves, will extract most of the value.

RICH PRODUCT INFORMATION

It's generally difficult for manufacturers to use rich customer information competitively because retailers are more directly connected to customers. But manufacturers have distinct advantages when it comes to rich product information.

In the music industry, for example, most of the major companies—Universal, Sony, BMG, Warner—are developing information-rich performer biographies, recording history, chat rooms, and discographies. They are using them in a number of ways: as stand-alone Web sites, as information feeds to electronic retailers, and as enhanced CDs sold directly to the consumer. Part of their aim is to cross sell from their catalog of products. Part is to build a cult following for the performer. Part is to give to the electronic retailing industry the marketing capabilities that might otherwise be available only to Tower Records or to Amazon, and thereby to discourage retailer concentration and the attendant shift in bargaining power.

When this kind of material is presented as a stand-alone Web site, it suffers limitations of reach: consumers cannot find it easily and the product range is narrow. It also has limitations in affiliation: corporate Web sites are generally not a credible source for picks and pans or for the funky, antiestablishment rumor mill that endows performers' lives with mythic significance. But as a low-cost way to build a channel of communication that circumvents the retailers, the strategy has powerful potential.

Rich product-information strategies work well for manufacturers in some circumstances, not so well in others. If the product is continually evolving, as cell phones and software are, the product supplier has state-of-the-art information that retailers and navigators can't match. These strategies are also effective when innovation is more cosmetic than real but consumers like the "sizzle." Products like stereo components, cars, even kitchen knives, boast features that people want to believe in. The impressive, if inscrutable, technical claims presented in stereo literature or, potentially, on Web sites—"*Uni-Q Technology* with its exceptional capacity to unify *co-planar* and *co-axial* directivity factors in the critical *crossover* region"—may not withstand the objective scrutiny of engineering bench tests. But many an audiophile would rather read and believe such material (and brag about it to friends) than confront a cold review in *Consumer Reports* suggesting that those $3,000 loudspeakers sound no better than a $300 pair available at Circuit City.

Rich product information is thus a powerful but uncertain weapon for the product supplier. Wherever consumers welcome evangelism, enthusiasm, and a strong connotative context, rich product-information strategies can be effective. Nokia's 8800 phone. The next insanely cool product from Apple. But when detachment, objectivity, and comprehensiveness matter more, that approach may prove counterproductive. Hot news and breathless excitement about mortgages or groceries will impress nobody. And, as with the automotive example, a single purchase may have some components (the virtual reality demo) where rich information successfully trumps reach and affiliation, and others (price, availability) where it proves totally irrelevant.

BRANDS

Manufacturers use branding all the time, of course, to communicate rich, product-specific information to their consumers. But there are two different types of brands, and we believe that one is far better suited to e-commerce than the other.

Some companies attempt to convey facts or beliefs about product attributes through branding. Sony, for example, persuades consumers to believe that it will deliver superior technology, high manufacturing quality, and miniaturization at a modest but warranted price premium. Each of these things is a *belief* about Sony products—perhaps true, perhaps not.

Other marketers use branding to communicate an experience: feelings, associations, and memories. "Coca-Cola" cannot be paraphrased as a set of propositions *about* the drink. The brand is the taste, the curvy bottle, the logo, and the set of emotional and visual connotations that the drink carries by merit of a century of advertising.

Rich information channels have very different effects on brand-as-belief and on brand-as-experience. To the extent that a brand is a matter of belief, the brand message is fundamentally a *navigator* message. Buy a Sony and you get better technology that weighs less and has higher manufacturing quality. Because an objective navigator could provide those messages, the brand-as-belief competes with the navigator. If a credible navigator repeatedly demonstrated that specific Sony products did not, in fact, have better technology, weigh less, and so forth, that would undermine the brand. Indeed, even if the navigator validated Sony's claims, if people came to respect Sony products *because* of the navigator's endorsement, then the brand would become redundant. Thus to the extent that the product is amenable to independent navigation, brand-as-belief is vulnerable also.

Brand-as-experience is a different story. Barbie is not a brand defined by Mattel's statements about it or by its product specifications. Barbie is a fantasy world for young girls and a collectible for adults. Mattel devotes enormous resources to creating and preserving the consistency with which that fantasy world is presented. Barbie-as-experience will be magnified by richer channels of communication. When Mattel can reach young girls in a broadband, interactive, customized environment (as will be commonplace in a few years), it can enrich the Barbie fantasy world with dress up, storytelling, and conversations. This enhances the brand, but it also enhances the product and the experience of owning it. Indeed the brand, the product, and the experience are really one and the same.

Today, category killer retailers such as Toys R Us stand between toy manufacturers and consumers. Mattel's ability to deliver the Barbie experience is constrained not just by the static nature of merchandising displays but also by shelf space limitations and the retailer's unwillingness to favor one toy company over another. Direct presentation of the Barbie experience will enable the company to circumvent the retailer and create a brand-as-experience far more compelling than that in the physical store. Power shifts back to the product supplier.

An electronic retailer such as eToys or Toysrus.com might respond on reach by creating an interactive fantasy world featuring characters that are drawn from multiple vendors. Such a world may be closer, in fact, to the way a girl actually plays with her toys. They might respond on affiliation by allying with educational broadcasters to create a more "uplifting" site, calculated to win parental approval. If mixing up dolls or adding doses of political correctness is how young girls want to imagine the experience, those would be smart strategies. But we suspect not. Really strong brands-as-experience transcend tinkering.

Where brands are already defined in terms of experience rather than belief, the evolving medium will strengthen them. Brands that have elements of both (as most do) must play up their experiential aspects. Rich, product-centered information, supporting a brand defined as experience, is the product supplier's counter to the superior reach and affiliation of retailers and navigators. (See "From Your Perspective.")

From Your Perspective

If You Are a Pure Navigator . . .

- Never take your business definition for granted. You must compete with other navigators on richness and reach within a search domain whose boundaries are constantly moving.

- Recognize that close affiliation with consumers is a major competitive advantage for you. It is part of your Web identity. Cultivate it. Do not compromise consumer interests for your own short-term gain. Never do anything you would not want all your users to know, because within a few days, they will.

- Build richness fast. When the incumbent suppliers get serious, that is where they will attack.

If You Are an Electronic Retailer . . .

- Define your business in terms of a coherent consumer search domain, not an irrelevant physical category.

- Be very skeptical of exclusives with product suppliers. The sacrifice of reach and consumer affiliation is likely to cost you more in competitive advantage than the gain in margin is worth.

- Beware of category killer physical retailers: they often have better consumer information and better logistics. Their only handicap is an inability to think differently. That could change.

If You Are an Incumbent Product Manufacturer . . .

- Adding richness—especially product-specific richness—is the most powerful way for you to compete. Concentrate on enhancing brand as experience.

- Mentally deconstruct your own business. Look at its informational components as businesses in their own right. Develop independent strategies for them. Create an organization that takes those strategies seriously.

- Reach for you is a two-edged sword: it might enable you to escape the stranglehold of your retailers, but it simultaneously exposes you to new navigators whose potential reach is far greater than yours.

- Look seriously at alliances to address the affiliation and reach problems: a group of suppliers may be able to create a navigator that is more comprehensive and credible than any of its members.

If You Are an Incumbent Category Killer Retailer . . .

- You have been beating department stores and general merchandisers in the reach game through overwhelming selection and mastery of logistics. But that is all economics of physical things. The new reach game is about information. If you play it seriously, it will force you to redefine your business.

- You are going to be attacked, so do it to yourself before somebody does it to you. And understand the multiplicative effects that even slight revenue erosion can have on the profitability of a high-fixed-cost physical business. You will need to make those fixed costs variable.

- You ought to win in the new world of e-commerce. You start with reach, a high measure of consumer affiliation, physical distribution, rich consumer data, options for multichannel marketing, brands, and many of the right merchandising skills. You just have to be willing to compete against yourself.

- Know that your operating managers, if left to themselves, will never make the necessary changes. The threat to their core business is simply too great. Create a separate entity and give its managers the authority to exploit the assets of the traditional business. Synergy must be a one-way street, from the old business to the new.

The Incumbent's Dilemma

The logic of reach, affiliation, and richness poses a profound organizational dilemma for incumbent product suppliers and retailers. They have to recognize that their value chain is being deconstructed. Aspects of navigation are no longer functions; they are becoming businesses. And if incumbents choose to compete in any of those emerging businesses, they must do so by building reach, affiliation, and richness and redefining strategy and scope as the business evolves beyond its physically defined origins. They can do all this only if they mentally break down the current business into its components, understand the evolution of new business models from the outside-in, and free their new-business managers from any obligation to prop up the old. Indeed, the new businesses will quite properly compete against the old, buy from or ally with traditional competitors, and take risks that may prove to be costly errors. Every aspect of organization, incentive, and operating style will change.

This is an enormous challenge to an established organization. Its competencies, procedures, and power structures stand in the way. The only answer, many incumbents have found, is to separate the new venture as much as possible from the established organization, perhaps even to spin it out. If the aim is to compete on reach or affiliation, that is probably the only answer. But we have argued that richness is the incumbent's greatest strength. How can an incumbent achieve the autonomy, motivation, and freshness of an Internet start-up and simultaneously exploit its uniquely rich customer- and product-centered information? That may require a far more threatening corporate transformation—the kind of reinvention that Schwab undertook when it halved its brokerage fees, committed to navigation as its business definition, and started selling its competitors' products. But Schwab—like Ford, like Sony—has a history of reinventing itself. For many incumbents, their first attempt to reinvent themselves may also be their last.

7
The Future of Commerce

A Note from the Editors at the *Harvard Business Review*

As we enter the twenty-first century, the business world is consumed by questions about e-commerce. While the electronic sale of goods still represents only a small fraction of economic activity, the Internet seems at this moment in history to present almost unlimited possibilities—as both a conduit and a disrupter of business. To shed light on the changes we may see as the early years of our new century unfold, we asked some close observers of electronic commerce to share their thoughts and speculations about the future.

Adrian J. Slywotzky, a management consultant and author, has written extensively on the evolution of business models. He believes that electronic commerce will accelerate the shift of power toward the consumer, which will lead to fundamental changes in the way companies relate to their customers and compete with one another. Harvard Business School professors Clayton M. Christensen and Richard S. Tedlow view the Internet as a classic example of a disruptive technology, one that will alter the basis of competition in retailing. They examine past retailing disruptions, and they find patterns that appear to be recurring, at least in part, today. Finally, HBR senior editor Nicholas G. Carr, who has edited a number of the articles on electronic commerce that we've published over the last two years, examines the fragmentation of economic activity taking place on the Web. He foresees a future of "hypermediation," in which profits derive more from clicks than from sales.

It should be no surprise that our authors offer very different visions of what's to come. Out of such intellectual friction comes insight.

The Age of the Choiceboard
Adrian J. Slywotzky

The last time I bought a car, I looked at a number of different models on dealers' lots. Not one of them precisely met my needs. Even the car I ultimately purchased represented a compromise, providing some features that I wanted (antilock brakes and a spacious trunk, for instance), some that I was neutral about (a sunroof and power mirrors), and a lot of others that I had no need for whatsoever (from cruise control to fog lamps to heated seats). I bought it, even with all the unwanted features, because I liked the way the car looked and handled, and because it was available at that moment. I didn't want to wait a month to get a car with a marginally better mix of features.

What I went through is what all customers go through. Indeed, customer frustration is designed into our business system. Companies create fixed product lines that represent their best guesses about what buyers will want, and buyers make do with what they're offered. There may be some minor tailoring at the point of purchase—a few optional features or add-ons—but by and large the set of choices is fixed long before customers even begin to shop. Whether they're purchasing cars or clothes or computers, people always get too little of what they want and too much of what they don't.

Of course, the fixed product-line system is no joy for suppliers, either. Predictions of future demand, no matter how well grounded, are inevitably inaccurate. That's why the pages of newspapers and catalogs teem with announcements of sales, factory rebates, and dealer incentives, and why off-price stores are always plentifully stocked. Frustrated retailers and manufacturers spend tens of billions of dollars in discounts every year to help dispose of merchandise that isn't moving the way they thought it would.

So why does a system that's bad for both customers and companies hold sway? Historically, there hasn't been an alternative. The slow, imprecise movement of information up the supply pipeline and of goods down it has meant that the manufacturing process must begin long before accurate information about demand exists. Our entire industrial sector operates on guesswork.

From Product Taker to Product Maker

Now for the good news. Thanks to the Internet, an alternative to the traditional unhappy model of supplier-customer interaction is finally becoming possible. In all sorts of markets, customers will soon be able to describe exactly what they want, and suppliers will be able to deliver the desired product or service without compromise or delay. The innovation that will catalyze this shift is what I call the *choiceboard.* Choiceboards are interactive, on-line systems that allow individual customers to design their own products by choosing from a menu of attributes, components, prices, and delivery options. The customers' selections send signals to the supplier's manufacturing system that set in motion the wheels of procurement, assembly, and delivery.

The role of the customer in this system shifts from passive recipient to active designer. That shift is just the most recent stage in the long-term evolution of the customer's role in the economy. For most of the twentieth century, customers were "product takers" and "price takers," accepting suppliers' goods at suppliers' prices. Over the past two decades, as customers became more sophisticated and gained greater power over the buying process, they stopped being price takers. Armed with more options and more information, they looked further, bargained harder, and eventually found lower prices. But customers are still product takers. Even though suppliers have tailored their offerings to finer and finer slices of the customer base, buyers are ultimately forced to settle for the best approximation of what they want. With the choiceboard system, however, customers are product takers no longer. They're product makers.

The Coming Dominance of Choiceboards

Choiceboards are already in use in many industries. Customers today can design their own computers with Dell's on-line configurator, create their own dolls with Mattel's My Design Barbie, assemble their own investment portfolios with Schwab's mutual-fund evaluator, and even design their own golf clubs with Chipshot.com's PerfectFit system. But the choiceboard model is still in its infancy. Despite its enormous benefits, it's involved in less than 1% of the $30 trillion world economy. Even where it's well established, such as in the PC business, it accounts for only a small fraction of overall industry sales.

Three things are holding choiceboards back. The first is simply their newness: many manufacturers can't even imagine doing business through a choiceboard model. It would mean restructuring their entire manufacturing and sales systems. The second is the lack of highly responsive supply networks that can deliver components and services as needed. The third, and most important, is the lack of a critical mass of customers able to use choiceboards. Digital readiness, which I define as the number of PCs times the degree of PC literacy times the breadth of broadband access, remains low. Some industrial markets have an abundance of digital-ready customers, but in most markets, especially consumer sectors, the digital-ready segment is still a tiny sliver of the customer base.

But that last roadblock will be dismantled quickly. PC sales are strong; digital literacy is spreading rapidly, particularly among the young; and the expansion of broadband access is inevitable. And as soon as the customers are there, you can bet that choiceboards and the supporting infrastructure will be in place. By the end of this decade, I anticipate that choiceboards will be involved in 30% or more of total U.S. commercial activity, as our economy moves from a supply-driven to a demand-driven system. The big question isn't, Will choiceboards dominate commerce? It is, Who will control the choiceboards?

Changing the Terms of Competition

Because choiceboards collect precise information about the preferences and behavior of individual buyers, they enable companies to secure customer loyalty as never before. With each transaction, a company becomes more knowledgeable about the customer and hence better able to anticipate and fulfill that customer's needs. That knowledge can be used to tailor, in real time, the design of the choiceboard itself, customizing the options presented to the buyer and promoting up-selling and cross-selling. Once aggregated, moreover, the customer information can be used to guide the evolution of entire product lines and to spot new growth opportunities at their earliest stages. In such an environment, it becomes very difficult for a competitor, lacking the in-depth customer information, to displace the existing provider.

As we are only in the early stages of the choiceboard revolution, first movers stand to gain enormous advantages. As Dell's experience has shown, successful choiceboards act as magnets. They not only exert a strong pull over existing customers but also draw in each new wave of digital-ready buyers. And with each new customer, the company's market knowledge grows stronger, propelling it ever further ahead of the pack. Equally important, choiceboards attract key suppliers, which are also hungry for accurate and timely information about demand. Dell's far-reaching supply contracts with IBM, for example, will help it endure periods of restricted component supplies far better than many of its competitors.

For all those reasons, the rise of choiceboards promises to redistribute power within industries. I foresee three types of competitors vying for early choiceboard control. First is the individual manufacturer or assembler, such as a Dell or a Schwab. Second is a consortium of existing manufacturers; an example is the MetalSite choiceboard launched by a group of leading metals producers. Third, and most threatening to existing players, is the new intermediary. Because choiceboards are essentially design tools and conduits of information, they needn't be controlled by the companies that produce the products. Point.com, for instance, uses a choiceboard to help customers research and buy wireless phones, service plans, and accessories. As it amasses more and more customer information and refines its choiceboard, it will pose an ever greater threat to entrenched telecommunication companies, particularly those that are slow to launch their own choiceboards.

What's abundant in most industries today is production capacity. What's scarce is the ownership of customer relationships. Because the companies that control choiceboards will also control customer relationships, they will be the ones that hold the power in an industry and reap the lion's share of the profits.

The War of the Choiceboards

Once a company controls a choiceboard in an industry, it can use its store of customer information to expand into new industries. This pattern is already playing out with Dell. It first used its choiceboard simply to sell computers. It subsequently expanded into selling computer peripherals and related services such as Internet access. And Michael Dell's investment in CarsDirect.com last year suggests an intent to extend beyond computing. Information-rich customer relationships need not—and will not—end at the traditional boundaries between industries.

In the not-too-distant future, therefore, I expect to see a war of the choiceboards. It's impossible to predict exactly how this war will play out, but it seems clear that the victors will be those with the best-designed choiceboards, the most responsive supplier networks, and the closest customer relationships. Today, choiceboards are essentially transaction devices; information is a by-product. Tomorrow, choiceboards will be primarily information-collection devices and customer relationship-builders. Companies will use their choiceboards to actively solicit from customers information about their satisfaction levels, their buying intentions, and their requirements and preferences. And, by means of sophisticated analytical techniques like collaborative filtering, they will use the information to predict customers' needs and behavior across virtually all product and service categories. One-stop shopping will take on a whole new meaning, and commerce will take on a whole new look.

Patterns of Disruption in Retailing
Clayton M. Christensen and Richard S. Tedlow

The entire retailing industry is in an acute state of uncertainty. Within every company, at every trade association meeting, in every product category, electronic commerce and its implications dominate the conversation. Fearful of missing an epochal opportunity, investors and executives are rushing to place huge bets on Internet retailing, at what appear to be very high odds. But despite all the talk and frenzied activity, the future of retailing remains decidedly cloudy.

It would be foolish to try to predict which companies' Internet strategies will prove profitable in the end. Yet it seems clear that electronic commerce will, on a broad level, change the basis of competitive advantage in retailing. The industry has, of course, undergone transformations in the past. By examining those transformations and identifying patterns in the way they unfolded, we can discover clues about how retailing is likely to evolve in the Internet era.

The essential mission of retailing has always had four elements: getting the right product in the right place at the right price at the right time. The way retailers fulfill that mission has changed as a result of a series of what we call *disruptive technologies*.[1] A disruptive technology enables innovative companies to create new business models that alter the economics of their industry. In retailing, the first disruption arrived in the form of department stores. The second was the mail-order catalog. The third was the rise of discount department stores. Internet retailing marks the fourth disruption. A diverse group of Internet companies—retailers such as Amazon.com and Autobytel.com, distributors such as Chemdex, travel agencies such as Travelocity.com, and auction sites such as eBay—are poised to change the way things are bought and sold in their markets. These newcomers pose powerful threats to competitors with more conventional business models.

While disruptions change the economics of an industry, they don't necessarily change companies' profitability. In retailing, profitability is largely determined by two factors: the margins stores can earn and the frequency with which they can turn their inventory over. The average successful department store, for example, earned gross margins of approximately 40% and turned its inventory over about three times per year. In other words, it made 40% three times, for a 120% annual return on the capital invested in inventory. Compare that with the business model of the average successful discount department store, which earned 23% gross margins and turned its inventory over five times annually. It achieved a similar return on inventory investment by changing the balance between margins and turnover rates. Internet retailers' profit margins haven't yet converged into a standard range. But if businesses such as Amazon.com continue to turn inventory at present rates of 25 times annually, they could achieve traditional returns with margins of 5%.

Department Stores as Disruptive Innovators

Retailing was originally dominated by local merchants who provided value to their customers by keeping large inventories, extending credit, and offering personalized advice. The merchants' high-inventory, service-intensive business model resulted in slow turnover— evidence suggests that many of these retailers struggled to turn their inventories over twice a year—and involved high costs. As a consequence, these retailers were forced to charge high prices to earn the margins necessary to stay in business.

The industry changed dramatically in the late nineteenth and early twentieth centuries as a result of the first retailing disruption: the launch of department stores by men like Marshall Field and R.H. Macy. These stores tended to underperform the existing retailers in many aspects of customer service—a classic characteristic of an industry disruption—but their other qualities gave them advantages. In particular, they did a superior job of getting the right products into the right place. They brought together an enormous number of different goods in one location, making it much easier for shoppers to find what they needed. In effect, the department stores served as the portals of their day: you knew that if you walked into a good department store, you were likely to find what you wanted. The aggregation of customers and products enabled department stores to outperform local stores in pricing. By accelerating inventory turnover rates, they could earn the same returns on much lower gross margins.

The department stores also found a way to mitigate their disadvantage in customer service. Because their clerks could not be as knowledgeable about individual customers' needs and preferences as local specialty shop owners, department stores initially tended to focus their merchandise mix on simple, familiar products. Then, as customers grew accustomed to the new format, the department stores introduced more complex products at higher price points. The brand of the retailer became a surrogate for product reliability.

The reason that department stores blossomed when they did can be traced to a new technology—the railroad. With an infrastructure of rails in place, department stores could aggregate goods from all over the country, and rail trolleys could transport customers from their homes at the fringes of town to the department stores at the center. Site location became a source of competitive advantage and was managed scientifically. Chains hired squads of "traffic counters" to tabulate the number of potential customers walking past busy street corners. (The busiest corner in America in 1914 was State and Madison in Chicago, which 142,000 people passed between 7:00 AM and midnight.)

At the same time that department stores were springing up in cities throughout the country, another very different disruption was also taking place—catalog retailing. Originally targeted at rural customers who could not easily visit department stores, mail-order catalogs were made possible by the introduction of rural free mail delivery. Sears touted its catalog as "the cheapest supply house on earth," and it compensated for the lack of personal service with money-back guarantees.

Catalogs were, in essence, an early equivalent of today's virtual department stores. And just as we are now beginning to see virtual retailers branch out into real stores—the so-called clicks-and-mortar strategy—so Sears expanded beyond its catalog to create a chain of physical outlets.

Trumped by Malls and Discounters

Another technological advance—the automobile—set in motion the next retailing revolution. First, the automobile made shopping malls possible. Although malls proved a real threat to department stores, they didn't alter the fundamental business model. They were a *sustaining* innovation, not a disruptive one. Malls did the same thing that department stores did, only better. They attracted enough customers to enable a collection of focused retailers such as the Gap, Abercrombie & Fitch, and Williams-Sonoma to achieve similar margins and inventory turns as department stores, but with deeper product lines within each category. For the first three decades after shopping malls appeared, department stores continued to play crucial roles as anchors, using their strong brands to draw shoppers. But by making shoppers comfortable with malls, the department stores sowed the seeds of their own obsolescence. Today, many strip and outlet malls are simply aggregations of category-focused retailers, which thrive in the absence of department stores.

A similar transformation took place in catalog retailing. As customers became accustomed to making purchases through the mail, hundreds of specialty catalogs appeared. They chipped away at the sales of the generalist catalogs, like those of Sears' and Ward's. In 1985, Ward closed down its catalog operations. Eight years later, Sears followed suit.

The automobile also made a second wave of innovation possible: the establishment of the discount department stores in the early 1960s. The increased mobility of shoppers enabled discounters like Kmart to set up shop in less expensive real estate at the edge of town, effectively voiding department stores' competitive advantage of prime locations in city centers. Unlike malls, discount stores were a disruptive innovation. They made money through a completely different business model—a low-cost, high-turnover model that enabled suc-cessful discounters to achieve five inventory turns a year with gross margins of between 20% and 25%.

Repeating department stores' early strategy, the discounters seized their beachhead by initially concentrating on simple products that could sell themselves. About 80% of the floor area of the leading dis-count stores during the 1960s and 1970s was devoted to branded hard goods such as hardware, kitchen utensils, books, luggage, and pack-aged personal care products. Because the key attributes of such mer-chandise could be communicated easily—by pictures on the package, the brand of the manufacturer, and a few numbers—the discounters were able to spend even less on customer service than the department stores did.

As the discounters invaded the low ground, the department stores systematically closed down their hard-goods departments and moved upmarket. They became retailers of soft goods such as clothing, home furnishings, and cosmetics—products whose key attributes are more complex and harder to communicate. Because soft goods were more difficult to sell in the low-service, discount format, department stores were able to maintain the higher margins required to sustain their business model.

Upending the Discounters

During their early years, the discounters were quite successful. As long as they priced their goods 20% below the prices of their common enemy, the department stores, they could make money. But when the discounters had driven the department stores from the lower tiers of the market, they were competing only against equally low-cost dis-counters. That competition drove pricing and profits in the branded hard-goods tiers of the market to subsistence levels.

And, in a continuation of the earlier pattern, another new set of highly focused retailers attacked the discounters. Specialty discounters such as Circuit City, Staples, Home Depot, Toys R Us, Barnes & Noble, CVS, and Tower Records carved up the hard-goods market. Like the malls, these category killers represent a sustaining innovation rather than a disruptive one. They offer broader, deeper selections of prod-ucts within their narrower categories, but they still have the volume to achieve the inventory turns required in the discounters' 23% × 5 profit model.

Faced with ever fiercer competition, many of the weaker discount department stores such as Korvettes, Venture, Woolco, Zayre, Grand Central, and Caldor have bowed out of the business. A few discounters, Wal-Mart, most notably, have been able to use their purchasing clout and logistics-management capabilities to continue to compete in hard goods. But most of the surviving discount department stores have followed the earlier path of the department stores: they've fled the hard-goods competition by migrating upmarket. Indeed, discounters such as Bradlees and Target have flipped their original merchandise mix: 60% to 80% of their floor space is now devoted to soft goods. Competing against full-price department stores is much easier than competing against the cutthroat category specialists.

Repeating Patterns?

A fourth retailing disruption, instigated by the Internet, is now under way, and it promises to alter the retailing landscape as fundamentally as the three earlier disruptions.

Of the four dimensions of the retailer's mission—product, place, price, and time—Internet retailers can deliver on the first three remarkably well. The right products? In categories ranging from books to chemicals, Web stores can offer a selection that no bricks-and-mortar outlet can match. The right price? Internet retailers enjoy unparalleled margin flexibility. To earn a 125% return on inventory investment, an Internet retailer such as Amazon.com, which can turn its inventory 25 times each year, needs to earn only 5% gross margins.

And the right place? It is here—location—that the Internet is most revolutionary. The Internet negates the importance of location. Anyone, at any time, can become a global retailer by setting up a Web page.

With such advantages, it's no wonder electronic commerce is attracting so much attention. But how should we expect this revolution to evolve?

As we've seen, there are two clear patterns in the way the earlier retailing disruptions unfolded. First, generalist stores and catalogs dominated retailing at the outset of the disruptions, but they were eventually supplanted by specialized retailers. The specialists emerged once the market for the new form of retailing had grown large enough to generate enough sales volume for a narrower but deeper product mix. Second, the disruptive retailers weighted their initial merchandise mix toward products that could sell themselves—simple, branded products whose key attributes could be comprehended visually and numerically. They then shifted their merchandise mix toward higher-margin, more complex products to maintain their profits in the face of intense competition at the low end of their businesses.

We appear now to be seeing a repeat of the early stages of both those patterns in Internet retailing. Let's look at each one.

Generalist to Specialist

Leading Internet retailers like Amazon.com have rapidly migrated toward the department store strategy. The logic is clear. The Web is a vast and confusing place, and it is currently very difficult to know who is selling what. Anybody with a few thousand dollars can set up a Web-based business, just as almost anybody with a little money in the 1850s could set up a small shop. The best Internet search engines today can locate only a fraction of the Web sites that exist in a category, and they are frustratingly inaccurate. And with such intense advertising noise about us, it is next to impossible to remember which dot-com name is associated with which product or service. Hence, Amazon seems to sense the same opportunity that Richard Sears and Marshall Field saw. If you need to find a product, you don't need to search in the thicket of the Internet. You only need to remember how to type "Amazon.com"—or better yet, click on its bookmark—and you'll be guided to whatever you need.

It's less clear, though, whether this pattern will unfold as it did in the past. Even the largest bricks-and-mortar department stores could stock only the items with the highest turnover rates within each product category. That limitation opened the door for the specialists. Internet department stores face no such physical limits. They can, in theory, offer the depth of the specialist with the breadth of the generalist.

It is possible, therefore, that the Internet department stores will not yield market share to specialized retailers as the volume of purchases in individual categories grows. But there is a counterforce. The inevitable emergence of better search engines, together with the availability of greater bandwidth into homes, will make it increasingly easy for consumers to find specialized e-tailers. We would like to be able to predict the future of Internet department stores and category-focused retailers based on the patterns of the past, but the future simply cannot be known at this point. The technological and economic factors that drove the historical patterns are different in this wave. Our bet, however, is that the pattern will play out: the managerial benefits of focus and the ultimate ease of travel across Web sites will give a slight edge, eventually, to focused players. The odds will tilt toward specialists even more if cyber-malls emerge that rent space to a collection of specialist retailers whose category brands are strong—akin to the way today's physical shopping malls have evolved.

Upmarket Momentum

As with the earlier disruptions, Internet retailing has initially focused on the simple end of the merchandise spectrum—books, CDs, publicly traded stocks, personal care products, commodity chemicals, and so on. The question is, How fast will the disruptors move upmarket into more complex products and value-added services?

Already we see signs of upmarket migration. The transformation of some Internet-based retailers into "clicks-and-mortar" retailers—establishing warehouses and physical stores to give customers faster access to inventory and to handle returns and service issues conveniently and personally—is not an admission that the Internet-retailing model doesn't work. Rather, just as we saw with Sears years ago, it is a perfectly predictable step. As competition in the simplest tiers heats up, good managers migrate toward higher price points and value-added services to keep their profit margins attractive.

The upmarket migration is likely to happen much more rapidly today than it did in the earlier disruptive waves. Traditional retailers have always had to make a trade-off between the richness of information they could exchange with customers and the number of customers they could reach. Although local merchants could exchange rich information about products, the economics of providing such expertise meant that they could cater to only a narrow set of customers. To reach a mass market, department stores could not afford to employ expert staff to sell a broad range of complex products. They were forced to provide less rich information. The Internet seems capable of breaking this trade-off. It can enable retailers to communicate rich information about a broad set of complex products to a very large set of customers.[2] That capability should help e-tailers move upmarket more quickly than their predecessors did.

Of course, some products are less suited to electronic sale than others. While Internet retailers excel at getting the right product in the right place at the right price, they're at a disadvantage when it comes to delivering physical products at the right time. When shoppers need products immediately, they'll head for their cars, not their computers. There are also certain experiences that the Internet cannot deliver. Even with a lot of bandwidth, communicating the feel of clothing and home furnishings will be difficult. And in those customer segments where the social experience of shopping is an important element of value, the homebound nature of on-line commerce offers little appeal.

Although such constraints appear daunting, they are unlikely to slow the momentum of Internet retailing. Historically, experts have underestimated the ultimate reach of disruptive technologies. Blinded by their perception of the initial limitations of the new technology, they failed to appreciate the strength of the innovators' motivation to move from the fringes of commerce to its mainstream.

Notes

1. The concepts of *disruptive technologies* and *sustaining technologies* were first introduced in Joseph L. Bower and Clayton M. Christensen's "Disruptive Technologies: Catching the Wave" (*HBR* January–February 1995) and explored more deeply in Christensen's *The Innovator's Dilemma* (Harvard Business School Press, 1997).

2. This theme is developed by Philip Evans and Thomas S. Wurster, in chapter 5, "Getting Real About Virtual Commerce," and in their book *Blown to Bits* (Harvard Business School Press, 1999).

Hypermediation: Commerce as Clickstream
Nicholas G. Carr

When the notion that you could sell things over the Internet first arose, there was a widespread belief that it would mean the death of the middleman: Producers of goods and services would use their Web sites to connect directly with consumers, bypassing wholesalers and retailers altogether. We'd enter a great era of "disintermediation," which would drain profits from distributors and redirect them back to manufacturers.

Like many of the early assumptions about electronic commerce, this one has proved laughably wrong. With few exceptions, manufacturers have not been able to do much direct selling over the Web. In the virtual world as in the physical world, people want a broad selection of goods when they go shopping; they don't want to be limited to a single product line. Even Levi Strauss, whose launch of a sophisticated e-commerce site back in 1994 made it a poster child for disintermediation, has thrown in the towel. It recently announced that it will stop selling jeans through its site.

It is now becoming clear that, far from experiencing disintermediation, business is undergoing precisely the opposite phenomenon—what I'll call *hypermediation*. Transactions over the Web, even very small ones, routinely involve all sorts of intermediaries, not just the familiar wholesalers and retailers, but content providers, affiliate sites, search engines, portals, Internet service providers, software makers, and many other entities that haven't even been named yet. And it's these middlemen that are positioned to capture most of the profits.

Clicks as Transactions

A simple, everyday example of Internet shopping will show how hypermediation works. Let's say that an occasional Web user—I'll call him Bob—becomes interested in the ubiquitous *Harry Potter* books. He thinks that he'd like to read them, but he wants to learn a little more about them. So he goes onto the Web and, since he's never bothered to change his browser's default home page, he ends up at the Netscape portal. In the search box he types the phrase "Harry Potter," and from a list of available search services he chooses, on a whim, GoTo.com. He's transported to the GoTo site, where his search results are posted. He chooses a promising-sounding site near the top called "Nancy's Magical Harry Potter Page."

Nancy's site, a personal home page with an unsophisticated but friendly design, is full of information that Bob finds useful. There are glowing reviews of the books by Nancy and a few of her friends, detailed plot summaries and character descriptions, and a discussion board where readers share their comments. There's also a link to a special Harry Potter page at eToys. Bob clicks on the link, and he finds that eToys is selling the first book in the series for 50% off its list price—just $8.97. He can't resist that kind of a bargain, so he takes out his Visa card and places an order. Three days later, the book is in his mailbox.

A fairly routine buying expedition on the Web, right? But consider the complex array of intermediaries that made money off Bob's modest purchase. There are the usual suspects, of course—the retailer eToys, the book distributor that eToys buys from, the bank that issued Bob's Visa card, the U.S. Postal Service. But there are less obvious players as well. First is Netscape. Netscape puts various search services on its home page and, in return, the services pay Netscape a penny or two every time a visitor clicks through to their sites. So when Bob was transferred to GoTo.com, Netscape received a little money. GoTo, for its part, auctions off its top search results to the highest bidders. Nancy, for instance, agreed to pay GoTo one cent for every searcher who clicks on her link. So when Bob chose Nancy's site, GoTo made a penny. GoTo didn't get to keep all of it, though. Because GoTo contracts with an outside provider, Inktomi, to conduct its searches, it had to pay Inktomi a fraction of that penny for processing Bob's search.

Then there's Nancy herself. Like thousands of other individuals who have personal Web pages, Nancy has signed up to be an affiliate of eToys. When she sends someone to eToys through a link on her page, the e-tailer pays her 7.5% of any resulting purchases. So Nancy made a cool 67 cents when Bob bought the book. What's more, eToys doesn't run its own affiliate program. It outsources the job to a company named Be Free. Be Free, in turn, takes a small cut on the purchases it administers. So it, too, got a little of Bob's money.

Add them up, and you'll find that no fewer than nine intermediaries had their fingers in Bob's $8.97 purchase. (And that doesn't even include the people who posted reviews on Nancy's site—they just haven't realized that they could be charging for their words.) In fact, every single time Bob clicked his mouse, a transaction took place: a little bit of value was created, and a little bit of money changed hands. Yes, the money usually amounted to only a penny or two, but it seems a safe bet that far more profit was made by the intermediaries that took those pennies than by eToys when it sold the book for half-price. Bob's transaction is a microcosm of the emerging economic structure of e-commerce: the profits lie in intermediate transactions, not in the final sale of a good.

Volume and Efficiency

Two characteristics of electronic commerce make hypermediation possible and even inevitable. First is the sheer volume of activity. People make billions of clicks on the Web every day, and because each click represents a personal choice, each also entails the delivery of value and thus an opportunity to make money. A penny isn't a lot of money in itself, but when you start gathering millions or billions of them, you've got a business.

The second characteristic is efficiency. Most physical businesses wouldn't be able to make money on penny transactions; it would cost them more than a penny to collect a penny. But the incremental cost of an on-line transaction is basically zero. It doesn't cost anything to execute a line or two of code once the code's been written. The pennies taken in by many intermediaries are almost pure profit.

If volume and efficiency make microtransactions attractive, they make microbusinesses attractive, too. Take Nancy's Magical Harry Potter Page. (I made up that site, but there are millions just like it all over the Web.) It doesn't cost Nancy much to maintain her site. She spends an hour or two on it a week, adding text and images using a site-design program that came bundled with her home PC. Her ISP hosts the site for free on its servers. And she didn't have to pay eToys anything to become an affiliate. The commission checks she receives from eToys are small—80 bucks a month, say—but they're all profit for Nancy. She brags about the income to her acquaintances, and now they're all launching small sites focused on everything from gardening to sports to education to doll collecting. Through affiliations with various e-tailers, they're pulling in a few extra dollars a month, too. Some are earning hundreds or even thousands.

Just as microtransactions don't look like much individually, so microbusinesses seem insignificant at first glance. But, again, volume changes everything. One microbusiness is no big deal. Millions of them, sucking billions of dollars of profit out of the e-commerce system, is a very big deal. After all, there's not a whole lot of profit in selling stuff on the Web to begin with.

Geeks Rule

So what does hypermediation mean for the future of on-line business? I would argue that the lion's share of the profits in e-commerce will likely flow to two very different types of intermediaries. One type is represented by Nancy—the owners of specialized content sites. These content sites will draw people interested in the particular subjects they cover, often using discussion boards or other interactive features to encourage return visits. As affiliates of big e-tailers, they will also serve as gateways to purchases, gaining a share of all sales. Some of these content sites will be large—America Online has long pursued such a business model—but most will be small and intimate. When people first venture onto the Internet, they tend to head for the big-name sites—Amazon, Yahoo!, and the like—because those are the easiest to find. But as they become used to the Web and more familiar with searches and other navigation aids, they start to seek out sites tailored to their particular interests—sites that might get only a few dozen visitors a day. For content sites, specialization is more important than scale.

The second type of intermediary is the infrastructure company—the search engines like Inktomi and Google, the advertising networks like DoubleClick and Engage, the affiliate networks like Be Free and LinkShare, the backbone providers like Akamai and Exodus. Here, scale will often be important. In some cases, the network effect will lock out small new competitors—at least for a time. But even more important than scale will be technical prowess. The technologies underpinning the Web are still in their infancy. Every day we see the arrival of some new company with a neat piece of code that changes something about the way the Web works. Those companies are well aware that every click is a potential source of profit. They are focusing their energy and creativity, not to mention millions of dollars of venture capital, on figuring out new ways to turn clicks into transfers of cash.

Just as it was once assumed that disintermediation was an inevitable result of e-commerce, so it has been assumed that the power over e-commerce will inevitably shift from the geeks to the suits: good, well-disciplined business sense will supplant enthusiasm and technical know-how as the key determinant of success. I don't see it that way. In a world of hypermediation, the enthusiasm that gives rise to specialized content sites and the engineering skill that underpins technological advances will continue to trump B-school smarts. While many big, highly visible Web retailers will vainly struggle to sell products above cost, a whole slew of anonymous businesses will be quietly collecting pennies behind the scenes.

8

Contextual Marketing: The Real Business of the Internet

David Kenny and John F. Marshall

Time for a painful admission: the Internet has been a letdown for most companies. Certainly, the Web is at the top of corporate America's priority list—the $10 billion that large U.S. companies spent on Web site development in 1999 is evidence enough of that. Yet in any given month, only about half of the largest U.S. consumer businesses attract more than 400,000 site visitors—and a similar percentage of sites generate no commercial revenue at all.

If the economic return is minimal, the strategic payoff is even lower. Less than half of these corporate sites capture any self-reported customer data. The few sites that manage to gather any information do a pretty poor job of it—we estimate that they compile meaningful profiles on less than 1% of their customers. And despite all assurances to the contrary, the Web is rarely a low-cost customer acquisition channel. Most companies using standard "drive-to-site" Web marketing approaches, such as banner advertisements, quickly learn that their customer acquisition costs are greater than those in the physical world — often 1.5 to 2.5 times greater.

Most corporate Web sites fall short of managers' high expectations because of a fundamental mismatch—the dominant model for Internet commerce, the destination Web site, simply doesn't suit the needs of most companies or their customers. For a destination Web site to make economic sense, it must attract repeat visits from customers, with each visit adding ever greater increments of information to a customer's profile. For example, Amazon.com's business model is based on retaining each customer for a significant number of years—up to an astonishing 12 years by some analysts' forecasts. That is considered sufficient time to develop the deep, continuing relationships that will justify the company's heavy investment in its site. Such a model is well suited to providers of financial services and travel services, whose dynamic, information-driven offerings generate repeat site visits that yield an increasingly detailed customer profile. But at the other extreme, most consumer product companies face an insurmountable challenge in adopting the destination site model; they don't provide enough value to induce consumers to make repeat visits, much less disclose intimate information.

Does this mean the Internet is of no value to all but a handful of well-positioned companies? Not at all. What it does mean is that most companies need to discard the notion that a Web site equals an Internet strategy. Instead of trying to create destinations that people will come to, they need to use the power and reach of the Internet to deliver tailored messages and information to customers at the point of need. They need to become what we call *contextual marketers.*

The Ubiquitous Internet

Hastening the demise of the destination site model is the phenomenon we call the *ubiquitous Internet.* Within three to five years, the Internet will begin to be accessible from almost anywhere. Consumers will be linked to the Net via wireless telephones, personal digital assistants, interactive television, always-on DSL or cable, or laptop computers with wireless connections. Consumers will be constantly enveloped in a digital environment—a personal digital bubble, as it were. And the phenomenon extends well beyond personal devices. Car makers, shopping mall operators, plane manufacturers, retailers, airport officials, and bus station managers all have plans on the drawing board —or under way—to provide Internet access to their customers. A quick look outside the United States confirms that this ubiquity is approaching at warp speed: already in Japan, the largest Internet service provider is a wireless carrier.

As the Internet becomes ubiquitous, companies will gain many new ways to connect with customers. This explosion of access will open up enormous marketing opportunities, but it will also pose big challenges. Designing a compelling Web site may be hard, and using personalization software to customize what individual consumers see may be

Table 8-1   Before and After: What Lies Ahead for Web Marketing

In three to five years, the ubiquitous Internet will begin to unfold. Consumers will be constantly enveloped in a digital environment, and marketing strategies will have to change radically. Web sites, the centerpiece of most of today's strategies, will be only one piece of a much larger and more complex puzzle.

	Today's Internet	Ubiquitous Internet	
Intermediary	The destination Web site	The mobilemediary	

Access points	PC equipped with Web browser	• PDA
		 • wireless phone
		 • interactive TV
		 • always-on
		   broadband
			• e-wallet
			 • kiosks
			 • Internet-enabled
			   POS terminal

Consumers Can Be Reached	Only when they're sitting at their PCs browsing the Web	24 hours a day, seven days a week, anywhere on the planet—in their cars, at the mall, on an airplane, at a sports arena	
Customer Focus	Price-conscious comparison shoppers	Anyone with an immediate need, who will spend money to save time	
Strategic Mandate	• Focus on content • Build destination Web site • Personalize Web pages • Wait (and wait) for customers to show up	• Focus on context • Build ubiquitous agent that travels alongside your customer • Master technology that lets you know when you're needed • Be there when and where your customer is ready to buy	

tougher still. But these tasks pale in comparison to managing a pervasive electronic presence that senses and responds not only to who the customer is but where she is and what she's doing. (See Table 8-1 "Before and After: What Lies Ahead for Web Marketing.")

Think about airlines—they need Web sites so their customers can make reservations and check schedules on-line. But the airlines will also need much more. When a traveler needs to change plans midjourney, an airline must be able to provide for him an Internet-enabled mobile device while he's still in the air or a computer terminal while he's in the departure lounge or airline club. The passenger may also require related services—hotel reservations and ground transportation, for instance—that change as his plans change.

For their part, retailers may use kiosks, Internet-enabled point-of-sale (POS) terminals, or mobile devices to digitally recognize loyal customers while they're in a store. Then, before the customer has even reached the checkout counter, the retailer can devise special offers based on the customer's purchase history and preferences.

The companies that master the complexity of the ubiquitous Internet will gain significant advantages: greater intimacy with customers and more efficient targeting of market segments. And by offering customers a more valuable, more timely product, they'll be able to charge a premium price. The crucial step is to recognize that the ubiquitous Internet will further reconfigure value chains that have already been shattered by the Internet's first wave. As the ubiquitous Internet becomes a reality, a new kind of intermediary role emerges—we call it the *mobilemediary.*

The mobilemediary will be able to break into the value chain at any point, bringing information and transaction capabilities to customers whenever and wherever they're ready to buy a product or avail themselves of a service. Mobilemediaries might serve up your spouse's wish list when you're in the mall shopping for a birthday present. They might enable you to trade stocks when the market is plunging and your commuter train is stalled. When you're with your family at a theme park, they might let you know that it's your turn to ride the roller coaster. But whatever form these intermediaries take, they'll be less about content and more about context.

The Rise of Contextual Marketing

Contextual marketing opens up opportunities for companies that, for various reasons, can't form the ongoing digital relationships that are the lifeblood of a successful destination Web site—for example, makers of consumer packaged goods, single-product companies, and infrequent service providers.

The most innovative of these companies are already adapting their marketing strategies to take advantage of the ubiquitous Internet. Take Mobil's Speedpass: the digital wand can be attached to a keychain and lets customers pay for gas and other purchases by waving it in front of an electronic reader at the gas pump or at the checkout counter. It has proved so convenient that some drivers go miles out of their way to find a filling station that accepts Speedpass. In Japan, wireless carrier NTT DoCoMo has signed up a staggering 10 million consumers for its i-mode service over the past 12 months. I-mode offers subscribers wireless access to restaurant locators, ski-condition reports, hotel reservations systems, on-line auctions, and thousands of other services. Some of this information is already available on the World Wide Web, but with i-mode, consumers can tee up the information they want when they want it, not just when they're sitting at their PCs. Japanese consumer marketers are taking advantage of this situation—there are now almost 10,000 i-mode sites.

As these examples suggest, the ubiquitous Internet will vastly expand marketers' opportunities to reach customers. At the same time, it will destabilize the "four Ps" of traditional marketing: price, product, placement, and promotion will all be thrown into constant flux, depending on the customer and the context. The marketing goal will be the same as ever: deliver the right product to the right customer at the right time. Companies will still have to form a deep understanding of their customers' needs and desires. But in many cases, instead of owning customer data or individual customer relationships, successful contextual marketers will borrow them.

Recent initiatives by Johnson & Johnson demonstrate this kind of contextual marketing in action. Accepting that it was unlikely to develop a meaningful dialogue with most consumers about headache remedies, skin care products, and the like, the health-care-product manufacturer has chosen not to focus its strategies and investments on a Web site alone. Instead, it places its products in the most fruitful digital context possible. Banner ads for J&J's Tylenol headache reliever unfurl on e-brokers' sites whenever the stock market falls by more than 100 points. The brokerage firms own the customer relationships, but J&J breaks into the dialogue at the moment when its marketing opportunity is greatest.

Or consider J&J's campaign for Clean & Clear, a skin care product line for teenage girls. Resisting the temptation to create yet another ill-fated destination site, such as the definitive on-line source for all things acne-related, J&J establishes a presence within preexisting on-line teen communities. The company gives teenage girls, many of whom spend their free time chatting on-line, the chance to send one another talking electronic postcards that offer a free skin analysis and a sample of Clean & Clear. The campaign's viral component—friend-to-friend referrals that multiply exponentially—significantly increases the product's exposure at little additional cost. The result: a response rate that's several times higher than standard Web levels, without any significant site investments. Once again, J&J inserts itself into a preexisting relationship at the optimal moment.

Even companies with flourishing destination sites can benefit from contextual marketing. Dell Computer, whose own site is an e-commerce leader, recognizes that most on-line computer shoppers bypass Dell's site and go straight to ZDNet and CNET for in-depth product information—combined, those two sites have almost ten times the number of site visitors that Dell has. So instead of using costly and ineffective banner ads to divert sales prospects to its own site, Dell posts its detailed product information on ZDNet's and CNET's sites. Visitors at those sites can then compare the latest offerings from Dell and Compaq, pick the Dell machine, and launch the ordering process directly from the CNET or ZDNet site. By piggybacking on CNET's and ZDNet's relationships, Dell has significantly improved its customer acquisition economics.

Beyond the Web Site

For all their innovation and ingenuity, J&J's and Dell's contextual marketing efforts are still defined by, and confined to, the PC. But the "tethered" Web is just a limited slice of the Internet, and it is ill suited to the marketing needs of many companies. The latest Internet technologies expose points of contact that are infinitely more timely and relevant. The convergence of the Internet with broadband connectivity and with TV will let marketers integrate commerce and entertainment: if you like Regis's suit, order it with a couple of clicks of your remote. Don't laugh—although early experiments with interactive TV were an expensive bust, recent trials have been more encouraging. When an interactive TV performance by pop artist Melissa Etheridge included an on-screen promotion for her latest CD, it generated an astonishing 46% click-through rate. The average click-through rate for a Web-based banner ad is only 0.5% at best.

Opportunities for contextual marketing extend well beyond the home. Mobile devices and Internet access in a broad range of public venues will let contextual marketers link real-life situations to virtual information and offerings. For instance, Unilever's mobile recipe book concept, which will be available on digital phones in Europe, should influence consumers' packaged-goods decisions far more than the company's Web site ever could. Intended for use while shopping, the mobile tool suggests recipes and breaks them down into their ingredients—identified, wherever possible, by their Unilever brand name. Rather than try to establish an ongoing Web site relationship with European grocery shoppers, U.K.-based Unilever plans to give them a digital tool precisely when and where they need it, helping shoppers and promoting Unilever brands at the same time.

Conceivably, the mobile recipe book could be used in connection with mobile e-coupons—electronic sales promotions that take into account the customer's identity and location, among other variables, and that are issued as close to the point of sale as possible. These time-sensitive contextual promotions can influence consumer purchasing decisions. At the same time, they let companies vary their pricing in real time in response to market and supply conditions.

These are just some of the ways that consumer product companies can harness the power of the ubiquitous Internet. But however they reach customers, whatever the mobilemediary, these companies should be guided by the following imperative: don't try to bring the customer to the site; instead, bring the message directly to the customer at the point of need.

The Ubiquitous Relationship

Even companies with enduring customer relationships and heavily trafficked Web sites need to master the tools of contextual marketing: electronic wallets, smart cards, mobile shopping lists, Internet-enabled POS systems, and many other electronic utilities and access technologies. These tools can extend the reach of relationship-oriented companies beyond their Web sites, capturing more information and improving customer service in the virtual and the physical worlds.

Consider FedEx. The company never fell into the trap of designating its Web site as its only mechanism for managing digital customer relationships—not surprising given that FedEx was practicing contextual marketing before the Web even existed. As early as 1988, its proprietary PowerShip terminals, installed in customers' mail rooms, brought digital interactions to the point of need. Today, FedEx is creating even deeper relationships. Its customers can use mobile devices to track packages or to locate the nearest spots to drop them off. Soon it will be possible for customers anywhere in the world to use a mobile phone to create a shipping label or a digital tracking record for a package.

The FedEx mobilemediaries could alert the company's customers to shipping problems encountered in transit. For instance, if a time-sensitive package is being held up at customs for lack of documentation, the mobilemediary could inform the customer and route the appropriate electronic forms to the customs office. FedEx also envisions customers using chip-embedded smart cards that can generate shipping labels and tracking information when swiped through a service terminal. Eventually, ubiquitous intelligence could move into the packages themselves; "smart packages" embedded with location-sensitive chips could transmit real-time tracking information to shippers and recipients, further expanding loyalty and raising competitors' barriers to entry.

American Express, for its part, recognizes that there's far more to the digital relationship than the customer's occasional visit to the company's site to review a bill. Ideally, the relationship should deepen every time the customer uses his or her Amex card. That's why the company has developed an e-wallet that automates the process of entering a customer's on-line purchasing data, such as her credit card number and shipping information. The e-wallet fosters loyalty by relieving the customer of that tedious chore. Even more important, it could become a tool for capturing data and cross-selling at the point of purchase. With explicit consent from customers, their e-wallet could follow them as they surf the Web or access the Internet through their mobile devices. The result would be a trove of customer intelligence.

Amex's recently launched Blue card is a potential predecessor to the ubiquitous e-wallet. With its embedded smart chip, the Blue card could extend beyond the Web site to the physical point of sale, bringing customer profile data not just to American Express, but also to the more than six million merchants that accept the company's cards.

But digital relationship management will involve far more than simply multiplying the points of contact. Ubiquity will enable bricks-and-mortar companies to convert physical customer traffic into digital relationships, introducing new combatants to the already fierce war for eyeballs. These companies will be able to use their physical access to customers to deliver precisely targeted messages—their own as well as those of companies that borrow the point of contact. Airlines, for instance, have a captive audience in the terminal club, the departure lounge, and the plane itself. They can exploit this advantage to offer contextual services beyond the reach of virtual agents such as Travelocity or Trip.com.

Even quintessential bricks-and-mortar businesses such as parking garages and shopping malls will be able to turn their traffic into personal relationships and incremental revenue. The best-conceived Web sites in the world wouldn't significantly improve the fortunes of those businesses. But ubiquity now allows garages and malls to manage customer relationships directly. In Sweden, garages now accept payment from the "digital wallet" of a Sonera cell phone. Embedded in the digital money is significant information about garage customers, including their names and when and how often they park. Garage owners can use the data to turn frequent visitors into monthly customers and to engage in dynamic pricing, charging more when the garage is nearly full and less when business is slow.

For shopping mall operators, ubiquity creates an opportunity to manage the customer relationships previously owned by individual retail tenants. Simon Properties, the largest retail mall developer in the United States, gives some shoppers mobile devices that they can use to generate electronic wish lists or to order products for home delivery. Simon eventually will be able to track shoppers as they move through the mall, feeding tenant retailers the purchase data they need to offer timely and relevant promotions. No longer an anonymous provider of retail space, Simon can now add value to the retail experience by helping store owners better match their products and services with customers' needs.

Ubiquity creates opportunities wherever there is customer traffic. As an extension of its existing FastPass electronic ticketing system, Disney could win loyalty in its theme parks by creating virtual lines. Using a Disney-supplied mobile device, a customer could reserve a seat on a popular ride hours in advance, eliminating the time spent waiting in line. That would increase customer enjoyment (and spending) while deepening the information-based relationship. Drawing on the information gathered during the customer's visit to the park, Disney could follow up with carefully targeted catalogs or promotions for movies, games, or merchandise. In similar fashion, some pretty unlikely candidates—from sports stadiums to movie theaters to taxicabs—suddenly emerge as digital intermediaries.

The automobile may present the richest new opportunity for digital relationship management. The ubiquitous Internet could enable GM, the world's largest manufacturing company, to transform itself from an automaker to a communications intermediary. After all, drivers spend an average of 8.5 hours a week inside the approximately 70 million GM vehicles on the road today. By comparison, America Online's 22 million subscribers spend 7.5 hours a week on-line. The information in every one of GM's vehicles is immensely valuable to other marketers. Shell and Texaco, for instance, would pay good money to know how much gas is left in a car's tank. Retailers and restaurateurs would pay to know when a vehicle is passing nearby. Mechanics would pay for access to a GM vehicle's service history. By reconceiving the car as an information device, GM dramatically increases the amount of value it can capture from each vehicle, while providing services that tie car owners closer to the company.

The New Corporate Agenda

It's tempting to take a wait-and-see attitude to the ubiquitous Internet. Wireless technologies are still in development. Interactive TV is years away from mass adoption. E-coupons and other methods of reaching the customer at the point of sale are in their infancy. But now is the time to begin building the skills needed to win in the age of ubiquity.

Senior managers need to start by honestly assessing their business. Does it offer a service or a product that will generate repeat visits to a Web site? Does it stand a chance of forming an ongoing relationship with customers? If so, the company should spend what it takes to design and build a destination Web site. But for most companies, the customer relationship is a series of contextual interactions. Those companies shouldn't be afraid to define an Internet strategy that deemphasizes the site itself; there are better ways for them to spend their marketing dollars.

Ubiquity will allow businesses to accompany their customers 24 hours a day, but not every business will be invited along for the ride. Customers will admit only the most relevant messages into their lives, so the concept of adding value to customers' lives will change significantly in an always-on world. The companies that can anticipate and meet the real needs of their customers—based on where they are located, what they do, and which communities of interest they belong to—will be valued partners. The companies that can't will be dismissed as pesky nuisances.

The winning companies will be the ones that master a few critical disciplines. First, database marketing tools will be essential. Whatever their industry, mass marketers will have to become direct marketers because the ubiquitous Internet will require companies to constantly retarget and retailor their messages. Second, new technology skills need to be mastered quickly: the companies that build new databases, upgrade their legacy systems early, and create the middleware necessary to tailor their messages to customers' ever-changing needs and situations will move ahead of the competition. And finally, companies need to adopt the discipline of measurement. Winners will measure everything, constantly refining their messages to meet ever-heightening consumer demands for relevance.

Mastering the contextual possibilities of the ubiquitous Internet will require a significant commitment of corporate resources. But the payoff is just as significant: Internet strategies that are truly relevant to companies and their customers. It will be neither cheap nor easy, but it will be a far better investment than pouring $10 billion into Web sites that few people visit.

9
Beyond the Exchange:
The Future of B2B

Richard Wise and David Morrison

The use of the Internet to facilitate commerce among companies promises vast benefits: dramatically reduced costs, greater access to buyers and sellers, improved marketplace liquidity, and a whole new array of efficient and flexible transaction methods. But if the benefits are clear, the path to achieving them is anything but. The B2B market is still in its infancy, and its structure and players remain in rapid flux. Despite breathless press coverage, very little is known about how business-to-business commerce will evolve on the Internet.

The high level of uncertainty is causing widespread anxiety among executives—and for good reason. Whether as buyers, sellers, or both, all companies have substantial stakes in the business-to-business marketplace. Their supply chains, their product and marketing strategies, their processes and operations—even their business models—will be shaped by the way B2B relationships are formed and transactions are carried out. Yet at this moment even the most basic questions remain difficult for companies to answer: Which exchanges should we participate in? Should we form a trading consortium with our competitors? Should we demand that our suppliers go on-line? What software should we invest in? Executives understand that the wrong choices could have dire consequences, but they also know that in the fast-paced world of the Internet they need to act soon or they'll be left behind.

Fortunately, there is a model for the future shape of B2B: the financial services industry. Characterized by information-based transactions, large and liquid exchanges, and intense competition, financial markets closely resemble the new B2B markets. But unlike their B2B counterparts, the financial markets have been around for centuries. Their evolution provides important clues to the likely evolution of B2B. In particular, the recent restructuring of the financial industry suggests that, counter to the common wisdom about B2B today, exchanges are not the primary source of value in markets that are information intensive. Rather, value tends to accumulate among a diverse group of specialists that focus on such tasks as packaging, standard setting, arbitrage, and information management.

We will use the financial services industry as a window into the future of B2B. We will show why the current exchange-based model is structurally flawed, examine the major trends that will influence the strategies of both entrepreneurs and established companies, and describe the key market players that are likely to emerge and the roles they'll play. The future we envision is already coming into being. New B2B players are now emerging with business models that mirror those that have come to define and dominate the financial industry.

The Flaws in the Exchange Model

Most B2B activity to date has centered on on-line exchanges and auctions, and most observers have assumed that these electronic marketplaces would come to dominate the B2B landscape. Once you look beyond the hype, however, you quickly see that most Internet exchanges are floundering. They suffer from meager transaction volume and equally meager revenues, and they face a raft of competitors. One of the leading chemical exchanges, for example, has seen its postings grow considerably since its launch in early 1998, but it's still processing less than one trade per day. The hard truth is that few of these exchanges will ever create the liquidity needed to survive.

The current B2B model has three fatal flaws. First, the value proposition offered by most exchanges—competitive bidding among suppliers allows buyers to get the lowest possible prices—runs counter to the best recent thinking on buyer-supplier relations. Most companies have come to realize that getting supplies at the lowest price may not be in their best economic interest. Other factors, such as quality, timing of deliveries, and customization, are often more important than price in determining the overall value provided by a supplier. (That's particularly true for the many manufacturers that have adopted lean, low-inventory production systems that depend on reliable, precisely scheduled shipments of supplies and components.) Many companies have spent the last two decades methodically forging tighter, more strategic relationships with suppliers—many such affiliations have involved joint product-design efforts, integration of complex processes, and long-term service contracts. The on-line exchanges' focus on arm's-length, price-driven transactions flies in the face of all this hard work.

Second, the exchanges deliver little benefit to sellers. Yes, suppliers have access to more buyers with only a modest increase in marketing cost, but that benefit is overwhelmed by pricing pressures. Few suppliers want to be anonymous contestants in ruthless bidding wars, and for the highest-quality, most innovative suppliers, price battles are anathema. As a result, the buyer-biased exchanges that characterize B2B today will not be able to achieve a critical mass of participants and transactions—they will be forever starved of liquidity. To be successful in the long run, B2B markets need to offer strong incentives to both buyers and sellers.

Finally, the business models of most B2B exchanges are, at best, half-baked. In their rush to get on-line, the companies that run the exchanges haven't taken the time to study their customers' priorities in-depth, create distinctive offerings, or even map out paths to profitability. They've simply used off-the-shelf software to set up simple auctions as quickly as possible. Because the software is readily available and relatively cheap, the barriers to entry are low, and the resulting proliferation of new exchanges is undermining the margins of all players. Indeed, the influx of new entrants is leading to the same type of market fragmentation that exchanges were designed to overcome in the first place.

The current B2B model, propped up by cheap investment capital, is not sustainable. As the markets mature, they will have to evolve in ways that fix the problems of the existing system. New structures will enable buyers and suppliers to form tight relationships while still enjoying the reach and efficiency of Internet commerce. Rewards will begin to flow to sellers as well as buyers. And new business models will provide profits in a world of dirt-cheap transactions. The B2B business will, in other words, reshape itself to resemble the financial services industry.

Four Formative Trends

Until recently, business-to-business markets had little in common with financial markets. But with the spread of digitization and, in particular, the Internet, B2B commerce has taken on many of the characteristics of financial trading. Greater market liquidity and transparency have enabled more efficient pricing and more effective matching of buyers and sellers, and, most important, value has shifted from the product itself to information about the product. While the transfer of physical goods may remain the end result of a business transaction, the information that shapes the transaction—price, availability, quality, quantity, and so on—can now be separated and exchanged electronically. And that information is often more valuable to companies than the underlying goods.

Over the last two decades, as deregulation and digitization have swept through financial services, the industry has gone through a radical restructuring. Traditional brokerage and banking channels have been dismantled, and transaction fees have fallen precipitously. As a result, power and profit have migrated away from centuries-old business models toward a wide variety of innovative and often highly specialized new models. Four major trends—good predictors of how B2B commerce will evolve—have combined to reshape the industry.

FROM SIMPLE TO COMPLEX TRANSACTIONS

To fulfill complicated financing needs, a company once had to forge a close working relationship with a major bank that could offer tailored loans. Even though the process of customizing a financing package was time consuming, expensive, and restricting, there was often no alternative. In recent years, however, highly complex financial transactions have been successfully packaged as securities that can be freely bought and sold. Securitization has vastly increased the financing choices available to companies—and vastly reduced the fees earned by traditional banks.

Standards made securitization possible. By adopting universal standards for loan terms and lending parameters, the financial industry enabled more customization within open marketplaces. Consider the mortgage market. Traditionally, mortgages were customized loans handled by local banks. Rates, terms, and lending requirements varied greatly. But spurred by the advent of lending agencies such as Fannie Mae and Ginnie Mae, the mortgage business has evolved into an efficient national marketplace of securities, with arm's-length transactions between dispersed buyers and sellers. The traditional bank's role of generalist, in which it handled every aspect of a mortgage, has been split into three specialist roles: origination, a customer relationship task still handled by local banks or mortgage brokers; securitization, a financial task handled by Fannie Mae and Ginnie Mae working with investment banks; and loan servicing, a processing task handled by large-scale service companies.

We expect to see a similar fragmentation of roles in the B2B world as markets are restructured to accommodate the complex goods and services that account for the bulk of most companies' spending. Already, some exchanges are repositioning themselves to play narrower but more lucrative roles. FreeMarkets, best known for running Internet auctions, is rapidly turning itself into what might be called a *specialist originator*—a company that helps buyers gather and analyze the information necessary to purchase complex products and services electronically. FreeMarkets knows that its greatest value lies not in conducting auctions, which is rapidly becoming a commodity service, but in identifying and qualifying bidders and in creating detailed, standardized requests for proposals that enable the bidders to provide comparable quotes even on highly specialized products. Auctions are becoming adjuncts to FreeMarkets' primary role of providing structure, standards, and liquidity for complex transactions.

As FreeMarkets handles more transactions, its product descriptions will become more refined and standardized, reducing the investment it has to make in subsequent auctions and expanding the range of auctionable items. It is unlikely, however, that FreeMarkets will be able to retain proprietary control over the standards it is helping create. The experience of the financial industry provides another clear lesson here: while many securitized products, from auto leases to credit card receivables, started out as proprietary inventions, they eventually became routine, widely traded offerings. In much the same way, the standards for describing products for on-line sale will become universal as other exchanges copy FreeMarkets' templates or as industry-specific standards emerge for describing product and transaction attributes.

As this happens, FreeMarkets' focus will likely shift to two areas: providing on-line expertise in sorting out which product features best meet a particular buyer's needs and leveraging its knowledge of quali-fied suppliers to serve buyers as a demand aggregator. Like a mortgage originator, FreeMarkets will concentrate on the initial qualification, specification, and packaging role, handing off the transaction itself to larger, more liquid exchange partners. (For a business-to-consumer version of this model, see "Learning from B2C: MySimon.")

Learning from B2C: MySimon

Most business-to-business exchanges focus on relatively simple transactions involving commodities, common maintenance items, or basic services like cargo transport. Yet the vast majority of business spending lies in the more complex categories of components, services, and capital goods. Here, pur-chase decisions hinge on many variables beyond price, and, as a result, compa-nies usually rely on salespeople and other traditional channels, such as distrib-utors and value-added resellers.

Can the Internet provide a mechanism for enabling complex transactions? MySimon, a consumer shopping service, suggests how specialized shopping intermediaries may emerge in B2B markets to fill this need.

Using decision-support software from Active Research, MySimon offers tailored purchasing advice in a variety of product categories while allowing buyers to compare the offerings of many vendors. It helps consumers sort through an array of purchase dimensions, decide which areas are important to them, and then see how well the available offerings match up with their requirements.

Here's how you buy a DVD player through MySimon. First, the Web site provides an overview of DVD players, highlighting key specifications and the most important ways that each model varies from the others. Then, through Active Research's proprietary recommendation engine, MySimon walks you through a real-time trade-off survey assessing the value you place on various features and brands and testing different bundled attributes—all to assess what you care about in a DVD player.

The Active Buyer's Guide then recommends several DVD players that best fit your needs, lists sites on the Web where those models are available, and shows the prices. You can click through to place an order.

MySimon renders obsolete the value-added role of the trained salesper-son and goes beyond the role of the typical e-retailer. Rather than selling the product, MySimon acts as a personal adviser to guide the customer to a source for purchase. The company generates revenues from vendor slotting fees and advertising.

With similar decision-support tools, more complex B2B sales will become feasible on-line. This trend will likely be accelerated by the advent of extensible markup language (XML), a set of software standards for displaying and sharing detailed information such as pricing and product specifications over the Web. Purchase support could become a unique source of value and customer loyalty, with the actual transactions handed off to sites that compete solely on price and availability. Companies such as General Electric and Milacron are already moving to provide more of this decision-making information on their Web sites.

FROM MIDDLEMEN TO SPECULATORS

As financial markets became more competitive, transaction fees steadily eroded. Stock trades that used to generate fat commissions, for example, are now executed for a few dollars—or even for free. The disappearance of transaction income has set off an intense search for new sources of revenue, which has in turn given rise to a new set of business models. Instead of extracting fees from transactions, a number of financial services players now make their money by actively trading in the underlying market. Several of the leading investment banks, for instance, have increasingly dedicated their capital and people to investing for their own accounts, and these investments generate a large and growing share of their overall profits. The companies still need to be closely involved in client transactions, but mainly for the information about market trends they provide.

As the profit margins of B2B exchanges get pushed down by competition, some exchanges will start to take their own speculative positions, buying and selling large quantities of the goods traded in their markets. In this "e-speculator" model, running the biggest exchange still provides a source of competitive advantage, but, just as in the financial markets, the advantage comes not from fees but from a superior window into the dynamics of the market. Ultimately, exchanges might even reduce their commissions to a price below zero; that is, they might pay for a flow of deals in order to gain valuable information about the market.

One pioneer in e-speculation can be found in the financial industry itself. Knight Trading Group, a wholesale market maker for stocks, executes trades behind the scenes for the largest on-line trading firms, including E*Trade and Ameritrade. Knight has invested in a highly automated system that can execute a large volume of trades efficiently, and roughly 40% of all on-line trading now flows through the company. Rather than earning profits through commissions on trades, however, Knight pays the on-line brokers for their order flows. The company uses the order information to analyze market movements and adjust its own positions accordingly. While most exchanges struggle to break even, Knight enjoyed a 35% operating margin and a 68% return on equity for the 12 months that ended with April 2000.

Enron is also using the e-speculator model. Originally a gas pipeline operator, the company steadily expanded to become a major provider of many other energy products. It has recently exploited its privileged position to establish a thriving on-line exchange in which it makes money not from commissions but from buying and selling a variety of energy products, including natural gas, electric power, pulp, and pollution credits, for its own account.

Following the lead of investment banks, Enron is now pursuing the logical extension of the e-speculator model: creating and selling derivatives such as options, futures, and swaps, which allow other market participants to mitigate their price risks. Enron currently transacts $1.5 billion in derivatives per day on-line, and it has been doubling its transaction volume each quarter. These instruments allow the company to profit in two ways. They are lucrative to sell, and they allow Enron to hedge its market positions, decreasing its exposure to trading losses.

FROM TRANSACTIONS TO SOLUTIONS

Decreases in transaction income have also led financial firms to emphasize comprehensive money-management services to enhance profit margins, cement customer relationships, and lock in predictable revenue streams. An early sign of this shift was the rise of mutual funds and asset management services in the late 1980s. More recently, we have seen a proliferation of sophisticated services such as investment planning, tax and estate planning, and tailored investment accounts. In addition to generating substantial returns for the providers, such integrated services have considerable appeal to well-heeled clients, who want to manage the overall costs and returns of their portfolios rather than maximize the value of any one transaction.

The B2B landscape is also well suited to solution providers. By using the Internet to bundle products with related information and services, creative companies can improve the effectiveness and efficiency of their clients' businesses. By doing so, they will be able to forge strong, long-lasting client relationships that will de-emphasize product price and exchange-based transactions. Early examples of solution sites are now appearing on the Internet. Some are operated by suppliers looking to counter the role of the exchanges; others are portals operated by third-party intermediaries.

An example of the first type is Milpro.com, a site operated by machine-tool manufacturer Milacron. Milpro sells high-margin Milacron coolants, cutting wheels, and drill bits directly to small machine shops. But the site also helps these customers handle a broad array of related business challenges, such as buying and selling used equipment, identifying new business opportunities, and troubleshooting problems. For example, the site includes a software "wizard" that guides customers through a set of questions about a process (such as grinding) and related problems (such as chatter marks) and then recommends particular products, much as an experienced sales representative would. Through such services, Milacron has been able to attract the attention and the business of small machine shops, a group that's difficult and expensive to reach through traditional channels. Those shops, in turn, gain access to expertise that they could not otherwise afford—and that would not be available through a transaction-focused exchange.

An example of a third-party solution site is Biztro.com, a portal for small-business transactions. Biztro aims to solve small-business managers' back-office headaches through an integrated suite of applications for such functions as payroll, benefits management, human resources management, and procurement. Biztro has signed deals with a group of product and service providers, including Dell and OfficeMax. The providers are able to sell through the portal, and Biztro earns a commission on the transactions. By providing a high level of convenience, Biztro shifts customers away from purely price-based purchases.

FROM BUYER-SELLER EXCHANGE TRANSACTIONS TO SELL-SIDE ASSET SWAPS

With the rise of large, sophisticated market makers and the emergence of digital networks, more and more securities trades are being executed without hitting the floor of a traditional exchange. Many financial companies, for example, are joining electronic communications networks, or ECNs, in which they can match trades with other participating members, saving them the cost of going through an exchange and allowing them to trade day or night. Charles Schwab has gone even further. It runs its own internal trading operation, enabling it to carry out many mutual fund transactions by simply swapping shares among its customers without involving or even notifying the mutual fund companies. Besides eliminating transaction costs, such internal trading preserves Schwab's control over client transactions and the resulting information.

Similar sell-side swap models are emerging in B2B e-commerce. In stark contrast to most existing exchanges, which tend to penalize sellers, asset swaps benefit suppliers by allowing them to better utilize their key assets—whether factories, trucks, warehouses, or containers for shipping. At the same time, they enable buyers to tap a broader, more efficient supply base.

The swapping model is particularly attractive in highly fragmented industries, where small-scale suppliers often lack a broad geographic reach and are highly vulnerable to fluctuations in demand. The trucking business is a perfect example. Many segments of the trucking market are populated by independents or small firms that cannot individually achieve scale economies, partly because of the unpredictability of their routes. Unable to coordinate pickups and deliveries among their own small sets of customers, truckers routinely return from deliveries without cargo. That means higher costs for the truckers and higher shipping fees and slower delivery times for their customers.

Most B2B Web sites in the trucking business don't help truckers address these problems. Instead, they use auctions to pit carriers against one another in cutthroat bidding wars, which only exacerbate an already bad situation. Transportal Network, in contrast, uses the Internet to allow carriers to trade capacity with other carriers, filling those empty trucks and creating a better system for all involved. In conjunction with its asset-swapping service, Transportal also offers truckers the ability to pool their purchases of employee benefits and insurance, parts and equipment, financing, and other products, enabling them to gain scale advantages without losing their independence. Customers, meanwhile, benefit from a stronger, more efficient base of carriers.

New Business Models

The restructuring of the financial services industry took two decades. The changes will happen much more quickly in B2B e-commerce,

Exhibit 9-1   The Emerging B2B Landscape

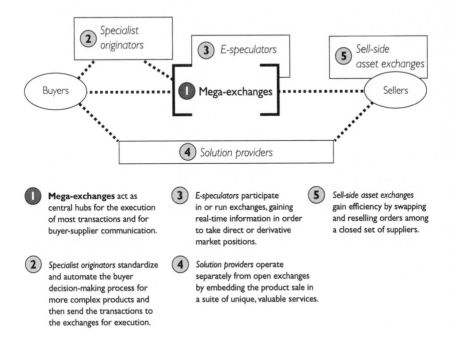

Mega-exchanges act as central hubs for the execution of most transactions and for buyer-supplier communication.

Specialist originators standardize and automate the buyer decision-making process for more complex products and then send the transactions to the exchanges for execution.

E-speculators participate in or run exchanges, gaining real-time information in order to take direct or derivative market positions.

Solution providers operate separately from open exchanges by embedding the product sale in a suite of unique, valuable services.

Sell-side asset exchanges gain efficiency by swapping and reselling orders among a closed set of suppliers.

where regulation is thin and competition is already intense. As the trends we've described play out, B2B commerce will be structured very differently from the way it is today. (See Exhibit 9-1 "The Emerging B2B Landscape.") Rather than being dominated by monolithic exchanges, it will encompass several distinct, interdependent business models.

Because scale and liquidity are vitally important to efficient trading, today's fragmented and illiquid exchanges will consolidate into a relatively small set of **mega-exchanges** that will occupy the center of the B2B universe. Although most transactions will flow through them, they will not generate much profit or shareholder value. As transaction fees fall or disappear entirely, the exchanges may turn into nonprofit collectives. (See "For the Traditional Exchange, a Collective Approach.") Many B2B players will maintain stakes in the exchanges for the benefit of more lucrative e-commerce endeavors such as origination or speculation.

For the Traditional Exchange, a Collective Approach

First-generation B2B exchanges, faced with boycotts by suppliers and anti-trust scrutiny from regulators, are likely to evolve in two important ways. First, since the best method of achieving sufficient market liquidity is to enlist every participant's support, the exchanges will move away from being for-profit entities and move toward being collective industry efforts run for the benefit of all.

Second, they will move beyond executing transactions to create the infrastructure and standards necessary to streamline communication between buyers and sellers. This will address pressing issues of efficiency, such as speeding up the flow of product information, automating billing and payment, and linking buyer and seller production processes more closely. And it will allow them to handle not only simple products but complex custom components and services, which account for most business purchases.

Covisint, the automotive mega-exchange hatched by General Motors, Ford, and DaimlerChrysler, is already moving down this path. Conceived as a for-profit enterprise that would earn commissions on the transaction volume generated by its founders, Covisint has changed that proposition in the face of resistance from suppliers. To ensure broad participation, Covisint has opened up its exchange to many other auto manufacturers as equity owners, and 40 suppliers have been given profit-sharing stakes. In their public comments, Covisint's owners are now talking less about sponsoring auctions and are instead trying to reduce the roughly $140 currently spent to process an average purchase order.

If the automotive industry—where buyers are concentrated and suppliers are fragmented—is moving toward a collaborative exchange model, other industries are bound to follow. Once again, this mirrors a similar evolution in financial markets. Over the past several decades, numerous subscale regional stock exchanges were replaced by two large exchanges, the NYSE and the NASDAQ. Both exchanges operate primarily for the benefit of members rather than to maximize the profits of the exchange, and both have played a key role in developing the information standards and infrastructure for electronic trading and funds exchange.

Surrounding the mega-exchanges and plugged into them in various symbiotic ways will be the specialist companies. **Originators** such as FreeMarkets will structure and take orders for complex transactions, aggregate them—bundle them into large order requests—and send them to mega-exchanges for execution. The originator role will be most valuable in markets with relatively expensive products that are neither commodities nor completely customized, such as automotive and aircraft components, industrial equipment subassemblies, and complex services such as insurance.

To be successful, an originator will need to concentrate initially on creating standards for trading complicated products and providing real-time support for customers on-line. An originator will be able to achieve an advantage by understanding a complex product category and customer decision-making parameters better than its competitors; it will also benefit by adeptly using configuration and decision-support software. Profits will come primarily from commissions and from slotting fees paid by vendors and exchanges in return for preferential positions with the originator, much as food manufacturers pay slotting fees to grocery chains for prime shelf space. Many of the niche portals already in operation will likely use their knowledge of narrow business communities to move toward an originator model.

Savvy **e-speculators,** seeking to capitalize on an abundance of market information, will tend to concentrate where relatively standardized products can be transferred easily among a large group of buyers. They'll also look for price volatility, which will provide trading spreads. Expect to see e-speculators in markets for specialty chemicals, paper, and certain basic auto parts.

To thrive, an e-speculator will need to develop strong financial and risk-management skills. A speculator's advantage will come from having better, more timely market information than other participants. To get that information, it will have to partner closely with at least one mega-exchange or operate as the profit-making arm of an exchange. Speculators will likely earn profits not only by trading but also by creating and selling various hedging instruments.

In many markets, a handful of independent **solution providers** with well-known brand names and solid reputations will thrive alongside mega-exchanges. Like Milacron, a good number of them will leverage distinctive technical expertise to become indispensable to customers—and thus reduce the importance of price in buying decisions. Many will derive a substantial proportion of their profits from high-margin add-ons and consumables. The solution model will be most common in markets where the product itself represents a small portion of a customer's overall costs but heavily influences those costs, as in specialty chemicals, engineered plastics, and cutting tools. For example, specialty chemical admixtures represent a small percentage of the cost of concrete, but the wrong admixture can cause an extremely costly problem: the cement won't cure properly.

Many B2B transactions will consist of **sell-side asset exchanges,** in which suppliers will trade orders among themselves, sometimes after initial transactions with customers are made on the mega-exchanges. Sell-side swapping will be most valuable where markets are highly fragmented, both on the buyer and seller sides—where, for geographic or information reasons, demand and supply are often mismatched and where suppliers can benefit greatly from keeping expensive fixed assets fully utilized. Industries with these characteristics include transportation, metalworking, plastic molding, farming, and construction.

A company seeking to pursue the asset-exchange model will need to have strong relationships with the supplier community, since success will hinge on its gaining a critical mass of supplier transactions. It will also need to be adept at understanding supplier problems; sales of products and services that solve them will likely be an important source of profits.

Investing in New Skills

Whether a company is hoping to play a role as a B2B service provider or simply needs to transact business with other companies, it will have to develop a deep knowledge of the emerging landscape and the various business models it will contain. (See Table 9-1 "An Overview of the New B2B Models.") As we've seen, the players' value and power will vary considerably depending on the industry and the products involved. Each company will have to create its own path to success—and not all products are suited to Internet transactions: very complex, very expensive items such as aircraft or merger-and-acquisition advisory services will continue to be sold primarily through personal relationships and multistep purchasing processes.

Many of the financial services companies that ultimately profited from the restructuring of the markets were not traditional banks or brokerage houses. They were companies that were able to spot disruptive trends and were willing to reconfigure their businesses, often at high cost and risk, to seize the new opportunities. Charles Schwab is perhaps the best example. Schwab reinvented itself not once but three times: it started as a discount broker, became a provider of asset

Table 9-1 An Overview of the New B2B Models

	Key enabling characteristics	Relevant industries or markets	Required capabilities	Sources of competitive advantage	Sources of profit
Mega-exchange	• Maximum liquidity • Common transaction standards	• Most vertical industries • Major horizontal purchase categories	• Large-scale transaction processing • Perceived neutrality	• Scope and liquidity • Standard setting	• Profits are slim or exchange is nonprofit
Specialist originator	• Complex products • Relatively expensive products	• Electronic and mechanical components • Automotive and aircraft components • Insurance	• Strong consultative sales skills • Deep product understanding • Strong customer relationships	• Deep knowledge of product category • Effective use of decision-support software • Access to qualified suppliers • Ability to bundle transaction volume	• Transaction commissions • Slotting fees from vendors, exchanges

Table 9-1 (continued)

	Key enabling characteristics	Relevant industries or markets	Required capabilities	Sources of competitive advantage	Sources of profit
E-speculator	• High degree of product standardization or fungibility • Moderate to high price volatility	• Electrical power • Chemicals • Replacement auto parts	• Financial engineering and hedging skills • In-depth knowledge of market and market dynamics	• Timely market information • Transaction scale • Alignment with a major buyer or seller	• Playing the spread • Selling hedging instruments to participants
Solution provider	• Product cost a small portion of overall costs • Product-related issues impact other costs	• Specialty chemicals • Engineered plastics • Cutting tools	• Strong technical skills • Problem-solving mind-set	• Brand strength • Rich set of offerings • Customer lock-in	• Higher product margins • Valuable add-ons and refills
Sell-side exchange	• High fixed costs • Relatively fragmented supplier and customer base	• Transportation • Metal machining • Construction	• Strong supplier relationships • Ability to offer additional relevant services • Perceived neutrality	• Liquidity • First mover with key suppliers	• Selling ancillary products/services to members

management and back-office services to financial planners, developed a mutual fund "supermarket," and then became a hybrid clicks-and-mortar solution provider combining Web-based transactions with personal advice. Each reinvention required significant investments—such as the recent purchase of U.S. Trust to fulfill the goal of providing asset management solutions—but ultimately increased Schwab's customer base, profits, and market valuation.

Managers contemplating their next B2B move should take the example of Schwab to heart. Radical changes in markets require radical responses. For many companies, traditional skills in such areas as product development, manufacturing, and marketing may become less important, while the ability to understand and capitalize on market dynamics may become considerably more important. Enron's experience illustrates the point. In building its e-commerce market-making capabilities, Enron has aggressively brought in new people with new skills. Engineers have been replaced by traders, economists, and risk managers. That kind of change is tough to make, but as Schwab and Enron understand, it's essential to success. Indeed, in the digital age, timidity is just another word for irrelevance.

PART
III
Reimagining Management

10
Bringing Silicon Valley Inside

Gary Hamel

It's a fact. In most industries, newcomers are creating much of the new wealth. Cisco, Amazon.com, Starbucks, Charles Schwab, America Online, the Gap, MCI WorldCom, Dell, Southwest Airlines, SAP—these companies didn't even exist a generation ago, yet by May 1999 their combined market capitalization had grown to nearly $800 billion. And they are hardly unique. In industry after industry, unorthodox start-ups are challenging complacent incumbents.

Stewardship versus entrepreneurship: that's the fundamental distinction between the mediocre mass and the revolutionary wealth creators. Stewards polish grandma's silver—they buff up the assets and capabilities they inherited from entrepreneurs long retired or long dead. Devoid of passion and imagination, they spend their time trying to unlock wealth by hammering down costs, outsourcing inefficient processes, buying back shares, selling off bad businesses, and spinning out good ones. But in the new economy, investors don't want stewards. They want entrepreneurial heroes—innovators who are obsessed with creating *new* wealth. Stewards conserve. Entrepreneurs create.

If you want your company to join the pantheon of wealth-creating superstars, you have to shift the balance of effort from stewardship to entrepreneurship in your organization. There's nothing wrong with stewardship—someone has to safeguard all those brands, skills, assets, and customers that underpin today's success. But in a world where strategy life cycles are increasingly measured in months, not decades, even the most skilled stewardship won't enable you to capture tomorrow's riches. It may not even enable you to survive.

Face it: Out there in some garage, an entrepreneur is forging a bullet with your company's name on it. Once that bullet leaves the barrel, you won't be able to dodge it. You've got one option: you have to shoot first. You have to out-innovate the innovators, out-entrepreneur the entrepreneurs. Sound impossible for a decades-old incumbent? It is. Unless you're willing to challenge just about every assumption you have about how to drive innovation and wealth creation in your company.

Your classroom is Silicon Valley—a sliver of real estate about 30 miles long and ten miles wide, nestled up against the Santa Cruz mountains. Here you'll find towering eucalyptus trees, verdant hills, a crisp Pacific breeze, and what may be the most perfect climate on earth. But in these bucolic surroundings lurks a raw and restless spirit.

The Valley is the distilled essence of entrepreneurial energy. Its ethos is simple: If it's not new, it's not cool; if it's not cool, it's not worth doing. If you don't own shares, you're getting screwed. If you've been in the same job for more than two years, your career is over. If you haven't been through an IPO, you're a virgin. This is where a $2 million house is a teardown. This is where a Porsche is just one more compact car and sushi's just another fast food. Never has so much wealth been created in so little time by so few people. If the Valley's residents pause to think about it for even a nanosecond, they know they're as blessed as those who lived in Italy during the Renaissance. Like the Florentines and Venetians, they're building a new age—an age of virtual presence, of globally interconnected communities, of frictionless commerce, of instantly accessible knowledge and stunningly seductive media.

If your company is going to grab more than its fair share of new wealth, it has to learn how to bring the energy and ethos of the Valley inside. The choice is simple, really. You can sit back and wait for the Valley or some other hotbed of innovation to spawn the revolutionary company that buries your business model. Or you can bring the Valley inside and capture the vast economic benefits that flow from unfettered imagination and unbridled ambition.

Big Stakes

What's the payoff to bringing Silicon Valley inside? Well, let's do a bit of arithmetic. Silicon Valley has about 2 million people. Let's say 50%

of them are at work in the private sector—the rest are kids, retirees, government employees, and the like. Of that million, let's say half are of the caliber you'd find in your company—people who haven't spent their entire careers working at 7-Eleven or Jiffy Lube. Let's call those 500,000 people the Silicon Valley gene pool. In 1998, that gene pool produced 41 IPOs, which by January 1999 had a combined market cap of $27 billion. If you divide $27 billion by 500,000, you get $54,000. That's $54,000 in new wealth creation per capita—in a single year.

Multiply $54,000 by the number of employees in your organization. Did your company create that much new wealth last year out of your employee gene pool? Let's see. At the end of 1998, General Motors had 594,000 employees. That's $32 billion in potential new wealth—if only GM could engender the passion and imagination of Silicon Valley. Kmart had 278,000 employees—that's $15 billion in potential new wealth. 3M had 73,000 employees—that's $4 billion.

Okay, so maybe it's unreasonable to aspire to match the heady performance of Silicon Valley. Maybe you can create new wealth at only half the pace or a quarter of the pace. But ask yourself this: Would the potential payoff of bringing Silicon Valley inside be any less than what you're getting with supply chain management or enterprise resource planning or some other stewardship program? If not, doesn't it deserve at least the same effort?

Many corporate leaders envy the success of Silicon Valley's entrepreneurs, but few have thought about how they might bring the Valley inside—how they might ignite the entrepreneurial passions of their own people. They assume the Valley is filled with brilliant visionaries while their own organizations are filled with witless drones. This assumption is, of course, self-fulfilling. Where employees are called on to do no more than service the existing business model, you will indeed find a company filled with witless drones.

Those who populate Silicon Valley don't have brains the size of basketballs. They don't live in some special energy field. What sets the Valley apart is not its people or its climate but its way of doing business. In the Valley, ideas, capital, and talent are allowed to circulate freely. They meld into whatever combinations are most likely to generate innovation and wealth. There are none of the numbing bureaucratic controls that paralyze creativity in traditional businesses. If you want to free the entrepreneurial spirit inside your company, you're going to have to figure out how to set up and sustain dynamic internal markets for ideas, capital, and talent. Sound implausible? There are companies that are already doing it.

Silicon Valley in Royal Dutch/Shell

Royal Dutch/Shell, the Anglo-Dutch oil giant headquartered more than 6,000 miles from Silicon Valley, is seldom mistaken for a lithe and nimble upstart. With $138 billion in revenues and 102,000 employees, it's the epitome of a lumbering industrial behemoth—the last place you'd expect to find entrepreneurial zeal. Within its balkanized organization, which one employee has compared to a maze of 100-foot-high brick walls, access to capital is tightly controlled, investment hurdles are daunting, and radical ideas move slowly, if at all. Shell's globe-trotting managers are famously disciplined, diligent, and methodical; they don't come across as wild-eyed dreamers. Indeed, employees with an entrepreneurial urge would probably prefer skinny-dipping in the North Sea to confronting Shell's conservative bureaucracy.

But a band of renegades, led by Tim Warren, the director of research and technical services in Shell's largest division, Exploration and Production, has been intent on changing all that. Warren and his team have been working hard to free up the flow of ideas, capital, and talent—to make E&P an innovation-friendly zone. Their initial success suggests that it is possible to imbue a global giant with the kind of damn-the-conventions ethos that permeates Silicon Valley. Here's their story.

By late 1996, it had become apparent to Warren and some of his colleagues that E&P was unlikely to meet its earnings targets without radical innovations. In recent years, his team had been under considerable pressure to align its R&D spending with the immediate needs of Shell's national operating units. Long-term projects had been reined in and short-term priorities given more weight. Warren understood the rationale for those moves, but he wondered whether the existing R&D process could be counted on to help Shell invent entirely new businesses and dramatically different business models. He sensed that a wealth of imagination was bottled up in Shell's employees—imagination that might help the company find its way into new, high-growth opportunities.

Looking to stir up some new thinking, he had already encouraged his people to devote up to 10% of their time to "nonlinear" ideas. The results were less than he'd hoped for. His frustration was the genesis for an entirely new approach to innovation, one that was both simple and slightly deviant.

He gave a small panel of freethinking employees the authority to allocate $20 million to rule-breaking, game-changing ideas submitted by their peers. Anyone could submit ideas, and the panel would decide which deserved funding. Proposals would be accepted not just from within E&P but from anywhere across Shell. In this way, unconventional ideas wouldn't have to run the usual approval gauntlet or justify their existence in terms of existing programs and priorities.

The GameChanger process, as it came to be known, went live in November 1996. At first, the availability of venture funding failed to yield an avalanche of new ideas. Though bright and creative, employees long accustomed to working on well-defined technical problems found it difficult to think revolutionary thoughts. Hoping to kick-start the process, the GameChanger panel enlisted the help of a team of consultants from Strategos who designed a three-day "Innovation Lab" to help employees develop rule-busting ideas and to dole out a half million dollars of seed money. Seventy-two enthusiastic would-be entrepreneurs showed up for the initial lab, a much larger group than the panel had anticipated. Many were individuals no one would have suspected of harboring an entrepreneurial impulse.

In the Innovation Lab, the budding revolutionaries were encouraged to learn from radical innovations drawn from outside the energy business. They were taught how to identify and challenge industry conventions, how to anticipate and exploit discontinuities of all kinds, and how to leverage Shell's competencies and assets in novel ways. Groups of eight attendees were then seated at round tables in front of networked laptop computers and encouraged to put their new thinking skills to work. Slowly at first, then in a rush, new ideas began to flow through the network. Some ideas attracted a flurry of support from the group; others remained orphans. By the end of the second day, a portfolio of 240 ideas had been generated. Some were for entirely new businesses, and many more were for new approaches within existing businesses.

The attendees then agreed on a set of screening criteria to determine which of the ideas deserved a portion of the seed money. Twelve ideas were nominated for funding, and a volunteer army of supporters coalesced around each one. Invigorated by their participation in the Innovation Lab, the teams vowed to move quickly to turn their GameChanger ideas into concrete business plans. A second Innovation

Lab was held a month later with a new tranche of nascent entrepreneurs, and it produced a similar outpouring of fresh thinking.

Realizing that GameChanger had to be more than a brainstorming exercise, Shell put mechanisms in place to ensure that the ideas were turned into actions. At the conclusion of the Innovation Labs, internal transfer payments were made to cover the time of the employees serving on the idea development teams. A five-day "Action Lab," again designed with Strategos, was held to teach the teams to create credible venture plans. In the Action Lab, team members were taught how to scope out the boundaries of an opportunity space, identify potential partnerships, enumerate genuine sources of competitive advantage, and identify the broad financial implications. Next, they were coached in developing 100-day action plans: low-cost, low-risk ways of testing the ideas. Finally, each team presented its story to a "venture board" consisting of the GameChanger panel, a sampling of senior managers, and representatives from Shell Technology Ventures—a unit that funds projects that don't fall under the purview of Shell's operating units.

Since the completion of the labs, the GameChanger panel has been working hard to institutionalize the internal entrepreneurial process. It meets weekly to discuss new submissions—320 have come in so far, many through Shell's intranet—and its members serve as coaches and advocates for prospective innovators. An employee with a promising idea is invited to give a ten-minute pitch to the panel, followed by a 15-minute Q&A session. If the members agree that the idea has real potential, the employee is invited to a second round of discussions with a broader group of company experts whose knowledge or support may be important to the success of the proposed venture. Before rejecting an idea, the panel looks carefully at what Shell would stand to lose if the opportunity turned out to be all its sponsors claimed. Ideas that get a green light often receive funding—on average, $100,000, but sometimes as much as $600,000—within eight or ten days. Those that don't pass muster enter a database accessible to anyone who would like to compare a new idea with earlier submissions.

Some months later, each accepted project goes through a proof-of-concept review in which the team has to show that its plan is indeed workable and deserves further funding. This review typically marks the end of the formal GameChanger process, although the panel will often help successful ventures find a permanent home inside Shell. About a quarter of the efforts that get funded ultimately come to reside in an operating unit or in one of Shell's various growth initiatives. Others are carried forward as R&D projects, and still others are written off as interesting but unsuccessful experiments.

Several of the GameChanger ventures have themselves grown into major corporate initiatives. Indeed, of the company's five largest growth initiatives in early 1999, four had their genesis in the Game-Changer process. One team was granted a charter to work with people throughout Shell to explore an entirely new business focused on renewable geothermal energy sources. GameChanger has also had a significant impact on Tim Warren's own division. Fully 30% of E&P's 1999 R&D budget is focused on ventures that have emerged from the process.

Yet the GameChanger program is still fragile. The 1998 slump in oil prices threw Shell into a frenzy of cost cutting. Whether Game-Changer will survive in its current form remains to be seen. But it has demonstrated unequivocally that entrepreneurial passion lurks everywhere—even deep in the canyons of a 92-year-old oil company.

From Resource Allocation to Resource Attraction

Shell is just one of a number of companies, ranging from Monsanto to Virgin to GE Capital, that have internalized the principles of Silicon Valley. To gain a fuller understanding of those principles, we need to head back to the Valley. Let's pop in for breakfast at Buck's—a popular diner in Woodside that attracts cyber-CEOs, venture capitalists, and an unending stream of entrepreneurs on the make. In the parking lot you'll find some of the world's most exotic cars, and maybe a horse or two tied up at a well-used hitching rail. Inside you'll find a restaurant that can be charitably described as eclectic (imagine an explosion in the props department at Paramount Pictures). Now look around. These people are having *fun*. These people know they're creating the new economy. There's a buzz that goes beyond caffeine. No whining Dilberts here. Everyone should have this much fun. Everyone should have the chance to build something that will make a difference. Everyone should have the chance to create new wealth. So why doesn't it happen?

It doesn't happen because few executives can distinguish between Silicon Valley as a place and Silicon Valley as a way of doing business. Silicon Valley's not just an incestuous little cluster of universities, venture capitalists, and eager entrepreneurs perched on a peninsula. At its core are three interconnected markets: a market for ideas, a market for capital, and a market for talent. It is at the intersection of unbounded imagination, opportunity-seeking cash, and energetic freethinking people that wealth gets created. Ideas, capital, and talent whirl through Silicon Valley in a frenetic entrepreneurial dance. In most large companies, by contrast, ideas, capital, and talent are indolent. They don't move unless someone orders them to move. Where Silicon Valley is a vibrant market, the average big company is a smothering bureaucracy.

In fact, the last bastion of Soviet-style central planning can be found in *Fortune* 500 companies—it's called resource allocation. Big companies are not markets, they're hierarchies. The guys at the top decide where the money goes. Unconventional ideas are forced to make a tortuous climb up the corporate pyramid. If an idea manages to survive the gauntlet of skeptical vice presidents, senior vice presidents, and executive vice presidents, some distant CEO or chairman finally decides whether or not to invest. You wanna try something new, something out of bounds, something that challenges the status quo? Good luck. It's no wonder so many Silicon Valley entrepreneurs are corporate exiles. After all, the Valley is nothing more than a refugee camp for frustrated entrepreneurs who couldn't get a hearing elsewhere. (See "How Sun Nearly Torched Its Future.")

How Sun Nearly Torched Its Future

Resource allocation is just as likely to hobble creativity in large and vibrant Silicon Valley companies as it is in boring, old, industrial-age companies. Sun Microsystems is a Valley legend. In the early 1980s, its four founders created the high-end workstation business. Sun's early workstations sold for as much as $40,000. When one of the company's founders, Andy Bechtolsheim, suggested building a $10,000 workstation using a radical new chip technology, he ran headfirst into a wall of internal skepticism. The reason was simple: Sun's process for allocating product development resources heavily favored incremental improvements to existing products. Frustrated, Bechtolsheim left the company and used his own money to build a prototype. When they finally saw the elegant new computer, Sun's top managers quickly invited Bechtolsheim back into the fold. Within three months the new workstation, named the SPARCstation, was outselling every other product in the Sun line.

Not every entrepreneur is as single-minded as Andy Bechtolsheim, and most lack the resources to fund their dreams. If your company insists on trying to frog-march every new idea through a resource allocation process built for incrementalism, it will leave millions of dollars of potential wealth on the table for future-focused start-ups.

Silicon Valley is based not on resource *allocation* but on resource *attraction*—a crucial distinction. If an idea has merit, it will attract resources in the form of venture capital and talent. If it doesn't, it won't. There's no CEO of Silicon Valley. There's no giant brain making global allocation decisions. And there's also no reason resource attraction can't be made to work inside a General Motors, an AT&T, or a Procter & Gamble. Everyone doesn't have to work within 50 miles of one another for free markets to function. As we saw at Shell, there are other ways to link passion, imagination, cash, and competence in the service of new business ideas.

Resource allocation is well suited to investments in existing businesses. After all, the guys at the top built the business, and they're well placed to make judgments about investments aimed at perpetuating existing business models. But management veterans are not usually the best ones to judge the merits of investing in entirely new business models or making radical changes to existing models. In these cases, their experience is irrelevant at best. A senior officer at Monsanto put it bluntly: "You can't trust the judgment of a senior vice president to get resources behind the best new ideas."

It's not that top-down resource allocation, and the painstaking financial analysis that underlies it, has no place in companies. It does. But it can't be the only game in town. If the goal is to create new wealth, something much more spontaneous and less circumscribed is required—something much more like resource attraction. Shell's GameChanger process is totally unsuited to the problem of evaluating the investment case for a new multibillion-dollar offshore oil platform. But, conversely, Shell's comprehensive financial modeling is of no help in deciding whether to make an initial investment in some nontraditional energy venture.

Resource allocation is about managing the downside. Resource attraction is about creating the upside. Who can say which is more important? It's vitally important to manage the downside risk of big investments in the core business. It's equally important to unleash the ideas and passion that will create new businesses or transform the core. For this reason every company must become an amalgam of disciplined resource allocation *and* impromptu resource attraction. Hierarchies and markets must coexist.

Hierarchy—you understand that. But what about markets for ideas, capital, and talent. Just how do they work?

The Market for Ideas

An average-sized venture-capital firm in Silicon Valley gets as many as *5,000* unsolicited business plans a year. How many unsolicited business plans does the average senior vice president of a big company get? Five? Ten? Zero? There's not much chance of catching the next wave when your corner of the ocean is as placid as a bathtub.

In Silicon Valley everyone understands that innovation is the only way to create new wealth—both corporately and individually. New-economy billionaires like Jerry Yang, cofounder of Yahoo!, and Pierre Omidyar, chairman and founder of eBay, didn't get rich by wringing the last ounce of efficiency out of dying business models. Everyone in the Valley knows this. The proposition that innovation creates new wealth is so obvious as to be totally unremarkable. But employees in most large companies live in a world where operational efficiency is everything. Reengineering. Workout. Six sigma. Supply chain optimization. Enterprise resource planning. Whatever the name, the goal is the same—get better at what you're already doing. Their spirits crushed by a decade-long efficiency death march, few employees are able to even imagine another route to wealth creation.

If you doubt it, ask yourself how many people in your company believe, *really* believe, that rule-busting innovation is more likely to create shareholder wealth than, say, a flawless SAP implementation. Every successful company was built on radical innovations. But are those innovations still celebrated in your company, or are they relegated to dusty pages in some corporate archive?

And how many people in your company believe that radical innovation is the fastest route to *personal* wealth creation? Two years ago, the CEO of one of America's large information technology companies approached me with a simple question: "What will it take for my company to capture a bigger chunk of Internet-related opportunities?"

"For starters," I replied, "a willingness to create a slew of 30-year-old millionaires."

The CEO furrowed his brow and said, "I can't see us doing that." Not surprisingly, his company has missed the Internet bonanza.

All too often, the risk-reward trade-off for internal entrepreneurs is long on risk and short on reward. Why should employees risk a bruising battle with the defenders of the status quo when the potential payoff is so meager? Unless the champions of the new believe there is a chance for substantial personal wealth creation, the marketplace for ideas will be as barren as the shelves of a Soviet supermarket. It's ironic that companies pay CEOs millions upon millions to unlock shareholder wealth but seem incapable of funneling six- and seven-figure rewards to people who can actually create new wealth. The currency in Silicon Valley is equity. There are many, many companies where every employee is a shareholder and where success has made millionaires out of all those who took a risk and joined the company before it was a sure thing.

It used to be that the difference between working for a large company and working in a start-up was job security. You wouldn't get rich working in a big firm but, short of malfeasance, your job was secure. That bargain was shattered by the endless waves of restructuring that swept through corporate America in the 1990s. In 1998, there were more than 600,000 layoffs in large U.S. companies. That was a record. Recent years have also seen a record number of start-ups. These trends are not unrelated. If job security inside Giganticorp is as precarious as it is in a start-up, why not go for the start-up and the chance for a big personal payoff? Until senior executives spend as much energy fostering innovation as they do efficiency, and until individuals believe they have the opportunity for substantial wealth creation, the marketplace for ideas will remain closed.

There's a second reason large companies fail to spur much true innovation. Inside their walls, the marketplace for ideas is a monopsony—there's only one buyer. There's only one place to pitch a new idea—up the chain of command—and all it takes is one *nyet* to kill that idea. In the Valley, there's no one person who can say no to a new idea. Power is diffuse, and there are many sources of capital. It's rare to find a successful start-up whose initial business plan wasn't rejected by several venture capitalists before finding a sponsor. In an analogous way, Shell's GameChanger process invites protagonists to present their business plans to a wide cross section of senior executives. The hope is that if one says no, another will say yes.

The third reason why the market for ideas is much more vibrant in Silicon Valley is that there's no prejudice about who is or is not capable of inventing a new business model. The hierarchy of imagination counts for far more than the hierarchy of experience. As Steve Jobs puts it, "Silicon Valley is a meritocracy. It doesn't matter how old you are. It doesn't matter what you wear. What matters is how smart you are." In the Valley, no one assumes that the next great thing will come from a senior vice president running the last great thing.

There's an implicit belief in most large companies that strategy is the province of senior management. Not so long ago, a disaffected employee in one of America's largest companies caught up with me at a conference where I was speaking. In his hands was the company's glossy new performance-assessment manual, which had recently been distributed to all employees. He drew my attention to the fact that only "senior executives" were to be accountable for "creating strategy." The performance criteria for "managers" and "associates" said not a word about strategy. Vibrating with indignation, he accused his employer of being uniquely stupid in having excused 99% of its employees from any responsibility for strategic thinking. Surely, no other company would be so backward as to assume that only top executives could create strategy. Yes, I assured him, he had a right to be indignant. But no, his company was far from unique. What he faced was no different from what mavericks face in big companies everywhere.

Think about the corporate pyramid and ask yourself three questions. First, where in the pyramid will you find the least genetic diversity in terms of how people think about the business? Second, where in the organization will you find people who have most of their emotional equity invested in the past? And third, where will you find people who have, for the most part, already "made it"? The answer to all three questions is, "at the top." What's the chance, then, that a truly revolutionary idea will emerge from the ranks of top management? Jeff Bezos, the founder of Amazon.com, wasn't some big muckety-muck at Barnes & Noble or Borders. Wayne Huizenga, the founder of Blockbuster and AutoNation, got his start in the garbage business. And Anita Roddick, founder of the Body Shop, had no prior experience in the cosmetics industry.

Every day of the week, venture capitalists get pitched new ideas by kids who haven't reached their 30th birthday. When was the last time you saw a 20-something pitch a radical new business idea in your company with any kind of success? If it's not happening, your company has already relinquished most of its wealth-creating potential. (See "Virgin's Amazing Business-Making Machine.")

Virgin's Amazing Business-Making Machine

While most large companies have to work hard to stoke the fires of entrepreneurship, they burn with a ferocious intensity at the Virgin Group. Described by one senior executive as a "branded venture-capital company," Virgin would never be mistaken for a hidebound incumbent. But as a £3 billion company that has created nearly 200 new businesses, it stands as clear evidence that ideas, capital, and talent can flow as freely in big, far-flung organizations as they can among the start-ups of Silicon Valley.

Virgin's eclectic business mix includes entertainment megastores, cinemas, a funky fun-to-fly airline, an all-in-one consumer-banking arm, a hip radio station, and a passenger-train service. (At one time the company even hawked condoms, though in that case they wisely avoided using the Virgin brand.) Unlike other business visionaries, Virgin's chairman, Richard Branson, doesn't limit his vision to one particular industry; he has a vision about what it takes to spawn entirely new business models. He hasn't invented a new business so much as he's invented a business-making machine.

Business ideas can come from anywhere in Virgin. As the company has grown, Branson has remained accessible to employees who have novel proposals. There was a time when every employee had Branson's phone number, and he would receive two or three calls a day from workers wanting to try something new. Today he gets around 50 letters a day from employees. And the annual "house party" he hosts for employees, which has grown into a week-long 35,000-person extravaganza, is another occasion to buttonhole the chairman.

In one telling incident, a woman who believed the company's airline should offer passengers onboard massages camped on Branson's doorstep until she was allowed to give him a neck and shoulder rub. Now, an in-flight massage is a valued perk in Virgin Atlantic's Upper Class. On another occasion, a soon-to-be-married flight attendant came up with the idea of offering an integrated bridal-planning service—everything from wedding apparel to catering to limousines to honeymoon reservations. She became the first CEO of Virgin Bride. And Virgin's burgeoning Internet business was started by an employee who was working in another company within Virgin's Media Group.

Branson and his deputies have worked hard to instill a "speak up" culture at Virgin. There is no gleaming corporate headquarters, just a large and slightly tatty house in London's Holland Park, where meetings are often held in a small conservatory overlooking an equally small garden. There are no trappings of executive privilege to intimidate employees. There are no job descriptions because they're believed to limit what people can do. In the company's pancake-flat organization, senior executives work shoulder-to-shoulder with first-line employees. It's probably safe to say that the level of discourse between top executives and "ordinary" employees is unprecedented in an organization of Virgin's size. One example: the managing director of the company's financial services arm, Virgin Direct, regularly books eight seats at a local restaurant. Anyone with a new idea can apply for a spot.

In addition to all the informal conversations, Virgin has instituted formal mechanisms to ensure that good ideas come to light and receive adequate attention and funding. Its business development function, once led by a former venture capitalist, canvasses managers from across the company for ideas and pulls together ad hoc teams to evaluate the most promising ones. Virgin Management, the nearest thing Virgin has to a head office, is a small team of creative people who help launch new businesses and work to inculcate them with the company's values. The role of business development and Virgin Management is not all that different from the role a venture capital board would play in bringing a new business into existence. Indeed, Will Whitehorn, one of Branson's key aides, describes the chairman as an investment "angel" of the type who gives first-stage funding to Silicon Valley start-ups.

Virgin's approval process for new business ventures doesn't look much like the traditional corporate planning process. The investment screen essentially consists of four questions: What is the potential for restructuring the market and bringing new benefits to consumers? Is the opportunity radical enough to justify the Virgin brand? (Me-too strategies are anathema.) Will the opportunity benefit from the skills and expertise Virgin has accumulated in its other businesses? Is there a way to keep the investment risk within acceptable boundaries? As Gordon McCallum, the current director of Virgin's business development function, puts it, "The ultimate business case is not a financial one, but one that is based upon deep customer needs and an understanding of how to meet them in a new way. The numbers will take care of themselves if we get things right for our customers."

Virgin's model for business creation is as unique as it is productive. In how many companies does every employee know they're in the business of creating new businesses? In how many companies does everyone deeply believe that to succeed they have to shatter the rules? In how many companies does everyone know they have the opportunity to be heard at the highest levels? Outside Silicon Valley, you won't find many.

The explosive growth of GE Capital has come in large part from its ability to bring Silicon Valley inside. Like venture capitalists, executives running GE Capital's 28 businesses devote much of their time to hunting down opportunities outside current business boundaries. In the 1998 planning round, someone suggested that every business put together a team of lower- to midlevel managers, all of them under 30, and give them the task of finding opportunities that their "stodgy old managers" had missed. The young teams came back with a bunch of novel ideas, including several focused on how GE Capital could leverage the Internet. New wealth is created by new ideas. New ideas tend to come from new voices. Are you listening to those voices in your organization?

The Market for Capital

Over the last decade it would have been great to be a shareholder in Silicon Valley Inc., a holding company encompassing all the high-tech start-ups in the Valley. Look at the numbers. Of the 63 companies that received venture funding in the fourth quarter of 1993, 26 had gone public by the end of 1998. An investor who bought into each of those companies at the offer price would have achieved a return of 1,700% by the end of last year. The internal rate of return of the average venture capital firm is estimated to be about 40%—hardly shabby—and the best do substantially better than that.

Venture capitalists are not financially stupid people, but they sure don't think like CFOs. While both may be in the business of funding projects, the market for capital in Silicon Valley isn't anything like the market for capital in large companies. The first difference is access. How easy is it for someone seven levels down in a large company to get a few hundred thousand dollars to try out a new idea? Whether the sum is half a million or $50 million, the investment hurdles usually appear insurmountable to someone far removed from top management.

Most companies have a system of graduated approval limits, where senior executives have the authority to make bigger financial commitments than lower-level managers do. Yet whatever the level and dollar amount involved, the aversion to risk is the same. What is a trivial risk for the company as a whole may be a substantial risk for a small unit and for the career of a young manager. An eager entrepreneur wanting to risk a few hundred grand has to make the same airtight business case as a divisional vice president who's going to risk tens of millions of dollars. But does it really make sense to set the same hurdles for a small investment in a new experiment as for a large and irreversible investment in an existing business? Why should it be so difficult for someone with an unconventional idea to get the funding needed to build a prototype, design a little market trial, or merely flesh out a business case—particularly when the sum involved is peanuts?

In most companies, there's an assumption that anything nonincremental is high risk and anything incremental is low risk. But in a fast-changing world, the reverse is often true. Venture capitalists are risk takers, but they're not *big* risk takers. Motorola investing in Iridium, AT&T buying into the cable TV industry, Monsanto spending billions on seed companies, Sony betting a billion on a new video game chip— these are big risks. VCs look for opportunities that don't need a lot of cash to get started. The initial investment in Hotmail was $300,000; the company was sold to Microsoft for something north of $400 million. Silicon Valley runs on nifty new ideas, not zillions of greenbacks. VCs work hard to enforce a culture of frugality in the companies they back. And because they are intimately involved in those companies— helping to appoint the management team, sitting on the board, plotting strategy with the owners—they are well positioned to know when to double their bets and when to cut and run. Compared with VCs, the average CFO is a spendthrift.

Roughly two-thirds of Silicon Valley start-ups receive their initial funding from "angels"—wealthy individuals who pool their investments to fund new companies. The average angel puts in around $50,000, and the average first-round investment for a start-up is $500,000. That's a rounding error in the average annual report. Yet how easy would it be for an ardent entrepreneur in your company to find ten angels willing to invest $50,000 each?

Creative new business ideas seldom make it through traditional financial screens. If estimates of market size and market growth seem the tiniest bit fuzzy, the proposal gets canned. If key business assumptions seem a bit shaky, no funds are forthcoming. If financial projections can't be supported with reams of analysis, top management takes a pass. Typical is the logic a senior car-company exec gave me for his firm's initial reluctance to invest in minivans: "There was no segment there, so how could we invest? We couldn't make a business case." By the time the company amassed enough evidence to assure itself that the minivan opportunity was real, it was a million units behind Chrysler, the minivan pioneer.

The market for capital works very differently in Silicon Valley. Talk to Steve Jurvetson, who funded Hotmail and is one of the Valley's hottest young VCs. Ask him how he evaluates a potential business idea, and this is what he'll tell you:

> The first thing I ask is, Who will care? What kind of difference will this make? Basically, How high is up? I want to fund things that have just about unlimited upside. The second thing I ask is, How will this snowball? How will you scale this thing? What's the mechanism that drives increasing returns? Can it spread like a virus? Finally, I want to know how committed the person is. I never invest in someone who says they're *going* to do something; I invest in people who say they're *already* doing something and just want the funding to drive it forward. Passion counts for more than experience.

A VC has a very different notion of what constitutes a business plan than the typical CFO. Again, listen to Jurvetson:

> The business plan is not a contract in the way a budget is. It's a story. It's a story about an opportunity, about the migration path and how you're going to create and capture value.
>
> I never use Excel at work. I never run the numbers or build financial models. I know the forecast is a delusional view of reality. I basically ignore this. Typically, there are no IRR forecasts or EVA calculations. But I spend a lot of time thinking about how big the thing could be.

The point is this: in most companies the goal of capital budgeting is to make sure the firm never ever makes a bet-the-business investment that fails to deliver an acceptable return. But in attempting to guarantee that there's never an unexpected downside, the typical capital-budgeting process places an absolute ceiling on the upside. Dollars lost are highly visible (everyone knows whose projects have lost money), but dollars foregone are totally invisible.

Venture capitalists start with a very different set of expectations about success and failure. Out of 5,000 ideas, a five-partner VC firm may invest in ten, which it views as a portfolio of options. Out of that ten, five will be total write-offs, three will be modest successes, one will double the initial investment, and one will return the investment 50- to 100-fold. The goal is to make sure you have a big winner, not to make sure there are no losers.

In most large companies, someone with a vision of a radical new business model has to go to the defenders of the old business model to get funding. All too often the guy running the old thing has veto power over the new thing. To understand the problem this creates, imagine that every innovator in Silicon Valley had to go to Bill Gates for funding. Pretty soon everyone in the Valley would be working to extend the Windows franchise. Goodbye to Netscape. Goodbye to the Network Computer. Goodbye to Java and Jini. Goodbye to PalmPilot. And goodbye to anything else that might challenge Microsoft's current business model.

A VC doesn't ask how one venture plays off against the success of another venture. There's no search for synergy. Nobody asks, Is this new venture consistent with our strategy? Now, synergy is good, and consistency is a virtue. But in a world where the life span of the average business model is longer than a butterfly's but shorter than a dog's, one needs the chance to regularly consider a few opportunities that are *inconsistent* with the current strategy. One of those opportunities might just turn out to be a whole lot more attractive than what you're already working on. But how will you ever know unless you're willing to create a market for capital that puts a bit of cash behind the unorthodox? (See "Spin-Ups, Not Spin-Outs.")

Spin-Ups, Not Spin-Outs

The goal of bringing Silicon Valley inside is not only to create new businesses but also to reinvent existing business models. Too often companies think of internal entrepreneurship as focused solely on new businesses—ones that typically lie far outside the company's core. Once such businesses start to gain momentum, they're often spun out into separate companies with their own equity structures and stock market listings. But spin-outs do little to transform the base business. Xerox's Palo Alto Research Center has spun off a number of successful entrepreneurial companies while Xerox's core business has languished with less than double-digit growth.

Spin-ups are often more valuable than spin-outs. An idea that has the power to radically improve the economics of an existing business shouldn't languish in some backwater. Instead it should be spun up into a corporatewide initiative. A company that succeeds in bringing Silicon Valley inside should expect to create, as Shell has done, dozens of game-changing experiments inside existing businesses—a new pricing strategy here, an unconventional distribution model over there, a fresh approach to merchandising somewhere else. The experiments should be small and tightly bounded. But if they show promise, they can be spun up into major business-transforming programs.

New ideas get squashed when they threaten to cannibalize the sales of existing businesses—businesses protected by powerful constituents. Yet every company is told that it must cannibalize its own business before competitors do. Solving the cannibalization problem isn't difficult. You simply have to make sure that individuals seeking funding for nontraditional opportunities don't have to go cup in hand to the guardians of the past. That's what Shell did. In the GameChanger process, Shell created a market for capital that is entirely separate from the traditional capital-budgeting process, a process dominated by the investment needs of yesterday's businesses. Rather than wait for the annual budgeting cycle to roll around, innovators can go to the GameChanger panel at any time and present their business case. And they are guaranteed an almost immediate response. So yes, it is possible to create an innovation-friendly market for capital inside a big company.

The Market for Talent

Imagine what would happen if 20% of your best people up and left in a single year. It happens all the time in Silicon Valley. Valley workers change companies with less angst than most people change jobs within companies. Sure, they jump for money, but more than that they jump at the chance to work on the next great thing. Companies pursuing killer opportunities attract the best talent. As one venture capitalist bluntly puts it: "'A' people work on 'A' opportunities."

Every Silicon Valley CEO knows that if you don't give your people truly exhilarating work—and a dramatic upside—they'll start turning in their badges. In recent years, companies like Apple and Silicon Graphics hemorrhaged talent, while up-and-comers like Cisco and Yahoo! have been magnets for the cerebrally gifted. Scott Cook, the chairman of Intuit, understands the hard reality of the talent market:

"I wake up every morning knowing that if my people don't sense a compelling vision and a big upside, they'll simply leave." Not to worry. Intuit's restless innovators are busy turning the company into a dominant financial services player on the Internet.

The talent merry-go-round spins fast enough in Silicon Valley to make the average HR manager nauseous. In the old economy, employees are often viewed as something akin to indentured servants. Divisional vice presidents think they own their key people. And if those people work in South Bend, St. Louis, Des Moines, Nashville, or a hundred other cities that don't have the kind of superheated economy that exists in Silicon Valley, they may not find it so easy to jump ship. But that's no reason to chain ambitious and creative employees to the deck of a slowly sinking strategy.

Isn't it amazing that while every company has at least some kind of process for capital allocation, almost no company has a process for talent allocation—much less an open market for talent? Capital budgeting may be sclerotic and filled with nostalgia for old businesses, but at least there's a process for addressing the question of how much capital each business deserves every year. And there are measures like EVA that let one judge whether or not a particular business is using its capital wisely. Yet there's no knowing whether a company's very best people are lined up behind its biggest new opportunities or slowly suffocating in moribund businesses. You can look at retention rates, but that's only part of the story. People often quit emotionally long before they quit physically. Novelty, meaning, and impact are the oxygen that gives life to the entrepreneurial spirit. Denied that oxygen, even the most talented folks are soon brain dead.

As difficult as it is for a prospective entrepreneur to get seed capital in a large company, it's even harder to grab a few of the very best engineering or marketing folks. There's an enormous sense of entitlement among divisional vice presidents and business heads. "Hey, we make all the money, we ought to have the best people," they'll say. But the marginal value a talented employee adds to a business running on autopilot is often a fraction of the value that individual could add to a venture not yet out of the proverbial garage.

Disney understands this. The company has excelled at moving its very best talent into new and nontraditional business areas. Whether it's producing Broadway shows, starting a cruise line, or opening the company's first live-animal theme park, Disney's most capable "cast members" vie for the chance to work on the new and the unique.

Helping to break new ground is regarded as a career coup. For their part, Disney's senior executives have worked to soften the kind of narrowly parochial profit-center thinking that so often scuppers the movement of people out of existing businesses and into new ones.

Shell, too, has been working hard to lower the barriers to employee mobility. The company has recently moved to what it terms an "open resourcing" model for talent. Jobs are listed on Shell's intranet, and with a two-month notice, employees can go and work on anything that interests them. There are no barriers hindering people from going to work on whatever fires their imagination. Monsanto has adopted a similar approach. One of the architects of Monsanto's metamorphosis from chemical giant to biotech pioneer puts it this way:

> Because we don't have a lot of structure, people will flow toward where success and innovation are taking place. We have a free-market system where people can move, so you have an outflow of people in areas where not much progress is being made. Before, the HR function ran processes like management development and performance evaluation. Now it also facilitates this movement of people.

At Monsanto, everyone across the company can point to the few critical projects that are redefining the company and opening up new vistas. What about your company? Could your most creative people point to ten unconventional ventures within your organization aimed at reinventing the company and its industry? And how easy would it be for those people to nominate themselves onto those teams?

Sure, many companies post internal job openings. But a market for talent is more than that. Employees have to believe that the best way to win big is to be part of building something new. That means providing additional incentives for employees who are willing to take a risk on something out of the ordinary. It means celebrating every courageous employee who abandons the security of a legacy business for an untested opportunity. It's not enough to remove the barriers to migration—one must positively provide incentives for employees to abandon the familiar for the unconventional.

Mobility fuels commitment. When employees are truly attracted to the projects and teams they work on, commitment is a foregone conclusion. And while they may not stay committed forever, particularly if a business model is running out of gas, people who've voted with their feet, and their lives, aren't likely to join the ranks of disaffected Dilberts.

Many companies are already paying a price for having failed to create internal markets for talent. People who have the passion and the aptitude to create new wealth are abandoning the old economy for the new. When AT&T vice presidents start leaving for the left coast, something's up. Even America's best MBA grads—kids who've been groomed for corporate life—have been forsaking the old guard for the vanguard. Today, 20% of Harvard MBAs join companies with fewer than 100 people, and 20% of Stanford MBAs join companies with fewer than 50. Yeah, some still want to go into consulting and devote their lives to making the world safe for vice presidents, but more and more want to go kick incumbent butt. Confident in their talents and ambitious as hell, they're going to companies where the market for talent is brutally efficient. They're going to companies where there are no constraints on their contribution, where there are no apprenticeships to serve, no senior partners to carry, and no corporate posteriors to kiss. If you fail to create a vibrant and vital market for talent in your company, you're never even going to have the chance to hire these people, and your leaky tap of talent will become a torrent.

The bottom line is this: if you have highly creative and ambitious people who feel trapped in moribund businesses, they *are* going to leave. The only question is whether they leave to join some other company or whether they leave to join a GameChanger kind of team in your company. Or, to put it more simply, are they going to create wealth for themselves and somebody else or are they going to create wealth for themselves and your shareholders? Creating an internal market for talent won't happen until you have the courage to blow up the entitlement mentality that so often imprisons both talent and capital. And it won't happen until you come to believe, truly, that there's more wealth to be had by setting ambitious and capable employees free than by holding them hostage in businesses that have already reached their sell-by date.

The Innovation Frontier

We are at the dawn of a new industrial order. We are leaving behind a world in which scale, efficiency, and replication were everything. We are taking our first tentative steps into a world where imagination, experimentation, and agility are, if not everything, at least the essential catalysts for wealth creation. Resource allocation worked fine for the old world, but companies need something more, and quite different, if they are to capture their fair share of wealth in the new world. In concept and in reality, resource attraction is well tuned to the new world of self-organization, spontaneity, and speed.

Opportunities are fleeting in this new world. By the time some cautious vice president decides to pull the trigger, some hot, young entrepreneur is already a billionaire. So you'd best not wait any longer to start building your own internal markets for ideas, capital, and talent. Shell, Virgin, GE Capital, and Monsanto are setting the pace, but you shouldn't expect to distill a neat little guide from their experience. If there were a best-practice manual, you'd be even further behind the curve than you already are. Instead, recognize that resource attraction is not something as simple as a new process—this isn't knowledge management or data mining. It's a fundamentally new approach to the challenge of creating wealth.

Silicon Valley companies are challenging the industrial aristocracy in fields as diverse as auto retailing, insurance, bookselling, and broadcast media. But the real competition between the old economy and the new economy is occurring not between individual companies but between remarkably different regimes. Just as communism and capitalism were competing economic regimes, resource allocation and resource attraction are competing innovation regimes. Resource allocation works fine where innovation is largely incremental to the existing business model (think Cherry Coke versus regular Coke). But where the goal is the invention of novel business models (music downloaded off the Web versus CDs bought at Tower Records), or the radical redesign of existing business models (Dell's build-to-order direct-selling approach), resource allocation is wholly inadequate. The shift to a postindustrial economy, accelerating by the minute, is perhaps the greatest economic sea change in history. Any company that hopes to profit from this transition must first ask itself whether its innovation regime is up to the challenge.

There is a persistent yet unfounded belief that big companies must always lose to nimble start-ups, that no incumbent can ever match the entrepreneurial fervor of Silicon Valley or its analogues around the globe. I heartily disagree. In fact, when it comes to innovation, large companies have their own advantages that in many ways offset those of Silicon Valley. Large companies have resources. They have a ready source of capital—if they can learn how to supplement risk-averse resource allocation with opportunity-focused resource attraction. They often have brands and distribution assets that can give a new venture a quick start. Mighty Microsoft would still be a minnow if it hadn't found a way to tap into IBM's brand and distribution strengths. In theory, it should be easier for large companies to redeploy talent into new areas than it is for start-ups to induce prospective employees to endure the hassles of changing companies. And where a venture capitalist will often lose a hot idea to a rival source of funds, large companies should at least enjoy preferential access to the ideas that emerge from their own employees.

Silicon Valley exists not because large companies are incapable of innovation but because they have been unwilling to abandon the tightly knit safety net of resource allocation. A disciplined, top-down approach to allocating money and talent gives top management a sense of control. But in a world where the risk of being rendered irrelevant by an impertinent interloper is ever present, such control is illusory. Yes, you can do your best to ensure that you never put a dollar of capital or a great employee into anything that doesn't come wrapped in an ironclad business case. But in the process, you'll surrender the future and its wealth to more intrepid souls.

11
Meeting the Challenge of
Disruptive Change

Clayton M. Christensen and Michael Overdorf

These are scary times for managers in big companies. Even before the Internet and globalization, their track record for dealing with major, disruptive change was not good. Out of hundreds of department stores, for example, only one—Dayton Hudson—became a leader in discount retailing. Not one of the minicomputer companies succeeded in the personal computer business. Medical and business schools are struggling—and failing—to change their curricula fast enough to train the types of doctors and managers their markets need. The list could go on.

It's not that managers in big companies can't see disruptive changes coming. Usually they can. Nor do they lack resources to confront them. Most big companies have talented managers and specialists, strong product portfolios, first-rate technological know-how, and deep pockets. What managers lack is a habit of thinking about their organization's capabilities as carefully as they think about individual people's capabilities.

One of the hallmarks of a great manager is the ability to identify the right person for the right job and to train employees to succeed at the jobs they're given. But unfortunately, most managers assume that if each person working on a project is well matched to the job, then the organization in which they work will be, too. Often that is not the case. One could put two sets of identically capable people to work in different organizations, and what they accomplished would be significantly different. That's because organizations themselves—independent of the people and other resources in them—have capabilities.

To succeed consistently, good managers need to be skilled not just in assessing people but also in assessing the abilities and disabilities of their organization as a whole.

This article offers managers a framework to help them understand what their organizations are capable of accomplishing. It will show them how their company's disabilities become more sharply defined even as its core capabilities grow. It will give them a way to recognize different kinds of change and make appropriate organizational responses to the opportunities that arise from each. And it will offer some bottom-line advice that runs counter to much that's assumed in our can-do business culture: if an organization faces major change—a disruptive innovation, perhaps—the worst possible approach may be to make drastic adjustments to the existing organization. In trying to transform an enterprise, managers can destroy the very capabilities that sustain it.

Before rushing into the breach, managers must understand precisely what types of change the existing organization is capable and incapable of handling. To help them do that, we'll first take a systematic look at how to recognize a company's core capabilities on an organizational level and then examine how those capabilities migrate as companies grow and mature.

Where Capabilities Reside

Our research suggests that three factors affect what an organization can and cannot do: its resources, its processes, and its values. When thinking about what sorts of innovations their organization will be able to embrace, managers need to assess how each of these factors might affect their organization's capacity to change.

Resources. When they ask the question, "What can this company do?" the place most managers look for the answer is in its resources— both the tangible ones like people, equipment, technologies, and cash, and the less tangible ones like product designs, information, brands, and relationships with suppliers, distributors, and customers. Without doubt, access to abundant, high-quality resources increases an organization's chances of coping with change. But resource analysis doesn't come close to telling the whole story.

Processes. The second factor that affects what a company can and cannot do is its processes. By processes, we mean the patterns of interaction, coordination, communication, and decision making employees use to transform resources into products and services of greater worth. Such examples as the processes that govern product development, manufacturing, and budgeting come immediately to mind. Some processes are formal, in the sense that they are explicitly defined and documented. Others are informal: they are routines or ways of working that evolve over time. The former tend to be more visible, the latter less visible.

One of the dilemmas of management is that processes, by their very nature, are set up so that employees perform tasks in a consistent way, time after time. They are *meant* not to change or, if they must change, to change through tightly controlled procedures. When people use a process to do the task it was designed for, it is likely to perform efficiently. But when the same process is used to tackle a very different task, it is likely to perform sluggishly. Companies focused on developing and winning FDA approval for new drug compounds, for example, often prove inept at developing and winning approval for medical devices because the second task entails very different ways of working. In fact, a process that creates the capability to execute one task concurrently defines disabilities in executing other tasks.[1]

The most important capabilities and concurrent disabilities aren't necessarily embodied in the most visible processes, like logistics, development, manufacturing, or customer service. In fact, they are more likely to be in the less visible, background processes that support decisions about where to invest resources—those that define how market research is habitually done, how such analysis is translated into financial projections, how plans and budgets are negotiated internally, and so on. It is in those processes that many organizations' most serious disabilities in coping with change reside.

Values. The third factor that affects what an organization can and cannot do is its values. Sometimes the phrase "corporate values" carries an ethical connotation: one thinks of the principles that ensure patient well-being for Johnson & Johnson or that guide decisions about employee safety at Alcoa. But within our framework, "values" has a broader meaning. We define an organization's values as the standards by which employees set priorities that enable them to judge whether an order is attractive or unattractive, whether a customer is more important or less important, whether an idea for a new product is attractive or marginal, and so on. Prioritization decisions are made by employees at every level. Among salespeople, they consist of on-the-spot, day-to-day decisions about which products to push with customers and which to de-emphasize. At the executive tiers, they often take the form of decisions to invest, or not, in new products, services, and processes.

The larger and more complex a company becomes, the more important it is for senior managers to train employees throughout the organization to make independent decisions about priorities that are consistent with the strategic direction and the business model of the company. A key metric of good management, in fact, is whether such clear, consistent values have permeated the organization.

But consistent, broadly understood values also define what an organization cannot do. A company's values reflect its cost structure or its business model because those define the rules its employees must follow for the company to prosper. If, for example, a company's overhead costs require it to achieve gross profit margins of 40%, then a value or decision rule will have evolved that encourages middle managers to kill ideas that promise gross margins below 40%. Such an organization would be incapable of commercializing projects targeting low-margin markets—such as those in e-commerce—even though another organization's values, driven by a very different cost structure, might facilitate the success of the same project.

Different companies, of course, embody different values. But we want to focus on two sets of values in particular that tend to evolve in most companies in very predictable ways. The inexorable evolution of these two values is what makes companies progressively less capable of addressing disruptive change successfully.

As in the previous example, the first value dictates the way the company judges acceptable gross margins. As companies add features and functions to their products and services, trying to capture more attractive customers in premium tiers of their markets, they often add overhead cost. As a result, gross margins that were once attractive become unattractive. For instance, Toyota entered the North American market with the Corolla model, which targeted the lower end of the market. As that segment became crowded with look-alike models from Honda, Mazda, and Nissan, competition drove down profit margins. To improve its margins, Toyota then developed more sophisticated cars targeted at higher tiers. The process of developing cars like the Camry and the Lexus added costs to Toyota's operation. It subsequently decided to exit the lower end of the market; the margins had become unacceptable because the company's cost structure, and consequently its values, had changed.

In a departure from that pattern, Toyota recently introduced the Echo model, hoping to rejoin the entry-level tier with a $10,000 car. It is one thing for Toyota's senior management to decide to launch this new model. It's another for the many people in the Toyota system—including its dealers—to agree that selling more cars at lower margins is a better way to boost profits and equity values than selling more Camrys, Avalons, and Lexuses. Only time will tell whether Toyota can manage this down-market move. To be successful with the Echo, Toyota's management will have to swim against a very strong current—the current of its own corporate values.

The second value relates to how big a business opportunity has to be before it can be interesting. Because a company's stock price represents the discounted present value of its projected earnings stream, most managers feel compelled not just to maintain growth but to maintain a constant rate of growth. For a $40 million company to grow 25%, for instance, it needs to find $10 million in new business the next year. But a $40 billion company needs to find $10 billion in new business the next year to grow at that same rate. It follows that an opportunity that excites a small company isn't big enough to be interesting to a large company. One of the bittersweet results of success, in fact, is that as companies become large, they lose the ability to enter small, emerging markets. This disability is not caused by a change in the resources within the companies—their resources typically are vast. Rather, it's caused by an evolution in values.

The problem is magnified when companies suddenly become much bigger through mergers or acquisitions. Executives and Wall Street financiers who engineer megamergers between already-huge pharmaceutical companies, for example, need to take this effect into account. Although their merged research organizations might have more resources to throw at new product development, their commercial organizations will probably have lost their appetites for all but the biggest blockbuster drugs. This constitutes a very real disability in managing innovation. The same problem crops up in high-tech industries as well. In many ways, Hewlett-Packard's recent decision to split itself into two companies is rooted in its recognition of this problem.

The Migration of Capabilities

In the start-up stages of an organization, much of what gets done is attributable to resources—people, in particular. The addition or departure of a few key people can profoundly influence its success. Over time, however, the locus of the organization's capabilities shifts toward its processes and values. As people address recurrent tasks, processes become defined. And as the business model takes shape and it becomes clear which types of business need to be accorded highest priority, values coalesce. In fact, one reason that many soaring young companies flame out after an IPO based on a single hot product is that their initial success is grounded in resources—often the founding engineers—and they fail to develop processes that can create a sequence of hot products.

Avid Technology, a producer of digital-editing systems for television, is an apt case in point. Avid's well-received technology removed tedium from the video-editing process. On the back of its star product, Avid's stock rose from $16 a share at its 1993 IPO to $49 in mid-1995. However, the strains of being a one-trick pony soon emerged as Avid faced a saturated market, rising inventories and receivables, increased competition, and shareholder lawsuits. Customers loved the product, but Avid's lack of effective processes for consistently developing new products and for controlling quality, delivery, and service ultimately tripped the company and sent its stock back down.

By contrast, at highly successful firms such as McKinsey & Company, the processes and values have become so powerful that it almost doesn't matter which people get assigned to which project teams. Hundreds of MBAs join the firm every year, and almost as many leave. But the company is able to crank out high-quality work year after year because its core capabilities are rooted in its processes and values rather than in its resources.

When a company's processes and values are being formed in its early and middle years, the founder typically has a profound impact. The founder usually has strong opinions about how employees should do their work and what the organization's priorities need to be. If the founder's judgments are flawed, of course, the company will likely fail. But if they're sound, employees will experience for themselves the validity of the founder's problem-solving and decision-making methods. Thus processes become defined. Likewise, if the company becomes financially successful by allocating resources according to cri-

teria that reflect the founder's priorities, the company's values coalesce around those criteria.

As successful companies mature, employees gradually come to assume that the processes and priorities they've used so successfully so
often are the right way to do their work. Once that happens and employees begin to follow processes and decide priorities by assumption
rather than by conscious choice, those processes and values come to
constitute the organization's culture.[2] As companies grow from a few
employees to hundreds and thousands of them, the challenge of getting all employees to agree on what needs to be done and how can be
daunting for even the best managers. Culture is a powerful management tool in those situations. It enables employees to act autono-
mously but causes them to act consistently.

Hence, the factors that define an organization's capabilities and disabilities evolve over time—they start in resources; then move to visible, articulated processes and values; and migrate finally to culture. As
long as the organization continues to face the same sorts of problems
that its processes and values were designed to address, managing the
organization can be straightforward. But because those factors also define what an organization cannot do, they constitute disabilities when
the problems facing the company change fundamentally. When the
organization's capabilities reside primarily in its people, changing capabilities to address the new problems is relatively simple. But when
the capabilities have come to reside in processes and values, and especially when they have become embedded in culture, change can be
extraordinarily difficult. (See "Digital's Dilemma.")

Digital's Dilemma

A lot of business thinkers have analyzed Digital Equipment Corporation's
abrupt fall from grace. Most have concluded that Digital simply read the market very badly. But if we look at the company's fate through the lens of our
framework, a different picture emerges.

Digital was a spectacularly successful maker of minicomputers from the
1960s through the 1980s. One might have been tempted to assert, when
personal computers first appeared in the market around 1980, that Digital's
core capability was in building computers. But if that were the case, why did
the company stumble?

Clearly, Digital had the resources to succeed in personal computers. Its engineers routinely designed computers that were far more sophisticated than

PCs. The company had plenty of cash, a great brand, good technology, and so on. But it did not have the processes to succeed in the personal computer business. Minicomputer companies designed most of the key components of their computers internally and then integrated those components into proprietary configurations. Designing a new product platform took two to three years. Digital manufactured most of its own components and assembled them in a batch mode. It sold directly to corporate engineering organizations. Those processes worked extremely well in the minicomputer business.

PC makers, by contrast, outsourced most components from the best suppliers around the globe. New computer designs, made up of modular components, had to be completed in six to 12 months. The computers were manufactured in high-volume assembly lines and sold through retailers to consumers and businesses. None of these processes existed within Digital. In other words, although the people working at the company had the ability to design, build, and sell personal computers profitably, they were working in an organization that was incapable of doing so because its processes had been designed and had evolved to do other tasks well.

Similarly, because of its overhead costs, Digital had to adopt a set of values that dictated, "If it generates 50% gross margins or more, it's good business. If it generates less than 40% margins, it's not worth doing." Management had to ensure that all employees gave priority to projects according to these criteria or the company couldn't make money. Because PCs generated lower margins, they did not fit with Digital's values. The company's criteria for setting priorities always placed higher-performance minicomputers ahead of personal computers in the resource-allocation process.

Digital could have created a different organization that would have honed the different processes and values required to succeed in PCs—as IBM did. But Digital's mainstream organization simply was incapable of succeeding at the job.

Sustaining Versus Disruptive Innovation

Successful companies, no matter what the source of their capabilities, are pretty good at responding to evolutionary changes in their markets—what in *The Innovator's Dilemma* (Harvard Business School, 1997), Clayton Christensen referred to as *sustaining innovation*. Where they run into trouble is in handling or initiating revolutionary changes in their markets, or dealing with *disruptive innovation*.

Sustaining technologies are innovations that make a product or service perform better in ways that customers in the mainstream market already value. Compaq's early adoption of Intel's 32-bit 386 microprocessor instead of the 16-bit 286 chip was a sustaining innovation. So was Merrill Lynch's introduction of its Cash Management Account, which allowed customers to write checks against their equity accounts. Those were breakthrough innovations that sustained the best customers of these companies by providing something better than had previously been available.

Disruptive innovations create an entirely new market through the introduction of a new kind of product or service, one that's actually worse, initially, as judged by the performance metrics that mainstream customers value. Charles Schwab's initial entry as a bare-bones discount broker was a disruptive innovation relative to the offerings of full-service brokers like Merrill Lynch. Merrill Lynch's best customers wanted more than Schwab-like services. Early personal computers were a disruptive innovation relative to mainframes and minicomputers. PCs were not powerful enough to run the computing applications that existed at the time they were introduced. These innovations were disruptive in that they didn't address the next-generation needs of leading customers in existing markets. They had other attributes, of course, that enabled new market applications to emerge—and the disruptive innovations improved so rapidly that they ultimately could address the needs of customers in the mainstream of the market as well.

Sustaining innovations are nearly always developed and introduced by established industry leaders. But those same companies never introduce—or cope well with—disruptive innovations. Why? Our resources-processes-values framework holds the answer. Industry leaders are organized to develop and introduce sustaining technologies. Month after month, year after year, they launch new and improved products to gain an edge over the competition. They do so by developing processes for evaluating the technological potential of sustaining innovations and for assessing their customers' needs for alternatives. Investment in sustaining technology also fits in with the values of leading companies in that they promise higher margins from better products sold to leading-edge customers.

Disruptive innovations occur so intermittently that no company has a routine process for handling them. Furthermore, because disruptive products nearly always promise lower profit margins per unit sold and are not attractive to the company's best customers, they're inconsistent with the established company's values. Merrill Lynch had the resources—the people, money, and technology—required to succeed at the sustaining innovations (Cash Management Account) and the disruptive innovations (bare-bones discount brokering) that it has confronted in recent history. But its processes and values supported only the sustaining innovation: they became disabilities when the company needed to understand and confront the discount and on-line brokerage businesses.

The reason, therefore, that large companies often surrender emerging growth markets is that smaller, disruptive companies are actually more capable of pursuing them. Start-ups lack resources, but that doesn't matter. Their values can embrace small markets, and their cost structures can accommodate low margins. Their market research and resource allocation processes allow managers to proceed intuitively; every decision need not be backed by careful research and analysis. All these advantages add up to the ability to embrace and even initiate disruptive change. But how can a large company develop those capabilities?

Creating Capabilities to Cope with Change

Despite beliefs spawned by popular change-management and reengineering programs, processes are not nearly as flexible or adaptable as resources are—and values are even less so. So whether addressing sustaining or disruptive innovations, when an organization needs new processes and values—because it needs new capabilities—managers must create a new organizational space where those capabilities can be developed. There are three possible ways to do that. Managers can

- create new organizational structures within corporate boundaries in which new processes can be developed,
- spin out an independent organization from the existing organization and develop within it the new processes and values required to solve the new problem, or
- acquire a different organization whose processes and values closely match the requirements of the new task.

CREATING NEW CAPABILITIES INTERNALLY

When a company's capabilities reside in its processes, and when new challenges require new processes—that is, when they require different people or groups in a company to interact differently and at a different pace than they habitually have done—managers need to pull the relevant people out of the existing organization and draw a new boundary around a new group. Often, organizational boundaries were first drawn to facilitate the operation of existing processes, and they impede the creation of new processes. New team boundaries facilitate new patterns of working together that ultimately can coalesce as new processes. In *Revolutionizing Product Development* (The Free Press, 1992), Steven Wheelwright and Kim Clark referred to these structures as "heavyweight teams."

These teams are entirely dedicated to the new challenge, team members are physically located together, and each member is charged with assuming personal responsibility for the success of the entire project. At Chrysler, for example, the boundaries of the groups within its product development organization historically had been defined by components—power train, electrical systems, and so on. But to accelerate auto development, Chrysler needed to focus not on components but on automobile platforms—the minivan, small car, Jeep, and truck, for example—so it created heavyweight teams. Although these organizational units aren't as good at focusing on component design, they facilitated the definition of new processes that were much faster and more efficient in integrating various subsystems into new car designs. Companies as diverse as Medtronic for its cardiac pacemakers, IBM for its disk drives, and Eli Lilly for its new blockbuster drug Zyprexa have used heavyweight teams as vehicles for creating new processes so they could develop better products faster.

CREATING CAPABILITIES THROUGH A SPIN-OUT ORGANIZATION

When the mainstream organization's values would render it incapable of allocating resources to an innovation project, the company should spin it out as a new venture. Large organizations cannot be expected to allocate the critical financial and human resources needed to build a strong position in small, emerging markets. And it is very difficult for a company whose cost structure is tailored to compete in high-end markets to be profitable in low-end markets as well. Spin-outs are very much in vogue among managers in old-line companies struggling with the question of how to address the Internet. But that's not always appropriate. When a disruptive innovation requires a different cost structure in order to be profitable and competitive, or when the current size of the opportunity is insignificant relative to the growth needs of the mainstream organization, then—and only then—is a spin-out organization required.

Hewlett-Packard's laser-printer division in Boise, Idaho, was hugely successful, enjoying high margins and a reputation for superior product quality. Unfortunately, its ink-jet project, which represented a disruptive innovation, languished inside the mainstream HP printer business. Although the processes for developing the two types of printers were basically the same, there was a difference in values. To thrive in the ink-jet market, HP needed to be comfortable with lower gross margins and a smaller market than its laser printers commanded, and it needed to be willing to embrace relatively lower performance standards. It was not until HP's managers decided to transfer the unit to a separate division in Vancouver, British Columbia, with the goal of competing head-to-head with its own laser business, that the ink-jet business finally became successful.

How separate does such an effort need to be? A new physical location isn't always necessary. The primary requirement is that the project not be forced to compete for resources with projects in the mainstream organization. As we have seen, projects that are inconsistent with a company's mainstream values will naturally be accorded lowest priority. Whether the independent organization is physically separate is less important than its independence from the normal decision-making criteria in the resource allocation process. "Fitting the Tool to the Task" goes into more detail about what kind of innovation challenge is best met by which organizational structure.

Fitting the Tool to the Task

Suppose that an organization needs to react to or initiate an innovation. Exhibit 11-1 can help managers understand what kind of team should work on the project and what organizational structure that team needs to work within. The vertical axis asks the manager to measure the extent to which the organization's existing processes are suited to getting the new job done effectively. The horizontal axis asks managers to assess whether the organization's values will permit the company to allocate the resources the new initiative needs.

In region A, the project is a good fit with the company's processes and values, so no new capabilities are called for. A functional or a lightweight team

Exhibit 11-1

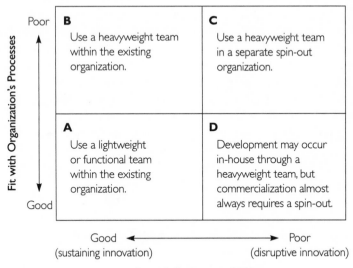

<table>
<tr><td>**B**
Use a heavyweight team within the existing organization.</td><td>**C**
Use a heavyweight team in a separate spin-out organization.</td></tr>
<tr><td>**A**
Use a lightweight or functional team within the existing organization.</td><td>**D**
Development may occur in-house through a heavyweight team, but commercialization almost always requires a spin-out.</td></tr>
</table>

Poor / Good — **Fit with Organization's Processes**

Good ←—————→ Poor
(sustaining innovation)   (disruptive innovation)

Fit with Organization's Values

can tackle the project within the existing organizational structure. A functional team works on function-specific issues, then passes the project on to the next function. A lightweight team is cross-functional, but team members stay under the control of their respective functional managers.

In region B, the project is a good fit with the company's values but not with its processes. It presents the organization with new types of problems and therefore requires new types of interactions and coordination among groups and individuals. The team, like the team in region A, is working on a sustaining rather than a disruptive innovation. In this case, a heavyweight team is a good bet, but the project can be executed within the mainstream company. A heavyweight team—whose members work solely on the project and are expected to behave like general managers, shouldering responsibility for the project's success—is designed so that new processes and new ways of working together can emerge.

In region C, the manager faces a disruptive change that doesn't fit the organization's existing processes or values. To ensure success, the manager should create a spin-out organization and commission a heavyweight development team to tackle the challenge. The spin-out will allow the project to be governed by different values—a different cost structure, for example, with lower profit margins. The heavyweight team (as in region B) will ensure that new processes can emerge.

Similarly, in region D, when a manager faces a disruptive change that fits the organization's current processes but doesn't fit its values, the key to success almost always lies in commissioning a heavyweight development team to work in a spin-out. Development may occasionally happen successfully in-house, but successful commercialization will require a spin-out.

Unfortunately, most companies employ a one-size-fits-all organizing strategy, using lightweight or functional teams for programs of every size and character. But such teams are tools for exploiting established capabilities. And among those few companies that have accepted the heavyweight gospel, many have attempted to organize *all* of their development teams in a heavy-weight fashion. Ideally, each company should tailor the team structure and organizational location to the process and values required by each project.

Managers think that developing a new operation necessarily means abandoning the old one, and they're loathe to do that since it works perfectly well for what it was designed to do. But when disruptive change appears on the horizon, managers need to assemble the capabilities to confront that change before it affects the mainstream business. They actually need to run two businesses in tandem—one whose processes are tuned to the existing business model and another that is geared toward the new model. Merrill Lynch, for example, has accomplished an impressive global expansion of its institutional financial services through careful execution of its existing planning, acquisition, and partnership processes. Now, however, faced with the on-line world, the company is required to plan, acquire, and form partnerships more rapidly. Does that mean Merrill Lynch should change the processes that have worked so well in its traditional investment-banking business? Doing so would be disastrous, if we consider the question through the lens of our framework. Instead, Merrill should retain the old processes when working with the existing business (there are probably a few billion dollars still to be made under the old business model!) and create additional processes to deal with the new class of problems.

One word of warning: in our studies of this challenge, we have never seen a company succeed in addressing a change that disrupts its mainstream values without the personal, attentive oversight of the CEO—precisely because of the power of values in shaping the normal resource allocation process. Only the CEO can ensure that the new organization gets the required resources and is free to create processes and values that are appropriate to the new challenge. CEOs who view spin-outs as a tool to get disruptive threats off their personal agendas are almost certain to meet with failure. We have seen no exceptions to this rule.

CREATING CAPABILITIES THROUGH ACQUISITIONS

Just as innovating managers need to make separate assessments of the capabilities and disabilities that reside in their company's resources, processes, and values, so must they do the same with acquisitions when seeking to buy capabilities. Companies that successfully gain new capabilities through acquisitions are those that know where those capabilities reside in the acquisition and assimilate them accordingly. Acquiring managers begin by asking, "What created the value that I just paid so dearly for? Did I justify the price because of the acquisition's resources? Or was a substantial portion of its worth created by processes and values?"

If the capabilities being purchased are embedded in an acquired company's processes and values, then the last thing the acquiring manager should do is integrate the acquisition into the parent organization. Integration will vaporize the processes and values of the acquired firm. Once the acquisition's managers are forced to adopt the buyer's way of doing business, its capabilities will disappear. A better strategy is to let the business stand alone and to infuse the parent's resources into the acquired company's processes and values. This approach truly constitutes the acquisition of new capabilities.

If, however, the acquired company's resources were the reason for its success and the primary rationale for the acquisition, then integrating it into the parent can make a lot of sense. Essentially, that means plugging the acquired people, products, technology, and customers into the parent's processes as a way of leveraging the parent's existing capabilities.

The perils of the DaimlerChrysler merger can be better understood in this light. Chrysler had few resources that could be considered unique. Its recent success in the market was rooted in its processes—particularly in its processes for designing products and integrating the efforts of its subsystem suppliers. What is the best way for Daimler to leverage Chrysler's capabilities? Wall Street is pressuring management to consolidate the two organizations to cut costs. But if the two companies are integrated, the very processes that made Chrysler such an attractive acquisition will likely be compromised.

The situation is reminiscent of IBM's 1984 acquisition of the telecommunications company Rolm. There wasn't anything in Rolm's pool of resources that IBM didn't already have. Rather, it was Rolm's processes for developing and finding new markets for PBX products that mattered. Initially, IBM recognized the value in preserving the informal and unconventional culture of the Rolm organization, which stood in stark contrast to IBM's methodical style. However, in 1987 IBM terminated Rolm's subsidiary status and decided to fully integrate the company into its own corporate structure. IBM's managers soon learned the folly of that decision. When they tried to push Rolm's resources—its products and its customers—through the processes that had been honed in the large-computer business, the Rolm business stumbled badly. And it was impossible for a computer company whose values had been whetted on profit margins of 18% to get excited about products with much lower profit margins. IBM's integration of Rolm destroyed the very source of the deal's original worth. DaimlerChrysler, bowing to the investment community's drumbeat for efficiency savings, now stands on the edge of the same precipice. Often, it seems, financial analysts have a better intuition about the value of resources than they do about the value of processes.

By contrast, Cisco Systems' acquisitions process has worked well because, we would argue, it has kept resources, processes, and values in the right perspective. Between 1993 and 1997, it primarily acquired small companies that were less than two years old, early-stage organizations whose market value was built primarily upon their resources, particularly their engineers and products. Cisco plugged those resources into its own effective development, logistics, manufacturing, and marketing processes and threw away whatever nascent processes and values came with the acquisitions because those weren't what it had paid for. On a couple of occasions when the company acquired a larger, more mature organization—notably its 1996 acquisition of StrataCom—Cisco did not integrate. Rather, it let StrataCom stand alone and infused Cisco's substantial resources into StrataCom's organization to help it grow more rapidly.[3]

Managers whose organizations are confronting change must first determine whether they have the resources required to succeed. They then need to ask a separate question: Does the organization have the processes and values it needs to succeed in this new situation? Asking this second question is not as instinctive for most managers because the processes by which work is done and the values by which employees make their decisions have served them well in the past. What we hope this framework introduces into managers' thinking is the idea that the very capabilities that make their organizations effective also define their disabilities. In that regard, a little time spent soul-searching for honest answers to the following questions will pay off handsomely: Are the processes by which work habitually gets done in the organization appropriate for this new problem? And will the values of the organization cause this initiative to get high priority or to languish?

If the answers to those questions are no, it's okay. Understanding a problem is the most crucial step in solving it. Wishful thinking about these issues can set teams that need to innovate on a course fraught with roadblocks, second-guessing, and frustration. The reason that innovation often seems to be so difficult for established companies is that they employ highly capable people and then set them to work within organizational structures whose processes and values weren't designed for the task at hand. Ensuring that capable people are ensconced in capable organizations is a major responsibility of management in a transformational age such as ours.

Notes

1. See Dorothy Leonard-Barton, "Core Capabilities and Core Rigidities: A Paradox in Managing New Product Development," *Strategic Management Journal* (Summer, 1992).

2. Our description of the development of an organization's culture draws heavily from Edgar Schein's research, as first laid out in his book *Organizational Culture and Leadership* (Jossey-Bass Publishers, 1985).

3. See Charles A. Holloway, Stephen C. Wheelwright, and Nicole Tempest, "Cisco Systems, Inc.: Post-Acquisition Manufacturing Integration," a case published jointly by the Stanford and Harvard business schools, 1998.

12
How We Went Digital Without a Strategy

Ricardo Semler

I own a $160 million South American company named Semco, and I have no idea what business it's in. I know what Semco does—we make things, we provide services, we host Internet communities—but I don't know what Semco is. Nor do I want to know. For the 20 years I've been with the company, I've steadfastly resisted any attempt to define its business. The reason is simple: once you say what business you're in, you put your employees into a mental straitjacket. You place boundaries around their thinking and, worst of all, you hand them a ready-made excuse for ignoring new opportunities: "We're not in that business." So rather than dictate Semco's identity from on high, I've let our employees shape it through their individual efforts, interests, and initiatives.

That rather unusual management philosophy has drawn a good deal of attention over the years. Nearly 2,000 executives from around the world have trekked to São Paulo to study our operations. Few, though, have tried to emulate us. The way we work—letting our employees choose what they do, where and when they do it, and even how they get paid—has seemed a little too radical for mainstream companies.

But recently a funny thing happened: the explosion in computing power and the rise of the Internet reshaped the business landscape, and the mainstream shifted. Today, companies are desperately looking for ways to increase their creativity and flexibility, spur their idea flow, and free their talent—to do, in other words, what Semco has been doing for 20 years.

I don't propose that Semco represents the model for the way businesses will operate in the future. Let's face it: we're a quirky company. But I do suggest that some of the principles that underlie the way we work will become increasingly common and even necessary in the new economy. In particular, I believe we have an organization that is able to transform itself continuously and organically—without formulating complicated mission statements and strategies, announcing a bunch of top-down directives, or bringing in an army of change-management consultants. As other companies seek to build adaptability into their organizations, they may be able to learn a thing or two from Semco's example.

Transformation Without End

Over the last ten years, Semco has grown steadily, quadrupling its revenues and expanding from 450 to 1,300 employees. More important, we've extended our range dramatically. At the start of the '90s, Semco was a manufacturer, pure and simple. We made things like pumps, industrial mixers, and dishwashers. But over the course of the decade, we diversified successfully into higher-margin services. Last year, almost 75% of our business was in services. Now we're stretching out again—this time into e-business. We expect that more than a quarter of our revenues next year will come from Internet initiatives, up from nothing just one year ago. We never planned to go digital, but we're going digital nonetheless.

You may wonder how that's possible. How do you get a sizable organization to change without telling it—or even asking it—to change? It's actually easy—but only if you're willing to give up control. People, I've found, will act in their best interests, and by extension in their organizations' best interests, if they're given complete freedom. It's only when you rein them in, when you tell them what to do and how to think, that they become inflexible, bureaucratic, and stagnant. Forcing change is the surest way to frustrate change.

Enough lecturing. Let me give you a concrete example of how our transformation has played out. Ten years ago, one of the things we did was manufacture cooling towers for large commercial buildings. In talking with the property owners who bought these products, some of our salespeople began to hear a common refrain. The customers kept complaining about the high cost of maintaining the towers. So our salespeople came back to Semco and proposed starting a little business in managing cooling-tower maintenance. They said, "We'll charge our customers 20% of whatever savings we generate for them, and we'll give Semco 80% of those revenues and take the remaining 20% as our commission." We said, "Fine, give it a shot."

Well, the little business was successful. We reduced customers' costs and eliminated some of their hassles, and they were happy. In fact, they were so happy that they came back and asked if we'd look after their air-conditioning compressors as well. Even though we didn't manufacture the compressors, our people didn't hesitate. They said yes. And when the customers saw we were pretty good at maintaining compressors, they said, "You know, there are a lot of other annoying functions that we'd just as soon off-load, like cleaning, security, and general maintenance. Can you do any of those?"

At that point, our people saw that their little business might grow into quite a big business. They began looking for a partner who could help bolster and extend our capabilities. They ended up calling the Rockefeller Group's Cushman & Wakefield division, one of the largest real-estate and property-management companies in the United States, and proposing that we launch a 50-50 joint venture in Brazil. Cushman wasn't very keen on the idea at first. People there said, "Property management by itself isn't a very lucrative business. Why don't we talk about doing something that involves real estate? That's where the money is."

We spent some time thinking about going into the real-estate business. We didn't have any particular expertise there, but we were willing to give it a try. When we started asking around, though, we found that no one in the company had much interest in real estate. It just didn't get anyone excited. So we went back to the Cushman folks and said, "Real estate sounds like a great business, but it's not something we care about right now. Why don't we just start with property management and see what happens?" They agreed, though not with a lot of enthusiasm.

We ponied up an initial investment of $2,000 each, just enough to pay the lawyers to set up a charter. Then we set our people loose. In no time, we had our first contract, with a bank, and then more and more business came through the door. Today, about five years later, the joint venture is a $30 million business.

It's also the most profitable property-management business within Cushman & Wakefield. The reason it has been so successful is that our people came into it fresh, with no preconceived strategies, and they were willing to experiment wildly. Instead of charging customers in the traditional way—a flat fee based on a building's square footage—they tried a partnership model. We'd take on all of a property owner's noncore functions, run them like businesses, and split the resulting savings.

One customer, for example, had been using 126 subcontractors for all sorts of maintenance and security tasks. It was a nightmare to manage, it resulted in poor or haphazard service, and it was ridiculously inefficient. We took over all 126 tasks, from changing lightbulbs to managing the car fleet to maintaining elevators, and we treated each as a separate business. We tore every task apart to see how it could be done better, and we made a series of improvement proposals to the client, ranging from relatively simple operating changes (reducing security personnel by installing video cameras) to highly technical systems installations (revamping the ATM architecture to dramatically reduce downtime). We outlined the investment and the expected gain and shared the cost reduction. The client reaped big savings and service improvements and got a single point of contact for doing everything necessary to run the building. And Semco made a heck of a lot more money than it would have by charging a flat fee.

Most manufacturers would probably consider a shift from making cooling towers to managing buildings pretty radical. Before making such a leap, they'd do a lot of soul-searching about their core businesses and capabilities. They'd run a lot of numbers, hold a lot of meetings, do a lot of planning. We didn't bother with any of that. We just let our people follow their instincts and apply their common sense, and it worked out fine.

Going to the Net

Our recent move into the digital space has proceeded in much the same way, with our people again taking the lead. In fact, some of the eight Internet ventures we've launched grew directly out of our earlier service initiatives. As our facility-management business expanded, for example, we extended it, through a joint venture with Johnson Controls, to managing retail facilities. As our people began to work closely with store managers, they began to notice the huge costs retailers incur from lost inventory. One employee came forward and asked for a paid leave to study opportunities in that area. We gave him a green light, and within a year he had helped us set up a joint venture with RGIS, the largest inventory-tracking company in the world. Less than two years later, the venture had become the biggest inventory-management business in South America. Now it is branching out into Web-enabled inventory control, helping on-line companies coordinate the fulfillment of electronic orders.

Our work in property management also brought us face to face with the disorganization and inefficiency of the construction business. Here, too, our people saw a big business opportunity, one that would build on the unique capabilities of the Internet. A number of the members of our joint ventures with Cushman & Wakefield and Johnson Controls banded together, with Semco's support, to set up an on-line exchange to facilitate the management of commercial construction projects. All the participants in a building project—architects, banks, construction companies, contractors, and project managers—can now use our exchange to send messages, hold real-time chats, issue proposals and send bids, and share documents and drawings. They can collaborate even if they're using different software, because the Web platform automatically does all the translation. The exchange is revolutionizing the construction process here in Brazil.

That business, which we're operating as a 50-50 joint venture with the U.S. Internet software company Bidcom, has itself become a springboard for further new initiatives. One of the most exciting is the creation of a South American Web portal for the entire building industry. The portal, called Edify, provides a single point of access for all the people, goods, and services required for a construction project. It's a place where contractors can hire tradesmen, hardware stores can sell lumber and fixtures, homeowners can buy insurance and cable television service, and real-estate agents and interior decorators can promote their offerings. We make money by charging transaction fees on all the business that takes place through the portal.

We're also partnering with a company called eTradeshow to host virtual construction fairs within the portal. As our people began to work closely with construction companies, they realized that many sectors of the South American building trade—flooring and masonry, for example—aren't large enough to pay the costs of physical trade shows. As a result, new ideas and products have been slow to enter the markets. We saw that on-line shows would be highly attractive to these sectors, providing them access not only to new products but to potential new partners all around the world. We'll be holding 60 different fairs on the site. In addition, we'll be hosting virtual versions of major international trade shows in such industries as automobiles, computers, and medical equipment. Visitors will be able to walk through a 3-D representation of the trade-fair space, collect business cards and brochures, watch presentations, and chat with sales representatives. These shows will generate fees for us while driving more traffic to the portal.

Management Without Control

Semco's ongoing transformation is a product of a very simple business philosophy: give people the freedom to do what they want, and over the long haul their successes will far outnumber their failures. Operationalizing that philosophy has involved a lot of trial and error, of taking a few steps forward and a couple back. The company remains a work in progress—and I hope it stays that way forever.

As I reflect on our experience, though, I see that we've learned some important lessons about creating an adaptive, creative organization. I'll share six of those lessons with you. I won't be so presumptuous as to say they'll apply to your company, but at least they'll stir up your thinking.

FORGET ABOUT THE TOP LINE

The biggest myth in the corporate world is that every business needs to keep growing to be successful. That's baloney. The ultimate measure of a business's success, I believe, is not how big it gets, but how long it survives. Yes, some businesses are meant to be huge, but others are meant to be medium-sized and still others are meant to be small. At Semco, we never set revenue targets for our businesses. We let each one find its natural size—the size at which it can maintain profitability and keep customers happy. It's fine if a business's top line stays the same or even shrinks as long its bottom line stays healthy. Rather than force our people to expand an existing business beyond its natural limits, we encourage them to start new businesses, to branch out instead of building up.

NEVER STOP BEING A START-UP

Every six months, we shut down Semco and start it up all over again. Through a rigorous budgeting and planning process, we force every one of our businesses to justify its continued existence. If this business didn't exist today, we ask, would we launch it? If we closed it down, would we alienate important customers? If the answers are no, then we move our money, resources, and talent elsewhere. We also take a fresh look at our entire organization, requiring that every employee—leaders included—resign (in theory) and ask to be rehired. All managers are evaluated anonymously by all workers who report to them, and the ratings are posted publicly. It has always struck me as odd that companies force new business ideas and new hires to go through rigorous evaluations but never do the same for existing businesses or employees.

DON'T BE A NANNY

Most companies suffer from what I call boarding-school syndrome. They treat their employees like children. They tell them where they have to be at what time, what they need to be doing, how they need to dress, whom they should talk to, and so on. But if you treat people like immature wards of the state, that's exactly how they'll behave. They'll never think for themselves or try new things or take chances. They'll just do what they're told, and they probably won't do it with much spirit.

At Semco, we have no set work hours, no assigned offices or desks, no dress codes. We have no employee manuals, no human resource rules and regulations. We don't even have an HR department. People go to work when they want and go home when they want. They decide when to take holidays and how much vacation they need. They even choose how they'll be compensated. (See "Eleven Ways to Pay.") In other words, we treat our employees like adults. And we expect them to behave like adults. If they screw up, they take the blame. And since they have to be rehired every six months, they know their jobs are always at risk. Ultimately, all we care about is performance. An employee who spends two days a week at the beach but still produces real value for customers and coworkers is a better employee than one who works ten-hour days but creates little value.

Eleven Ways to Pay

At Semco, we let employees choose the way they are paid. There are 11 compensation options.

1. Fixed salary
2. Bonuses
3. Profit sharing
4. Commission
5. Royalties on sales
6. Royalties on profits
7. Commission on gross margin
8. Stock or stock options
9. IPO/sale warrants that an executive cashes in when a business unit goes public or is sold
10. Self-set annual review/compensation in which an executive is paid for meeting self-set goals
11. Commission on difference between actual and three-year-value of company

And because the options can be combined in different ways, there is a vast number of possible permutations. We've found that by being flexible about rewards, we encourage our employees to innovate and take risks. In the end, people understand it's in their best interest to choose compensation packages that maximize both their own pay and the company's returns.

LET TALENT FIND ITS PLACE

Companies tend to hire people for specific jobs and then keep them stuck in one career track. They also tend to choose which businesses people work in. The most talented people, for instance, may be assigned automatically to the business unit with the biggest growth prospects. The companies don't take into account what the individual really wants. The resulting disconnect between corporate needs and individual desires shows up in the high rates of talent churn that afflict most companies today.

We take a very different approach. We let people choose where they'll work and what they'll do (and even decide, as a team, who their leaders will be). All entry-level new hires participate in a program called Lost in Space. They spend six months to a year floating around the company, checking out businesses, meeting people, and trying out jobs. When a new hire finds a place that fits with his personality and goals, he stays there. Since our turnover rate in the past six years has been less than 1%—even though we've been targeted heavily by headhunters—we must be doing something right.

MAKE DECISIONS QUICKLY AND OPENLY

The best way for an organization to kill individual initiative is to force people to go through a complicated, bureaucratic review and approval process. We strive to make it as easy as possible for Semco employees to propose new business ideas, and we make sure they get fast and clear decisions. All proposals go through an executive board that includes representatives from our major business units. The board meetings are completely open. All employees are welcome to attend—in fact, we always reserve two seats on the board for the first two employees who arrive at a meeting. Proposals have to meet two simple criteria that govern all the businesses we launch. First, the business has to be a premium provider of its product or service. Second, the product or service has to be complex, requiring engineering skills and presenting high entry barriers. Well-considered proposals that meet those standards get launched within Semco. Even if a proposed business fails to meet both criteria, we'll often back it as a minority investor if its prospects look good.

PARTNER PROMISCUOUSLY

To explore and launch new businesses quickly and efficiently, you need help; it's pure arrogance to assume you can do everything on your own. I'm proud to say that we partner promiscuously at Semco. Indeed, I can't think of a single new business we've started without entering into some kind of alliance, whether to gain access to software, draw on a depth of experience, bring in new capabilities, or just share risk. Partnerships have provided the foundation for our experiments and our expansion over the years. Our partners are as much a part of our company as our employees.

Staying Free

I travel a lot in my job, and recently I've been spending time in Silicon Valley. I've been visiting Internet companies, talking with technology visionaries, and participating in panel discussions on the future of business. The new companies and their founders excite me. I see in them the same spirit we've nurtured at Semco—a respect for individuals and their ideas, a distrust of bureaucracy and hierarchy, a love for openness and experimentation.

But I'm beginning to see troubling signs that the traditional ways of doing business are reasserting their hegemony. Investors, I fear, are starting to force young start-ups into the molds of the past—molds that some thought had been broken forever. CEOs from old-line companies are being brought in to establish "discipline" and "focus." Entrepreneurs are settling into corner offices with secretaries and receptionists. HR departments are being formed to issue policies and to plot careers. Strategies are being written. The truly creative types are being caged up in service units and kept further and further from the decision makers.

It's sad and, I suppose, predictable. But it isn't necessary. If my 20 years at Semco have taught me anything, it's that successful businesses do not have to fit into one tight little mold. You can build a great company without fixed plans. You can have an efficient organization without rules and controls. You can be unbuttoned and creative without sacrificing profit. You can lead without wielding power. All it takes is faith in people.

13
Managing for the Next Big Thing: An Interview with EMC's Michael Ruettgers

Paul Hemp

EMC is hardly a household name, but it is one of the most successful companies of the past decade. The best-performing stock of the latest bull market's first ten years—the period ending October 11, 2000—it topped companies such as Cisco Systems and Dell Computer with a share price that rose 84,000%. EMC's recent market value has roughly equaled that of competitor IBM, although EMC's estimated 2000 revenue of $8.5 billion is one-tenth that of its rival. Despite predictions that the company has become too big to maintain its torrid pace, EMC has posted 14 consecutive quarters of at least 20% revenue and profit growth.

To some extent, EMC's success comes from being in the right industry at the right time. Data storage, for years a conspicuously unglamorous business, is hot these days, especially with the rise of the Internet. Each on-line mouse click either creates new information, which must be stored somewhere, or taps an expanding repository of existing information, much of it data-rich material such as photo images and music files. The Internet has only accelerated the already rapid growth in data storage, as companies rush to gather increasingly detailed information on their customers and other aspects of their business. The demand for storage is expected to grow exponentially, because increasingly, individuals are saving all kinds of personal data, from family videos to medical records, in electronic formats.

But how has EMC come to dominate the industry at the expense of other once high-flying new entrants, not to mention established players such as IBM? The answer lies in an array of specific managerial practices that have repeatedly helped EMC anticipate and exploit profitable opportunities before competitors. For example, in the early 1990s, EMC stole the mainframe storage market from

IBM with a faster system featuring software that was capable of anticipating and moving to a temporary "cache memory" the data a user was likely to need next. Several years later, EMC foresaw and then capitalized on the trend toward replacing numerous isolated storage units attached to servers with a single storage system. More recently, it pioneered companywide data storage networks, in which a large number of servers can be connected to a large number of storage units. EMC's experiences provide lessons for any company striving to maintain growth in the face of unexpected, disruptive, and near-constant change.

Much of the credit for EMC's success goes to Michael Ruettgers, the company's CEO for the past eight years. By repeatedly leading the company into untested markets—once even abandoning a profitable business that at the time generated most of the company's revenue—he has turned a struggling maker of minicomputer memory boards into the dominant player in one of the new economy's fastest-growing industries.

Ruettgers, 58, didn't exactly get off to a roaring start on the way to becoming one of America's most successful CEOs. He flunked out of the University of California at Los Angeles his freshman year because, by his own account, he spent too much time at the beach girl-watching from his red Triumph TR3. But he regrouped, first at tiny St. Martin's College in Washington state and later at Idaho State University, from which he graduated in 1964. He worked for defense contractor LTV and then attended Harvard Business School, graduating in 1967. After stints at Raytheon, where he worked on the early development of the Patriot missile, and at several software consulting firms, he joined EMC in 1988 as executive vice president for operations.

At the time, EMC, based in Hopkinton, Massachusetts, was a $120 million company that was losing money because of quality problems with its memory boards. Ruettgers quickly took command. At an early meeting with top executives, he placed airsickness bags at each seat, a graphic reference to the way he felt about the company's products. As if any elaboration were needed, he told those assembled: "The quality of our products makes me puke." The event foreshadowed the atmosphere of accountability he later worked to cultivate. "No whining, no excuses, no surprises" is now a company credo. Indeed, though Ruettger's manner is casual—he occasionally wears cowboy boots to work and regularly eats in the employee cafeteria—he can wither underlings with a look or a tough question. "The easygoing boss from hell" is how one subordinate jokingly describes him.

Ruettgers ultimately solved the product quality problems, which had nearly bankrupted the company, and in 1989 he was promoted to president and chief operating officer. In 1992, he became CEO and accelerated EMC's move into the storage business. Since then, revenues and profits have grown at an average rate of more than 50% per year. In talking about the company's success—as well as the challenges and new competitors that lie ahead—Ruettgers often uses the analogy of a surfer spotting, catching, and riding successive waves, each one representing an opportunity created by a disruptive technology, new market, or business model.

Was there ever a moment when you suddenly turned and, heart in your throat, saw a wave that was closer and approaching much faster than you thought?

Yes, the one we're riding right now. In February 1999, I traveled to the West Coast and spent four days talking with dot-coms and other Internet companies. Suddenly it became clear that there was a surging demand that we hadn't seen and that we risked missing. In fact, Sun Microsystems had seen it and had already made inroads with its storage systems. We immediately established a dedicated sales force to focus on Internet companies. And we set out to identify the people who would have an influence on the purchase of our products. These were primarily venture capitalists—people who could live with the business risk of a start-up but didn't want the technical risk of a company losing all its data.

I remember one of our sales guys in Arizona saying he'd received a call from the CIO of a dot-com whose board had just approved the purchase of somebody else's storage system. The CIO mentioned that one of his venture guys had said, "How come you're not talking to EMC?" By that point, we were on the radar screen as the de facto standard in storage. The board reversed its decision, and we got the sale. Within six to eight months, we'd gone from essentially not having much visibility in this space to being considered one of the "four horsemen of the Internet": Oracle in databases, Sun in servers, Cisco in networking, and EMC in storage.

But wasn't it fairly obvious to you some time ago that the Internet revolution would create a big demand for storage?

Yes and no. Nearly four years ago, we formed our Internet Solutions Group, which includes a small Web-hosting business, because I wanted us to have firsthand experience with data storage on the Internet. We host the Web sites of 50 or 60 customers, and this allows us to advise our storage customers—for example, Internet service providers—on state-of-the-art technical issues.

At the same time, however, most of the dot-coms were falling through the cracks as we looked at potential customers. In our business, only a few large companies provided the majority of data storage, so we focused on companies with more than $500 million in revenue, 150 people in the IT department, and so forth. But suddenly there were companies with little or no revenue who were poised to immediately buy as much storage as some of our largest customers.

So yes, three or four years ago, we saw the Internet wave coming. But it turned out to be much bigger and faster than we initially thought. It could have crashed over us. The memory of almost missing it is a constant reminder that we always need to look beyond our current customers. The important thing, though, is that we quickly adjusted. And riding a wave is just as important as catching it. In fact, there were one or two times in the past year or two when sudden unexpected shifts threatened to knock us off balance, if not pull us under.

Let's return to those near misses in a minute. First, let's talk about how you've anticipated some of the big waves in your industry.

You have to view this in the context of the typical life cycle of a technology company. There's usually a period of growth—sometimes tremendous and rapid growth. Then there's surprise, as some disruptive technology or stealth competition appears out of nowhere. Then panic, with its accompanying loss of focus and paralysis. And then decline. Occasionally, a company will reinvent itself and start the cycle again. But how much better to simply stay in the growth stage.

Within a growth stage, there is the typical product adoption cycle, the one that Geoffrey Moore [author of *Crossing the Chasm* and *Inside the Tornado*] writes about. When a new product is introduced, a handful of innovators will try it, followed by a few more early adopters. And then there is that crucial chasm that must be crossed to get to the early majority of users and ever-wider acceptance. Then the growth tapers off until only the laggards are left to buy the product.

Staying in the growth stage requires both timing and speed. For example, we stagger our products rather than develop them one after the other: as one product peaks, the next one in the pipeline is poised to cross the chasm. One sign of our own success in this area is that, in recent years, as much as 80% of our annual revenue has come from products introduced during the year.

So concurrent product development involves timing. What about speed?

We get a new product to the very early adopters quickly—maybe not with all the bells and whistles in place, but with the expectation of full functionality in the near future. Then we can modify and refine the product for them—and for later users—based on actual use. So when we cross the chasm and roll the product out broadly, the product has already been in the hands of customers.

The drive to get something into the market as quickly as possible can be frustrating for engineers, who typically want to refine and refine to ensure that a product is perfect before letting it out the door. But left in their hands, a product might be released too late to catch the wave—if it ever leaves the factory at all. At the same time, the discipline of limiting these early shipments to a handful of early adopters can be frustrating to the salespeople, who want to roll it out and boost sales quickly.

I remember when we decided to take on IBM in the mainframe storage business. We had our product, but we weren't quite ready for prime time. Well, we knew there are always enough Mad Hatters among the innovators and early adopters who will buy one of almost anything. At the same time, we didn't want any high-profile failures, even among the Mad Hatters. So we sold most of these early systems in the boondocks. We had three accounts in Vermont—and today, ten years later, as the leading supplier in the world, I don't think we have any more than those original three accounts in the state. From there, we followed the New York State Thruway, with accounts in Rochester, Syracuse, and Albany. It was like having out-of-town tryouts for a Broadway show. I didn't want a major account in Boston to have a bad experience and then never be able to show up in Boston again.

We don't have to take these early product versions to Vermont anymore. Customers now have enough faith in us to know that we will offer them something of high quality and that full functionality will follow. One way we have gained that credibility is in our refusal to follow the common practice of "preannouncing" products months in advance of their release—the vaporware phenomenon, designed to get customers to hold off planned purchases of competing products. Because we don't do this, there is never that familiar delay in the launch. When we finally announce a product and offer it widely, it's already been used by customers and refined in response to their needs.

You talk about the importance of quickly getting products into the hands of your customers. How do you know what they want or, more important, what they are likely to want in the future?

We focus on the customers we call "lead users." These are early adopters who will try unconventional approaches and push us for customized solutions, which we can later modify for wider customer use. In every case, we try to understand not only their current needs but also their future, unarticulated ones. There are formal and informal ways of getting at this. For example, we hold what we call "customer councils" twice a year in North America and Europe and annually elsewhere in the world. These aren't sales meetings or conventional user groups. Customers don't bring golf clubs. They bring completed homework assignments.

The aim of these meetings is to methodically extract product requirements from customers, to test the validity of concepts we are considering for future products, and in general to create a climate of collaborative innovation. The meetings include 50 to 60 carefully chosen customers and our own product management and engineering executives. Twenty hours of intense discussions are spread over two and a half days. Customers commit to working with us in this role for at least 18 months and sign nondisclosure agreements. They willingly do this for the opportunity to help influence our priorities and get their storage problems solved sooner rather than later.

Typically, the session begins with a series of presentations that lays out our vision of the short- and long-term challenges facing the industry. Then we get feedback to see whether our understanding of where customers are feeling pain matches theirs. If it appears we're in sync, we then present a detailed look at EMC's "work-in-process" solutions to these problems—how to automate the management of a storage network, for example. This can lead to intense discussions about whether our proposed solution will indeed solve the problem and have a positive business impact. Customers have often told us, "Hey, don't do that. Another piece of software already solves that problem, so you'll be wasting your time." And so we can take that issue right off our list of priorities. This process also helps us determine what to include in the early versions of new products that we release to our lead users. We'll say, "What do you want first?"

One other thought here: getting too far ahead of your customers is just as dangerous as failing to anticipate their needs, because if you're too far ahead, you're unlikely to cross the chasm to widespread acceptance. Or to use the surfing image, you'll lose momentum and sink while waiting for the wave to catch up with you. So, again, you have to curb an engineer's instincts to give people the perfect product rather than what they actually need or can deal with. To use a familiar if somewhat simplistic analogy, look at how annoyed customers get when trying to program a videocassette recorder. Most people end up putting masking tape over the digital clock that continues to blink at the factory-set 12:00. We want to be sure that our products don't offer more than customers can cope with.

You also have talked about gleaning insights about customers from your customer service organization. In what way?

When we get a frantic call that someone's system has crashed, we don't ask if one of our products is at fault. We get there immediately and fix the problem. Besides earning the gratitude of numerous managers, we inevitably learn something new about that customer's present and future requirements.

Less dramatic but even more powerful, we build into every one of our storage systems an onboard self-diagnostic system that is linked by dedicated, high-speed telephone lines directly to our round-the-clock customer service center. This means that we know the minute-by-minute status of our more than 40,000 machines around the world, allowing us to detect errors before they become serious enough to threaten data availability. Besides providing customers with peace of mind, this enables our engineers to experience customers' daily problems and to translate that learning into future versions of software that will prevent those problems from recurring.

An added benefit is that such a support system, woven tightly into a customer's business, creates not only barriers to entry by competitors but also barriers to exit by customers. They simply find it hard to extricate themselves from the supportive infrastructure we have surrounded them with.

How often do you personally meet with customers?

I talk with about 500 customers and prospects a year, which accounts for maybe 20% of my time. Clearly, these conversations aren't systematic in the way that the customer councils are. But they can produce unexpected insights. I usually poke around with three or four questions, testing something I've just heard from one or two other executives: "Are you seeing this? What do you think about this? Is this true?"

For example, our aggressive move into open storage, where different types of servers are linked to a single storage system, grew out of a conversation I had in the early 1990s with the CIO at John Deere. I asked him whether he saw any signs that the management of data storage would return to corporate headquarters from the business units, where it had migrated as companies moved from mainframes to local area networks built around a server. And he started to turn red and he said, "Yeah. You know I told those"—and here a bunch of expletives referring to the company's business unit managers came pouring out—"I told them not to disperse our data storage capabilities. The servers are often down and, even when they aren't, the information sits in isolated data islands throughout the company." The guy's evident frustration reinforced our hunch that we were on to something: there was a desire to consolidate data storage, but it would require a reliable storage system able to communicate with the variety of computers that usually exist within an organization.

But obviously, I'm not the only one who talks to customers. Both our customer service and sales staffs constantly get insights from them. Somewhat atypically, so do our engineers. I read recently that Hewlett-Packard, as part of a reorganization, was separating its product development activities from its marketing activities, which would seem to isolate HP engineers from customers. Our engineers are always getting together with customers to see how emerging technologies might be able to solve customers' emerging problems.

Rivals like IBM, Hitachi, and Sun Microsystems all sell storage as a complement to other products. Doesn't this give them additional leverage with customers?

I think our focus on a single business actually helps us stay ahead of the curve. In some respects, this runs counter to what I learned in business school, where the prevailing wisdom was to diversify. But our single-minded focus creates a special lens through which to view and interpret customers' current and future needs. For example, our perspective allowed us to see that the computer industry had, in some ways, lost sight of its reason for being. It had become so consumed with the "T" in IT—the creation of faster processors and more efficient networks—that it had forgotten about the "I." Yet ultimately, it's information that customers care about: the speed of access to it, its availability, the ability to share it across an organization. Other companies, with the distractions of their different business areas, weren't as quick to see this.

Just look at IBM. Ten years ago, it had 80% of the data storage market; now it has 10 to 15%. There are probably a number of reasons why this happened, but focus must have had something to do with it. Today, IBM's storage system business is probably less than 1% of its business, so you know that only a few good people at IBM are likely to be working in this space.

Or look at Data General, which we acquired in 1999. The company faced terrific challenges as the minicomputer business collapsed, but it moved into the open-storage business about the same time we did. It had an excellent storage product and a relatively good position in certain segments of the storage marketplace. Still, its executives were never willing to give up their other business until we acquired them, even though their minicomputer revenue was declining and they understood their opportunities were on the storage side. Acting on an opportunity, as well as merely identifying it, is to some extent easier when you're committed to a single industry. (See "The Democratization of Data.")

The Democratization of Data
by Peter Lyman and Hal R. Varian

The declining cost of data storage and communications has led to an explosion in the volume of available information. Just as we've become comfortable with megabytes (the digital equivalent of a novel-length book, which can be stored on a computer floppy disk), we are being forced to think in terms of gigabytes (1,000 books) and terabytes (1 million books). The largest of today's data storage products—refrigerator-sized boxes made by companies such as EMC—hold nearly 20 terabytes of data, the rough equivalent of the U.S. Library of Congress.

But the amount of information is not the only thing that has changed; so has its accessibility. Material that was available only to an elite a few decades ago can now be retrieved and used by any person

with a network connection. In addition, individuals are largely responsible for the growing glut of data. With this unprecedented increase in the use and production of information by individuals, data
are becoming democratized—a development that has profound implications for business executives.

Anyone who surfs the Web knows that more and more information
is now widely available. Somewhat less obvious is the degree to which
individuals, rather than organizations, are responsible for generating
that information. Indeed, information technology increasingly allows
not only for mass production of information but also for production of
information by the masses.

In a recent study, we attempted to measure and analyze the total
amount of data produced every year. Some of the findings were surprising. For example, the world's film industry produces about 4,000
movies a year—the equivalent of about 16 terabytes of data. But that
number is dwarfed by the 410,000 terabytes of photographs or the
300,000 terabytes of videotapes produced by ordinary people. The
Web, which seems so huge, represents "only" 21 terabytes of information. This pales beside the 610 billion e-mail messages sent each year,
totaling about 11,000 terabytes. In a few years, an ordinary household
with a camcorder, a digital camera, a VCR, a DVD player, a personal
video recorder, and a computer could easily contain a terabyte of
data—and there are over 100 million households in the United States
alone.

The democratization of data will profoundly affect business. For one
thing, the explosion of individually generated data presents both opportunities and challenges for data storage providers. Our study found
that while the capacity of today's giant corporate data warehouses is
phenomenal, taken together it represents only about 16% of the
world's total digital storage. A whopping 56% of storage is in single-
user PCs.

If concerns about privacy can be overcome, people may well turn
over the management of their personal data to specialized data storage
businesses. After all, would you rather keep all your family photos on
your PC hard drive and risk losing everything if it crashes, or store
them on a secure site managed by Kodak? On the other hand, the
makers of data storage equipment, which typically focus on products
that offer ever-greater capacity, may ultimately find that individuals
would rather keep information about themselves in smaller systems
that only they control.

Business also will be affected by individuals' greater access to data. Today, information that just a few years ago was available only to department heads on a quarterly basis can be instantaneously provided to anyone in an organization. A foreman on the shop floor can access real-time order information from the sales force, something that was virtually inconceivable 20 years ago.

The difficulty comes in managing this information effectively: making sure that your suppliers, employees, and customers not only have access to the data they need but can also locate, manipulate, and understand it. This is no easy task, as our ability to store and communicate information has far outpaced our ability to search, retrieve, and present it. Information management—at the individual, organizational, and even societal level—is one of the key challenges we face.

Two hundred years ago, the economist Thomas Robert Malthus noted that the expansion of the food supply was linear, while the number of mouths to feed expanded geometrically. His forecast of widespread famine led to the reputation of economics as the "dismal science." The human race has survived—so far, at least—because technological advances in food production have kept pace with population growth.

But now the amount of information is growing exponentially while the time that people spend absorbing that information has stayed almost constant. Another Malthusian crisis is brewing. Will technology bail us out again?

PETER LYMAN AND HAL R. VARIAN *are professors at the School of Information Management and Systems at the University of California at Berkeley; Varian is the coauthor with Carl Shapiro of* Information Rules: A Strategic Guide to the Network Economy *(Harvard Business School Press, 1998). EMC provided financial support for the study mentioned in this sidebar. For more about this study, go to www.sims.berkeley.edu/how-much-info.*

People compare the intense atmosphere at EMC to that of a start-up. Can you describe the company's culture?

I think the defining characteristic is a sense of urgency. This primes us to seize opportunities that are only just emerging, as well as to execute our existing plans. For example, when we launched our open-storage product in 1995, I set a goal of $200 million in sales for the year. At the end of the first quarter, we were way behind our sales targets, even though we had built enough products to meet them. So to make sure everybody understood how important this was, we took all that extra inventory and put it in people's offices. People had to climb around crates to get to their desks. Miraculously, by the end of the next quarter, we had met our sales targets. And all of the offices were empty.

We help fuel this sense of urgency by setting quarterly goals for the 800 or so executives in the organization. We measure and pay people against those quarterly goals. I continue to be amazed at companies that still have annual goals for executives. I can understand having a profit target for the year, but I can't imagine just turning them loose and saying, "As long as you get this done by the end of the year, it's okay." We all know that it will probably be significantly more valuable to the company if it is done within two months. It's like the old farmer's rhyme about the value of a honey hive: "A swarm of bees in May is worth a load of hay. A swarm of bees in June is worth a silver spoon. A swarm of bees in July is not worth a fly."

Related to this is our emphasis on results and personal accountability. We're a very nonbureaucratic culture, and we give people a lot of responsibility. But they have to deliver. There are no excuses. I don't buy the "brother-in-law excuse"—that we can't make a sale because the brother-in-law of our contact works for a competitor. In the early days, honest to God, I used to hear that. Or if it's not the brother-in-law, it's the godfather. That was the reason that, for a couple of years, we couldn't get into this one bank in California. The guy's godfather worked for IBM. That's not acceptable. And this results-oriented focus applies to senior management, too. Employees know if senior managers make their goals or not.

How much does the company's culture reflect your own personality?

Well, I'm quite skeptical of success, which probably contributes to our sense of urgency and our constantly looking beyond our current success for the next thing. I always think of an experience I had when I was at LTV. We were testing a missile down at White Sands [Missile Range in New Mexico]. We put a stake out in the desert and the missile did the proverbial William Tell and landed right on it. But we never analyzed the telemetry. When we brought the second round of missiles down, they didn't hit the stake. We figured this must be an anomaly. But time and again, the missile didn't even go near the stake. So we went back and looked, and we learned that in the first test the guidance system wasn't even working. The missile had just landed on the stake by chance. Ever since then, I've been wary. People will come in and give me a piece of good news and I'm likely to say, "Great," but then follow it up by saying, "Why do you think that happened? Will it continue to happen?"

Most company cultures are resistant to change. But catching the next wave—as opposed to merely seeing it forming on the horizon—usually requires wrenching change. How do you foster the flexibility needed to do this?

Internal resistance to change is greatest when things seem to be going well. People will say to me, "Hey, if we're so screwed up, how come we're so successful?" You would think that a company like EMC, which has changed course at least four times during the last ten years, would be comfortable with it. But every time we initiate a change, there has to be a lot of pushing. We typically have fallout from people all through the organization, top to bottom, who simply can't do it again.

It was even more difficult ten years ago when we made our first big change. To immediately focus on our new business—mainframe storage devices—we decided to wind down our memory board business, which by this time was again profitable. In fact, within 90 days, we closed down most of that business, which accounted for about 80% of our revenue. And I'd have marketing guys come in and say, "You know, I happen to really agree with this decision. But my case is different because right now I'm trying to cut this deal with a customer." So there was all of this guerilla warfare between individuals and business units that, if you didn't stamp it out, would spread. Finally, I restricted the ability of the sales guys to sell anything but this one product, and they saw that the game was over. Of course, at times like these you must have faith in your convictions. If it's lonely at the top, it becomes even lonelier when you make this kind of decision.

Even if you convince people of the need for change, don't you have to equip them with new skills?

Each time we've made a big change, we've had to go out and recruit new people with the necessary skills. Those skills have become more sophisticated with each move we've made. This means that we're constantly upgrading big chunks of the company, which is difficult. And it's worth noting that the CEO isn't exempt from the retooling.

For example, our open-storage business is based on linking up different types of computers. Initially, these were servers using the UNIX operating system, but all we knew about at that point was the mainframe business. I can remember, pretty vividly, going on our first sales call here in the Boston area. It was at State Street Bank and there were three of us, two sales guys and myself. We expected the meeting to include three of us and two of them, or something like that. And we got into this big conference room, and there must have been 20 guys in there, all UNIX administrators. They started asking questions. We were able to handle the first three questions, and after that—well, they were finally forced to cut the meeting short.

We got on the elevator and we were white and we were shaky, and I don't think I went on another sales call for two weeks. After coming across the beaches of D day, the last thing you want to do is stick your head up again. But we went back, and the next time we could answer ten questions. And the next time after that, 15 questions. And eventually we could answer all the questions. But the learning curve was steep.

You mentioned earlier that there have been times when you've been successfully riding a big wave but could have wiped out because of an unexpected disruption to the business. How do you avoid such mishaps?

You have to be nimble enough to respond quickly to unexpected changes—for example, what we call the "HP divorce." At 8:15 on the morning of our 1999 annual meeting, I got a call from Lew [Platt, former CEO of Hewlett-Packard] saying that HP was ending our partnership agreement and teaming up with Hitachi. For some time, HP had been selling our storage systems to their server customers. We had expected the partnership to yield about $200 million in revenue for the quarter, or nearly 20% of total sales.

Within 48 hours of the call, we had changed our sales compensation system and refocused our sales force to contact HP server customers directly. We also determined that, with aggressive targeting of these customers, the end of the relationship wouldn't have any impact on revenue. And in fact, we finished the quarter with about $200 million in revenue from HP server customers, except that only $70 million came through HP. The remainder we made up through direct sales or our indirect channels.

How were you able to respond so quickly?

A number of our procedures help us respond quickly to changes. For example, our new six-quarter rolling budgeting process allows us to constantly adjust our budget allocations to meet changes in the market. But in the case of the split with HP, it was the discipline imposed by our monthly business review meetings, or BRMs, which we have perfected over the past decade.

These are planning and forecasting meetings in which we specify, for example, the number and type of units we expect to sell so that manufacturing will build the right amount. The meetings are run by our CFO and include senior executives and representatives from sales, manufacturing, and other departments. Attendance is pretty consistent. In fact, even the seating is preplanned. A supporting cast is also there, armed with backup data, so that we can get immediate answers to detailed questions. There is no "I'll get back to you next week on that." People understand that enough information must be available so we can make decisions on the spot. The regular and detailed sharing of information allows us to effectively look at our P&Ls on a monthly basis and make business adjustments on the fly.

When we heard from HP, the BRM process allowed us to quickly identify what revenue we could salvage. That's because we had at our fingertips detailed information about each HP account and its likely near-term needs—for example, whether the company was considering an upgrade or new applications requiring additional storage. Then we determined which ones were likely to buy directly from us. The attitude was, "Hey, I don't care if there's been an earthquake here. The sales organization has signed up to do this much revenue, and we'll do it." No excuses. (See "Five Ways to Exploit the Next Big Thing.")

Five Ways to Exploit the Next Big Thing

EMC has adopted numerous managerial practices that help the company anticipate and capitalize on profitable opportunities before their competitors do. These practices include:

Concurrent Product Development
Ensuring that the next-generation product is ready for trial as the current one ships and the previous one peaks helps EMC maintain momentum when introducing new technologies.

Customer Councils
Intensive two-day gatherings of top EMC engineers and 50 to 60 technologically savvy customers allow the company to pinpoint products and features that will address future customer priorities.

Aggressive Customer Service
A vigorous response to customer problems provides insight into latent customer needs, while diagnostic software—embedded in each product and linked to EMC's customer service center—delivers detailed, real-time information about product use and potential product glitches.

Quarterly Goal-Setting and Bonuses
Compression of the usual yearly cycle fosters a sense of urgency that encourages EMC employees to focus on future challenges rather than dwell on current success.

Frequent Forecasting
Monthly business review meetings, at which manufacturing output is synchronized with likely orders, and a six-quarter rolling budgeting process allow EMC to get early glimpses of changes in the market and respond to them quickly.

Despite EMC's success over the past decade, you describe a company that sounds as though it's still running to get ahead. How do you maintain that drive?

We're acutely aware that more companies fail because of their success than any other reason. I tell people, "What got us here won't keep us here." Technology leadership is not an entitlement, and we have to be constantly vigilant for signs of complacency. I get a chilling reminder of that every day on my way to work when I drive down Route 495, passing the tombstones of once high-flying technology companies. If you start up north, you'll pass Wang. Then Digital. Then Prime. Then Data General. If you come in a little bit, there's Computervision and others.

If you're looking to place blame for these casualties, you have to fault the management. And sometimes the top management. It's my job, more than anybody else's, to make sure that this doesn't happen to EMC. But I think healthy paranoia runs all the way through the company. Down in Milford, we occupy a building that Prime once leased. On the second floor, there's a big auditorium. In the back of the auditorium, against a red velvet background, is a giant sign that says Prime Computer. When we moved into the building, the employees asked us to leave the sign up as a reminder of what could happen if EMC ever became complacent.

Executive Summaries

Unbundling the Corporation

John Hagel III and Marc Singer

No matter how monolithic they may seem, most companies are really engaged in three kinds of businesses. One business attracts customers. Another develops products. The third oversees operations. Although organizationally intertwined, these businesses have conflicting characteristics.

It takes a big investment to find and develop a relationship with a customer, so profitability hinges on achieving economies of scope. But speed, not scope, drives the economics of product innovation. And the high fixed costs of capital-intensive infrastructure businesses require economies of scale.

Scope, speed, and scale can't be optimized simultaneously, so trade-offs have to be made when the three businesses are bundled into one corporation. Historically, they have been bundled because the interaction costs—the friction—incurred by separating them were too high.

But we are on the verge of a worldwide reduction in interaction costs, the authors contend, as electronic networks drive down the costs of communicating and of exchanging data. Activities that companies have always believed were central to their businesses will suddenly be offered by new, specialized competitors that won't have to make trade-offs.

Ultimately, the authors predict, traditional businesses will unbundle and then rebundle into large infrastructure and customer-relationship businesses and small, nimble product innovation companies. And executives in many industries will be forced to ask the most basic question about their companies: What business are we really in? Their answer will determine their fate in an increasingly frictionless economy.

Syndication: The Emerging Model for Business in the Internet Era

Kevin Werbach

Syndication has long been a fundamental organizing principle in the entertainment world, but it's been rare elsewhere in business. The fixed physical assets and slow-moving information that characterized the industrial economy made it difficult, if not impossible, to create the kind of fluid networks that are essential for syndication. But with the rise of the information economy, flexible business networks are not only becoming possible, they're becoming essential. As a result, syndication is moving from business's periphery to its center.

Within a syndication network there are three roles that businesses can play. *Originators* create original content, which encompasses everything from entertainment programming to products to business processes. *Syndicators* package that content, often integrating it with content from other originators. *Distributors* deliver the content to consumers. A company can play a single role, or it can play two or three roles simultaneously.

Syndication requires businesses to rethink their strategies and relationships in radical ways. Because a company's success hinges on its connections to other companies, it can no longer view its core capabilities as secrets to protect. Instead, it needs to see them as products to sell. FedEx, for example, is succeeding by distributing its sophisticated package-tracking capability to other companies on the Net.

Syndication promises to change the nature of business. As this new way of doing business takes hold, companies may look the same as before to their customers, but behind the scenes they will be in constant flux, melding with one another in ever-changing, self-organizing networks.

Where Value Lives in a Networked World

Mohanbir Sawhney and Deval Parikh

While many management thinkers proclaim an era of radical uncertainty, authors Sawhney and Parikh assert that the seemingly endless upheavals of the digital age are more predictable than that: today's changes have a common root, and that root lies in the nature of intelligence in networks. Understanding the patterns of intelligence migration can help companies decipher and plan for the inevitable disruptions in today's business environment.

Two patterns in network intelligence are reshaping industries and organizations. First, intelligence is decoupling—that is, modern high-speed networks are pushing back-end intelligence and front-end intelligence toward opposite ends of the network, making the ends the two major sources of potential profits. Second, intelligence is becoming more fluid and modular. Small units of intelligence now float freely like molecules in the ether, coalescing into temporary bundles whenever and wherever necessary to solve problems.

The authors present four strategies that companies can use to profit from these patterns: *arbitrage* allows companies to move intelligence to new regions or countries where the cost of maintaining intelligence is lower; *aggregation* combines formerly isolated pieces of infrastructure intelligence into a large pool of shared infrastructure provided over a network; *rewiring* allows companies to connect islands of intelligence by creating common information backbones; and *reassembly* allows businesses to reorganize pieces of intelligence into coherent, personalized packages for customers.

By being aware of patterns in network intelligence and by acting rather than reacting, companies can turn chaos into opportunity, say the authors.

Starting Up in High Gear: An Interview with Venture Capitalist Vinod Khosla

David Champion and Nicholas G. Carr

The current high level of venture capital investment is driving enormous innovation in business. Every conceivable experiment is being tried. About 40% of the growth in the U.S. GDP is coming out of the tech sector, and most of that can be traced to the vibrancy of entrepreneurial initiatives, according to accomplished entrepreneur and venture capitalist Vinod Khosla.

But in a wide-ranging interview, Khosla says greed is at a high level, too, and he's concerned about its effect on entrepreneurs and their infant businesses. Today, an entrepreneur with a plan for a new business can get funded within a week. But the entrepreneur doesn't get an honest, painstaking critique. The weaknesses of the plan are often ignored. The result is that great ideas don't reach their full potential.

Khosla says the environment in which entrepreneurs operate has changed—everything moves much faster than it did when he cofounded Sun Microsystems in the early 1980s. The idea of spending a lot of time creating a business plan, he says, is now absurd in most cases. Entrepreneurs have to change course all the time. The best an entrepreneur can do is intuit where the big opportunities are.

Khosla touches on the qualities required of today's entrepreneurs and the difficulties that established companies face in adapting to the Internet. He also offers some of his secrets for finding and exploiting the biggest new technologies.

Transforming Life, Transforming Business: The Life-Science Revolution

Juan Enriquez and Ray A. Goldberg

If you think the Internet has changed the shape of business, just imagine what genetic engineering is going to do. In this groundbreaking article, Juan Enriquez and Ray Goldberg explain how advances in genetics will not only have dramatic implications for people and society, they will reshape vast sectors of the world economy.

The boundaries between many once-distinct businesses, from agribusiness and chemicals to pharmaceuticals and health care to energy and computing, will blur, and out of that convergence will emerge what promises to be the largest industry in the world: life science. And as scientific advances continue to accelerate, more and more businesses will be drawn, by choice or by necessity, into the life-science industry.

Companies have realized that unlocking life's code opens up virtually unlimited commercial possibilities, but operating within this new industry presents a raft of wrenchingly difficult challenges as well. Companies must rethink their business, financial, and M&A strategies. They must make vast R&D investments with distant and uncertain payoffs. They must enter into complex partnerships and affiliations, sometimes with direct competitors. And perhaps most difficult, they must contend with a public that is uncomfortable with even the thought of genetic engineering.

The optimal structure of the life-science industry—and of the companies that compose it—is as yet unknown. But the actions that executives take now will go a long way toward determining the ultimate role their companies play in the world's largest and most important industry.

Getting Real About Virtual Commerce

Philip Evans and Thomas S. Wurster

In its first generation, electronic commerce has been a landgrab. Space on the Internet was claimed by whoever got there first with enough resources to create a credible business. It took speed, a willingness to experiment, and a lot of cybersavvy. Companies that had performed brilliantly in traditional settings seemed hopelessly flat-footed on the Web. And despite their astronomical valuations, the new e-commerce stars have appeared to be just as confused. Many have yet to make a profit, and no one has any idea when they will.

Now, the authors contend, we are entering the second generation of e-commerce, and it will be shaped more by strategy than by experimentation. The key players—branded-goods suppliers, physical retailers, electronic retailers, and pure navigators—will shift their attention from claiming territory to defending or capturing it. They will be forced to focus on strategies to achieve competitive advantage. Success will go to the businesses that get closest to consumers, the ones that help customers navigate their way through the Web. Indeed, the authors argue, navigation is the battlefield on which competitive advantage will be won or lost.

There are three dimensions of navigation: *Reach* is about access and connection. *Affiliation* is about whose interests the business represents. And *richness* is the depth of the information that a business gives to or collects about its customers. Navigators and e-tailers have the natural advantage in reach and affiliation, while traditional product suppliers and retailers have the edge in richness. The authors offer practical advice to each player on competing in the second generation of e-commerce.

The Future of Commerce

Adrian J. Slywotzky; Clayton M. Christensen and Richard S. Tedlow; and Nicholas G. Carr

As we enter the twenty-first century, the business world is consumed by questions about e-commerce. In this article, four close observers of e-commerce speculate about the future of commerce.

Adrian Slywotzky believes the Internet will overturn the inefficient push model of supplier-customer interaction. He predicts that in all sorts of markets, customers will use *choiceboards*—interactive, on-line systems that let people design their own products by choosing from a menu of attributes, prices, and delivery options. And he explores how the shifting role of the customer—from passive recipient to active designer—will change the way companies compete.

Clayton Christensen and Richard Tedlow agree that e-commerce, on a broad level, will change the basis of competitive advantage in retailing. The essential mission of retailers—getting the right product in the right place at the right price at the right time—is a constant. But over the years retailers have fulfilled that mission differently thanks to a series of *disruptive technologies*. The authors identify patterns in the way that previous retailing transformations have unfolded to shed light on how retailing may evolve in the Internet era.

Nicholas Carr takes issue with the widespread notion that the Internet will usher in an era of "disintermediation," in which producers of goods and services bypass wholesalers and retailers to connect directly with their customers. Business is undergoing precisely the opposite phenomenon—what he calls *hypermediation.* Transactions over the Web routinely involve all sorts of intermediaries. It is these middlemen that are positioned to capture most of the profits.

Contextual Marketing: The Real Business of the Internet

David Kenny and John F. Marshall

The painful truth is that the Internet has been a letdown for most companies—largely because the dominant model for Internet commerce, the destination Web site, doesn't suit the needs of those companies or their customers. Most consumer product companies don't provide enough value or dynamic information to induce customers to make the repeat visits—and disclose the detailed information—that make such sites profitable.

In this article, David Kenny and John F. Marshall suggest that companies discard the notion that a Web site equals an Internet strategy. Instead of trying to create destinations that people will come to, companies need to use the power and reach of the Internet to deliver tailored messages and information to customers. Companies have to become what the authors call "contextual marketers."

Delivering the most relevant information possible to consumers in the most timely manner possible will become feasible, the authors say, as access moves beyond the PC to shopping malls, retail stores, airports, bus stations, and even cars. The authors describe how the ubiquitous Internet will hasten the demise of the destination Web site—and open up scads of opportunities to reach customers through marketing "mobilemediaries," such as smart cards, e-wallets, and bar code scanners.

The companies that master the complexity of the ubiquitous Internet will gain significant advantages: they'll gain greater intimacy with customers and target market segments more efficiently. The ones that don't will be dismissed as nuisances, the authors conclude. They suggest ways to become welcome additions—not unwelcome intrusions—to customers' lives.

Beyond the Exchange: The Future of B2B

Richard Wise and David Morrison

Using the Internet to facilitate business-to-business commerce promises many benefits, such as dramatic cost reductions and greater access to buyers and sellers. Yet little is known about how B2B e-commerce will evolve. The authors argue that changes in the financial services industry over the past two decades provide important clues. Exchanges, they say, are not the primary source of value in information-intensive markets; value tends to accumulate among a diverse group of specialists that focus on such tasks as packaging, standard setting, arbitrage, and information management.

Because scale and liquidity are vitally important to efficient trading, today's exchanges will consolidate into a relatively small set of mega-exchanges. Originators will handle the origination and aggregation of complex transactions before sending them on to mega-exchanges for execution. E-speculators, seeking to capitalize on an abundance of market information, will tend to concentrate where relatively standardized products can be transferred easily among a large group of buyers. In many markets, a handful of independent solution providers with well-known brand names and solid reputations will thrive alongside mega-exchanges. Sell-side asset exchanges will create the networks and provide the tools to allow suppliers to trade orders among themselves, sometimes after initial transactions with customers are made on the mega-exchanges.

For many companies, traditional skills in such areas as product development, manufacturing, and marketing may become relatively less important, while the ability to understand and capitalize on market dynamics may become considerably more important.

Bringing Silicon Valley Inside

Gary Hamel

In 1998, Silicon Valley companies produced 41 IPOs, which by January 1999 had a combined market capitalization of $27 billion—that works out to $54,000 in new wealth creation per worker in a single year. Multiply the number of employees in your company by $54,000. Did your business create that much new wealth last year? Half that amount?

It's not a group of geniuses generating such riches. It's a business model. In Silicon Valley, ideas, capital, and talent circulate freely, gathering into whatever combinations are most likely to generate innovation and wealth. Unlike most traditional companies, which spend their energy in resource *allocation*—a system designed to avoid failure—the Valley operates through resource *attraction*—a system that nurtures innovation.

In a traditional company, people with innovative ideas must go hat in hand to the guardians of the old ideas for funding and for staff. But in Silicon Valley, a slew of venture capitalists vie to attract the best new ideas, infusing relatively small amounts of capital into a portfolio of ventures. And talent is free to go to the companies offering the most exhilarating work and the greatest potential rewards.

It should actually be easier for large, traditional companies to set up similar markets for capital, ideas, and talent internally. After all, big companies often already have extensive capital, marketing, and distribution resources, and a first crack at the talent in their own ranks. And some of them are doing it. The choice is yours—you can do your best to make sure you never put a dollar of capital at risk, or you can tap into the kind of wealth that's being created every day in Silicon Valley.

Meeting the Challenge of Disruptive Change

Clayton M. Christensen and Michael Overdorf

Why didn't a single minicomputer company succeed in the personal computer business? Why did only one department store—Dayton Hudson—become a leader in discount retailing? Why can't large companies capitalize on the opportunities brought about by major, disruptive changes in their markets?

It's because organizations, independent of the people in them, have capabilities. And those capabilities also define disabilities. As a company grows, what it can and cannot do becomes more sharply defined in certain predictable ways. The authors have analyzed those patterns to create a framework managers can use to assess the abilities and disabilities of their organization as a whole.

When a company is young, its resources—its people, equipment, technologies, cash, brands, suppliers, and the like—define what it can and cannot do. As it becomes more mature, its abilities stem more from its processes—product development, manufacturing, budgeting, for example. In the largest companies, values—particularly those that determine what are its acceptable gross margins and how big an opportunity has to be before it becomes interesting—define what the company can and cannot do. Because resources are more adaptable to change than processes or values, smaller companies tend to respond to major market shifts better than larger ones.

The authors suggest ways large companies can capitalize on opportunities that normally would not fit in with their processes or values; it all starts with understanding what the organizations are capable of.

How We Went Digital Without a Strategy

Ricardo Semler

Once you say what business you're in, you put your employees into a mental straitjacket and hand them a ready-made excuse for ignoring new opportunities.

So rather than dictate his company's identity, Ricardo Semler—the majority owner of Semco in São Paulo, Brazil—lets his employees shape it through their individual efforts and interests. "I don't know what Semco is," he writes in this first-person account of his company's expansion from manufacturing to Internet services. "Nor do I want to know."

Ten years ago, Semco employees who were selling cooling towers to owners of large commercial buildings heard customers complain about the high cost of maintaining the towers. The salespeople proposed a new business in cooling-tower maintenance, and the venture is now a $30 million property-management business. That initiative led to the creation, with Semco's support, of an on-line exchange to facilitate the management of commercial construction projects. The exchange is revolutionizing the construction process in Brazil and has become a springboard for further Web initiatives such as virtual trade shows.

The author shares some of the lessons he has learned along the way: Forget about the top line. Never stop being a start-up. Don't be a nanny (treat your employees like adults). Let talent find its place. Make decisions quickly and openly when it comes to reviewing proposals for new businesses. And partner promiscuously: "Our partners," Semler says, "are as much a part of our company as our employees."

Managing for the Next Big Thing: An Interview with EMC's Michael Ruettgers

Paul Hemp

In this HBR interview, CEO Michael Ruettgers speaks in detail about the managerial practices that have allowed EMC to anticipate and exploit disruptive technologies, market opportunities, and business models ahead of its competitors. He recounts how the company repeatedly ventured into untested markets, ultimately transforming itself from a struggling maker of minicomputer memory boards into a data storage powerhouse and one of the most successful companies of the past decade.

The company has achieved sustained and nearly unrivaled revenue, profit, and share-price growth through a number of means. Emphasizing timing and speed, Ruettgers says, is critical. That's meant staggering products rather than developing them sequentially and avoiding the excessive refinements that slow time to market.

Indeed, a sense of urgency, Ruettgers explains, has been critical to EMC's success. Processes such as quarterly goal setting and monthly forecasting meetings help maintain a sense of urgency and allow managers to get early glimpses of changes in the market. So does an environment in which personal accountability is stressed and the corporate focus is single-minded.

Perhaps most important, the company has procedures to glean insights from customers. Intensive forums involving EMC engineers and leading-edge customers, who typically push for unconventional solutions to their problems, often yield new product features. Similarly, a customer service system that includes real-time monitoring of product use enables EMC to understand customer needs firsthand.

About the Contributors

Nicholas G. Carr is an executive editor at the *Harvard Business Review,* where he writes and edits articles and interviews on business strategy and technology. Since December 1999, he has also written the monthly "Decoding Business" column for the *Industry Standard.* Before joining *HBR* in 1997, Mr. Carr was a principal with Mercer Management Consulting, Inc. His web site can be found at www.nicholasg carr.com.

David Champion is a senior editor at the *Harvard Business Review.* He has been with *HBR* since 1998 and is the author of an HBR Case Study on new ventures, "Too Soon to IPO?" which was published in the February 2001 issue.

Clayton M. Christensen is a professor of business administration at Harvard Business School, with a joint appointment in the Technology Operations Management and General Management faculty groups. His research and teaching interests center on the management of technological innovation, developing organizational capabilities, and finding new markets for new technologies. Before joining the HBS faculty, Professor Christensen served as chairman and president of CPS Corporation, a firm he cofounded with several MIT professors in 1984. Professor Christensen has received the Newcomen Society's award for the best paper on business history, the McKinsey Award for the best article published in the *Harvard Business Review* (1995), and the *Financial Times*/Booz•Allen and Hamilton Global Business Book Award (1997) for his book, *The Innovator's Dilemma.*

Juan Enriquez has served as CEO of the Mexico City Urban Development Corporation, coordinator general of economic policy, chief of staff to Mexico's secretary of state, and as member of the peace commission that negotiated a cease-fire in Chiapas. He worked in the war zone for six months. During the past four years he has held a number of positions at Harvard University, including senior researcher at Harvard Business School, fellow at the Center for International Affairs, and, currently, researcher at The David Rockefeller Center for Latin American Studies. He serves on over a dozen boards, including Cabot Microelectronics, the genetics advisory council of the Harvard Medical School, The State Department advisory committee on economic policy (biotechnology), the Chairman's Council of the Americas Society, The Brookings Council, *The Journal of BioLaw and Business*, and Tufts' EPPIIC.

Philip Evans is a senior vice president of the Boston Consulting Group in its Boston office and coleader of BCG's Media and Convergence Practice group. His practice is focused on strategy issues for clients in media, financial services, and consumer goods. A frequent speaker on the new economy, he is coauthor, with Thomas Wurster, of the bestseller *Blown to Bits: How the New Economics of Information Transforms Strategy*, which has been translated into ten languages. Prior to joining BCG he obtained the top double first class honours degree from Cambridge University in economics and was a Harkness fellow in the economics department at Harvard University.

Ray A. Goldberg is the George Moffett Professor of Agriculture and Business Emeritus at Harvard Business School where he chairs the agribusiness senior management seminars. Professor Goldberg also teaches a course on agribusiness and food policy at the John F. Kennedy School of Government. Together with John H. Davis he developed the agribusiness program at HBS in 1955. Professor Goldberg is author, coauthor, or editor of twenty-three books and over 110 articles on positioning firms and institutions in the global value-added food system. His most recent publications involve developing strategies for private, public, and cooperative managers as they position their firms, institutions, and government agencies in a rapidly changing global food-system. Professor Goldberg has served on over forty boards of directors of major agribusiness firms, farm cooperatives, and technology firms, and has advised financial institutions such as Rabobank, John Hancock, and Agriculture Technology Partners on their agribusiness investments. He is also one of the founders and first president of the International Agribusiness Management Association and an advisor and consultant to numerous government agencies and private firms.

John Hagel III is chief strategy officer at 12 Entrepreneuring, Inc., an operating company that builds and manages a select group of e-businesses. Prior to joining 12 in April 2000, Mr. Hagel spent sixteen years at McKinsey & Company, Inc., where he was founder and leader of their Global Electronic Commerce Practice. At McKinsey, he worked with a broad range of clients across many industries on e-commerce issues, with a focus on strategic management and performance improvement. Prior to joining McKinsey, Mr. Hagel served as senior vice president for strategic planning at Atari; as founder and president of Sequoia Group, a systems house that sells turnkey computer systems to physicians; and as a consultant with the Boston Consulting Group. Mr. Hagel is the author of *Net Gain: Expanding Markets through Virtual Communities* (with Arthur G. Armstrong) and *Net Worth: Shaping Markets When Customers Make the Rules* (with Marc Singer).

Gary Hamel is founder and chairman of Strategos, a company dedicated to helping clients develop revolutionary strategies. He is also a visiting professor of strategic and international management at London Business School. In his work Mr. Hamel helps many of the world's leading companies to first imagine and then to create the new rules, new businesses, and new industries that will define the industrial landscape of the future. He has published numerous articles in the *Harvard Business Review, Fortune, Sloan Management Review,* and the *Wall Street Journal.* He has introduced such breakthrough concepts as strategic intent, core competence, corporate imagination, expeditionary marketing, and strategy as stretch. Mr. Hamel's book *Competing for the Future* (with C.K. Prahalad) has been hailed by many journals as one of the decade's most influential business books, and by *Business Week* as Best Management Book of the Year. His most recent book, *Leading the Revolution,* was published by Harvard Business School Press in September 2000 and was Amazon.com's pick as Business Book of the Year.

Paul Hemp is a senior editor at the *Harvard Business Review.* He joined *HBR* from Mercer Management Consulting, Inc., where he was director of publications. He has been a writer or editor at the *Wall Street*

Journal, The Boston Globe, and *The Boston Globe Magazine.* He also worked for the nonprofit International Center for Journalists, training business journalists in developing countries.

David Kenny, chairman and CEO of Digitas, is one of the chief architects of global e-business transformation in the Internet Age. With perspective and insight, he has earned a coveted role as strategic partner to some of the world's most respected corporations, including American Express, AT&T, General Motors, Charles Schwab, Delta Air Lines, FedEx, L.L. Bean, Morgan Stanley Dean Witter, and the National Basketball Association. A former senior partner at Bain & Company, the global business strategy consulting firm, Mr. Kenny holds a BS from the General Motors Institute and an MBA from Harvard Business School. He is chairman of the board of Teach for America, and a director of Harvard Business School Publishing and The Corporate Executive Board. He is also an active member of the BOLD Diversity Initiative.

John F. Marshall is senior vice president and global head of the Digital Strategy group at Digitas, where his responsibilities include partnering with clients to determine how to use the Internet and emerging technologies to create new business models toward gaining competitive advantage. Mr. Marshall also leads the Digitas Wireless Practice and is responsible for the strategy and implementation of customer solutions for the "ubiquitous Internet" for the firm's clients. Prior to joining Digitas in 1999, Mr. Marshall had twelve years of experience in strategic consulting and technology investment banking. He was most recently a partner at MercerDelta Management Consulting. His current focus has been on corporate strategy development for *Fortune* 100 companies, with particular emphasis on designing new business models in response to major changes in technology. Mr. Marshall has worked extensively with companies such as AT&T, Sears, and Dow Chemical to define new customer-driven business models. A former venture capitalist and technology analyst, he has significant experience in capital markets, new technology venture development, and value-based management.

David J. Morrison is vice chairman of Mercer Management Consulting, Inc., and directs the firm's MercerDigital practice. In his twenty-one years of consulting, Mr. Morrison has worked with leading companies in the electronics, computer hardware and software, information services, e-commerce, Internet, health care, telecommunications, and financial services industries. Mr. Morrison is coauthor (with Adrian Slywotzky) of *How Digital Is Your Business?*, *Profit Patterns: 30 Ways to Anticipate and Profit from Strategic Forces Reshaping Your Business*, and *The Profit Zone: How Strategic Business Design Will Lead You to Tomorrow's Profits*, which *Business Week* named one of the Top 10 Business Books of 1998. He has also authored articles for the "Managers Journal" section of the *Wall Street Journal* and contributed to the development of the frameworks in Mr. Slywotzky's best-selling book *Value Migration*. An accomplished speaker, Mr. Morrison has been a lead presenter at The Conference Board's Strategic Management and Marketing conferences in New York and Los Angeles. He has also appeared as a guest on CNBC, the BBC, and CNNfn; been the keynote speaker at conferences for IDG, the NACDS, SAP Sapphire, and the Ziff Davis Internet Nextravaganza; and frequently presents Mercer's Value Growth and Business Design frameworks at executive forums for large corporations.

Michael Overdorf was one of Harvard Business School's first dean's research fellows. He worked with Professor Clayton Christensen to write and conduct research on the management processes and decision criteria that enable companies to effectively identify and manage disruptive innovations. Mr. Overdorf is currently chairman and CEO of Innosight, a company he cofounded with Professor Christensen to help companies improve their ability to manage innovation. Prior to his work at HBS, Mr. Overdorf worked for Alcoa where he held various managerial positions in operations and product development.

Deval (Dave) Parikh is a management consultant in the San Francisco office of Pittigglio Rabin Todd & McGrath, a leading management consulting firm to technology-based businesses. At PRTM, Mr. Parikh specializes in the areas of supply-chain management and e-business. Prior to joining PRTM, Mr. Parikh cofounded a satellite-based, data networking solutions firm in India. He also worked as a process engineer at VLSI Technology (Philips Semiconductor), where he was responsible for manufacturing application-specific semiconductors. Mr. Parikh graduated with honors from North Carolina State University with degrees in engineering and economics. He holds an MBA from Northwestern University's J.L. Kellogg School of Business.

Mohanbir Sawhney is the McCormick Tribune Professor of Electronic Commerce and Technology and the director of the Center for Research in Technology, Innovation, and E-Commerce at the Kellogg

School of Management, Northwestern University. Professor Sawhney is a globally recognized expert in business-to-business e-commerce and e-business strategy. *Business Week* named him one of the twenty-five most influential people in e-business. His research on e-business and marketing has appeared in *California Management Review,* the *Harvard Business Review, Management Science, Marketing Science,* and *Journal of the Academy of Marketing Science.* Professor Sawhney has also written extensively in the trade press for publications such as *Business 2.0, Context Magazine,* and *Financial Times.* His book on e-business, *The Seven Steps to Nirvana: Strategic Insights into eBusiness Transformation,* will be published by McGraw-Hill in 2001. Professor Sawhney has received several awards for teaching excellence, including the Outstanding Professor of the Year at the Kellogg School in 1998 and the Sidney Levy Award for Excellence in Teaching in 1999 and 1995. He speaks extensively to audiences worldwide, and advises several Global 2000 firms as well as start-up firms in technology and e-commerce.

Ricardo Semler, president of Semco S/A, the Brazilian marine and food-processing machinery manufacturer, is internationally famous for creating the world's most unusual workplace. Mr. Semler's management philosophy of empowering employees and looking at corporate structure in new ways is a serious departure from the ingrained model of the corporate pyramid. His two books, *Turning the Tables* and *Maverick,* are best-sellers in Brazil and Europe, and he has been profiled in more than 200 magazines and newspapers, including the *Wall Street Journal, Time, Financial Times,* and *Fortune.* Mr. Semler was also named one of the Global Leaders of Tomorrow by the World Economic Forum at Davos.

Marc Singer is a principal at the Redwood City, California, office of McKinsey & Company, Inc., and coleader of the firm's Continuous Relationship Marketing practice. He works mainly with clients in the financial services, software, media, retail, and health care businesses, with a focus on strategy and marketing. Mr. Singer has published articles in the *McKinsey Quarterly,* the *Harvard Business Review,* and other publications, and is the coauthor of *Net Worth: Shaping Markets When Customers Make the Rules* (with John Hagel III).

Adrian J. Slywotzky is vice president and member of the board of directors of Mercer Management Consulting, Inc., a global business strategy consulting firm that focuses on the development of strategies for growth in changing markets. Mr. Slywotzky is also responsible for the development of the firm's intellectual capital and for its corporate-marketing function. Mr. Slywotzky is the best-selling author or coauthor of *Profit Patterns: 30 Ways to Anticipate and Profit from Strategic Forces Reshaping Your Business, Value Migration: How to Think Several Moves Ahead of the Competition, How Digital Is Your Business?,* and *The Profit Zone: How Strategic Business Design Will Lead You to Tomorrow's Profits,* which *Business Week* named one of the Top 10 Business Books of 1998. As a frequent speaker on the changing face of business strategy, value migration, and business design, Mr. Slywotzky has been featured at the World Economic Forum at Davos (1997) and at numerous conferences sponsored by The Conference Board and The Planning Forum. In 1997 he was a keynote speaker at the Microsoft CEO Summit, in which he also participated in 1998. He has also been the keynote speaker at the *Forbes* CEO Forum (1998), the *Fortune* CEO Conference (1998), and the *Fortune* CIO Conference (1998).

Richard S. Tedlow is the Class of 1949 Professor of Business Administration at Harvard Business School, where he is a specialist in the history of business. He has also taught in numerous executive education programs both on and off the HBS campus, including programs in marketing and general management. Professor Tedlow is currently writing a book about changes in the leadership backgrounds and styles of corporate CEOs in the United States over the past century.

Kevin Werbach is editor of Release 1.0, a renowned monthly report that explores emerging trends in the Internet, communications, and computing worlds. He also co-organizes the annual PC Forum conference with Esther Dyson and Daphne Kis. Previously, Mr. Werbach served as counsel for new technology policy at the Federal Communications Commission, where he helped develop the U.S. Government's approach to the Internet and e-commerce and wrote *Digital Tornado: The Internet and Communications Policy.* He speaks worldwide and appears frequently in print and broadcast media as an analyst of technology, emerging business models, and policy issues.

Richard Wise is vice president with Mercer Management Consulting, Inc., and the leader of Mercer's North American e-commerce strategy practice. He has worked with both start-ups and traditional industry incumbents in the business-to-business and business-to-consumer e-commerce sectors, helping them identify and prioritize Internet business opportunities, define specific e-commerce business strategy requirements, and undertake key implementation activities such as organizational design, strategic alliance development, and funding procurement. Mr. Wise also played a key role in developing Mercer's value-driven business design process that helps companies to systematically identify and exploit opportunities, which create shareholder value growth. The author of several articles, Mr. Wise's work has appeared in the *Journal of Business Strategy, Marketing Management Journal, Business 2.0,* and the *Harvard Business Review.*

Thomas S. Wurster is a senior vice president in the Boston Consulting Group's Los Angeles office, where he is head of the office and coleader of BCG's Media and Convergence Practice group. His practice is focused on working with leading media and consumer products companies. Mr. Wurster writes on media and strategy and is coauthor, with Philip Evans, of the bestseller *Blown to Bits: How the New Economics of Information Transforms Strategy,* which has been translated into ten languages.

Note: *Information provided within the article about the contributors to "Managing the Next Big Thing: An Interview with EMC's Michael Ruettgers" was applicable at the time of original publication.*

Index

accountability, 204, 214
acquisitions. *See* mergers and acquisitions
Active Research, 136–137
Adams, Scott, 24
affiliation, 85, 86, 87, 89, 90, 95, 117. *See also* alliances; joint ventures
competition based on, 90–93
Affymetrix, 71
aggregation strategy, 46–47
agribusiness, 69, 70, 77–79
"agriceuticals," 70
airline industry, 126–127
Akamai, x, 118
alliances. *See also* affiliation; joint ventures
collective industry approach and, 142
internal innovation and, 201
life-science industry and, 76
network intelligence and, 44
pharmaceutical industry and, 12
reach and, 88
Amazon.com, 162
business model at, 119–120
core businesses at, 13–14
core capabilities at, 31–32
as navigator, 85, 86, 90
syndication strategy at, 30–31
valuation of, 83

zShops program, 31
American Airlines, 92
American Express, 126
American Home Products, 73
America Online, 13, 17
angel investors, 166
Apple Computer, 3, 4
arbitrage strategy, 45–46
asset exchange model, 139–140, 141, 144
AT&T, 17, 41
automobiles
digital relationship management and, 127–128
as disruptive technology, 109–110
automotive industry, 14–15
Avid Technology, 180
Avon, 44–45

bandwidth, 52–53, 112, 124
banking industry. *See* financial services industry
Bechtolsheim, Andy, 158–159
Be Free (company), 116
Bezos, Jeff, 30, 162
Bidcom, 197
"bioinformatics," 72
biotechnology. *See* life-science industry
Biztro.com, 139

brands
  contextual marketing and, 125
  e-commerce and, 96–99
Branson, Richard, 163–164
B2B commerce, xvii. *See also* contextual marketing
  entrepreneurship and, 53–54
  financial services as model for,
      131–132, 134–140, 144, 147
  flaws in exchange-based model
      and, 132–133
  future shape of, 131–147
  intelligence migration and, 44–45
  investment in new skills and, 129,
      144–147
  new business models and, 140–
      144, 145–146
business development process, and
      venture capitalists, 58–59, 60–
      61
business models
  definition of, ix–x
  early B2B exchanges and, 133
  emerging in B2B commerce, 140–
      144, 145–146
  versus strategies, viii–x
  venture capitalists and, 167–169
business opportunities. *See also* entrepreneurship; navigation
  anticipation of, 205–206, 217–218
  contextual marketing and, 124–125
  Internet entrepreneurship and, 52–
      54
  network intelligence and, 45–48
  resource attraction and, 172–174
business plan, 52
business processes. *See also* core
      businesses
  capacity for change and, 177, 184–
      185, 187, 189–190
  pace of new economy and, 62
business-to-business commerce. *See*
      B2B commerce

capital markets, xviii, 165–169. *See
      also* venture capital
Careerpath.com, 86
Carr, Nicholas G., xiv, 51–64, 101,
      114–118

catalog retailing, 90, 108–109
category killer retailers, 99, 110–111
CDNow, 94
Celera Genomics, 66, 68, 72
Chakrabarty, Ananda, 75
Champion, David, xiv, 51–64
Charles Schwab (company). *See*
      Schwab, Charles
chemical industry, 69, 70
chief information officer (CIO), 62
choiceboards, 103–106
Christensen, Clayton M., xviii, 101,
      106–114, 151–174
Chrysler, 185. *See also*
      DaimlerChrysler merger
CIO. *See* chief information officer
Cisco Systems, 40, 53, 190
Clark, Kim, 185
click-through rate, 124
CNET, 124
communication
  with customers, 208, 209–210
  hierarchy as block to, 63
  public education and, 79
Compaq, 72, 183
compensation, 199, 200
computer industry
  compared with Internet industry,
      54
  customer needs and, 210–211
  interaction costs and, 3–4
  life-science industry and, 72
  network intelligence and, 41–42
consolidation
  customer relationship businesses
      and, 17
  processing intelligence and, xiii
consortia, 44
consumers. *See also* customer
      relationships
  digital readiness and, 104
  information control options of, 94
  navigation affiliated with, 91–92
contextual marketing, xvi–xvii, 119–
      129
  customer relationships and, 125–
      128
  opportunities for, 124–125
  rise of, 122–124
Cook, Scott, 169–170

core businesses
  economic models and, 7–9, 16–18
  fracturing within industries by, 9–12, 16–17
  Internet organization and, 12–16
  types of, 4–7
  unbundling in traditional companies and, 16–18
core capabilities
  coping with disruptive change and, 175–176, 189–191
  creation of, 184–191
  "distributed capabilities" and, 43–44
  evolution in, 180–182
  identification of, 176–179
  internal creation of, 184–185
  lack of focus on, 175–176
  packaging of, 44
  syndication and, 31–33
corporate culture. *See also* Silicon Valley
  capacity for change and, 177–179, 181
  at EMC, 213–215
  entrepreneurship and, 63–64, 163–165
  traditional companies and, 63–64, 215
corporate relationships. *See* affiliation; alliances; industry organization; joint ventures; syndication
Covisint, 142
credit cards, 11
Crick, Francis, 67
"customer councils," 208, 218
customer information
  choiceboards and, 104–106
  contextual marketing and, 126
  e-commerce richness strategy and, 93–95
  Internet competition based on, 93–95
  service organization as source of, 209, 218
  Web sites as sources of, 119–120
customer needs
  destination site model and, 119–120

EMC and, 208–209, 210–211
  "ubiquitous Internet" and, 123, 128–129
customer relationships, xii. *See also* customer information
  borrowing of, 123–124
  contextual marketing and, 125–128
  as core business within companies, 3, 4
  customer-interface intelligence and, xii
  e-commerce strategy and, 90–95
  economies of scope and, 7, 17
  Internet entrepreneurial opportunity and, 53–54
  personal meetings and, 208, 209–210
customer role
  choiceboards and, 103–106
  at EMC, xix
  in markets, xvi
cyber-malls, 113

DaimlerChrysler merger, 189–190
database marketing tools, 129
Data General, 211
decision-making
  corporate values and, 177–179
  decision-support software and, 136–137
  speed and, 201
delivery. *See* distribution
Dell Computer
  choiceboards and, 105–106
  contextual marketing and, 124
  e-commerce strategy and, 92–93
department stores, 107–109. *See also* discount department stores
destination site model, 119–120
Digital Equipment Corporation, 181–182
digital readiness, 104
discount department stores, 109–111
Disney, 127, 170–171
disruptive change, xviii, 54, 175–191
  EMC and, 216–217
  financial services industry and, 144, 147

disruptive change (*continued*)
    fit between organization tools and,
        186–188
    organization capabilities and, 175–
        182
    retailing industry and, 106–114
    versus sustaining innovation, 182–
        184
disruptive technologies, 107, 111–
    112, 114n1
distribution
    e-commerce and, 114
    life-science industry and, 72
    syndication and, 22
distributors, xiii, 24, 26–27
divestitures, 17
dot-com bubble, bursting of, vii–viii
Dow Chemical, 69, 73
DuPont, 69, 72, 76

ECNs. *See* electronic communications
    networks
e-commerce. *See also* B2B commerce;
    contextual marketing; Inter-
    net; new economy; *entries for
    specific companies*
    brands and, 96–99
    clicks as transactions and, 115–116
    competition on affiliation and, 90–
        93
    competition on reach and, 86–90
    competition on richness and, 93–99
    disruptive technology patterns and,
        111–112
    doomsday scenario for, 88–89
    efficiency and, 117
    electronic market evolution and, xv
    hypermediation and, xi, 102, 114–
        118
    interaction costs and, 12–14
    navigation as business and, 84–86
    power over, 118
    syndication and, 23
e-coupons, 125, 128
Edify (portal), 197
education
    genetic engineering and, 79
    network intelligence and, 44
efficiency, and e-commerce, 117

eLance.com, 53
electronic commerce. *See* e-commerce
electronic communications networks
    (ECNs), 139–140
electronic retailers. *See also*
    e-commerce
    hypermediation and, 114–118
    navigation strategies and, 96–97, 98
EMC, xix, 203–219
    corporate culture at, 213–215
    managerial practices at, xix, 203–
        204, 217–218
    success of, 203
employee empowerment, xviii–xix
    compensation options and, 199–
        200
    floating employees and, 200–201
    as management philosophy, 193–
        194, 198
    transformation and, 194–196
energy business, 72
Enriquez, Juan, xiv–xv, 65–80
Enron, 138
environmental service companies, 72
entertainment industry, 21, 212
entrepreneurship. *See also* Khosla,
    Vinod; Silicon Valley
    B2B and, 53–54
    development process and, 58–59
    hegemony of tradition and, 202
    Internet and, ix, 52–54
    keys to success and, 51–52
    people mix and, 59, 60–61, 169–
        172
    resource allocation and, 157–160
    within traditional companies, 151–
        174, 193–202
    venture capital patterns and, 55–57
    Virgin's model for, 163–165
environmental service industry, 72
Epinions, x
e-speculation model, 137–138, 141,
    143, 146
Etheridge, Melissa, 124
eToys, 97, 116
E*Trade, 23, 26
eTradeshow, 197
e-Trak system, 47
Europe, public fears in, 78
Evans, Philip, xv, 83–100

EveryCD, 86
e-wallet, 126
Excite (company), 13, 18n2

Federal Express (FedEx), xiii, 32–33,
    125–126
Field, Marshall, 108, 112
film industry, 212
financial services industry
    as model for B2B, 131–132, 134–
        140, 144, 147
    unbundling and, 11, 15–16
FireDrop, 58–59
forecasting, 218
FreeMarkets, 135–136, 142

GameChanger process, 155–157, 159,
    161–162
GE Capital, 165
General Motors Corporation, 127–
    128, 142
genetic code, xiv–xv, 67–68. *See also*
    life-science industry
genome-mapping process, 67–68
Genzyme Transgenics, 70
GetMusic.com, 88
goal-setting, 218
Goldberg, Ray A., 65–80

Hagel, John, III, xii, 3–19
Hamel, Gary, ix, xvii, 151–174
Haseltine, William, 71
health care industry, 71, 74
"heavyweight teams," 185
Hemp, Paul, xix, 203–219
Hewlett-Packard, 40, 186, 216
Holliday, Chad, 80n2
Home Depot, 29
Hotmail, 166, 167
Huiqenga, Wayne, 162
human genome project, 66, 67–68.
    See also life-science industry
Human Genome Sciences, 71, 75
human resources. *See also* employee
    empowerment; talent
    retention
    employee mobility and, 169–172

entrepreneurship and, 59, 60–61
    Silicon Valley and, 153
    traditional companies and, 63
hypermediation, xi, 102, 114–118

IBM, 72, 190, 211
ideas, market for, xviii, 160–165
India, 43
industrial economy, ix, x–xi, 21
industry structure. *See also* core
        businesses
    boundaries of, 86–87, 184–185
    changes in interaction costs and, 3–
        4
    choiceboards and, 105, 106
    collective industry efforts and, 142
    life sciences and, xiv–xv, 69–70,
        74–75
    network intelligence and, 41–42
infomediaries. *See also*
        hypermediation;
        mobilemediary; syndicators
    in automotive industry, 14–15
    defined, 12
    in financial services industry, 15–
        16
    Internet portal companies and,
        18n2
    traditional companies and, 16–18
information, democratization of, 211–
        213
information era. *See* new economy
information goods, and syndication,
        22. *See also* network
        intelligence
information technology spending, 54–
        55
infrastructure management, xii
    aggregation strategy and, 46–47
    collective approach and, 142
    as core business within companies,
        3, 4
    economies of scale and, 8, 17
    hypermediation and, 118
    in industrial vs. digital era, x–xi
    network intelligence and, 44, 46–
        47, 118
    traditional companies and, 63–64
Inktomi, 25

innovation, xii
  as core business within companies,
    3, 4
  disruptive technologies and, 107
  organization tools for, 186–188
  personal wealth creation and, 160–
    165
  product-information strategies and,
    95–96
  proposal-approval process and, 201
  Silicon Valley and, xvii–xviii, 160–
    165
  size of company and, xviii
  speed and, 207
  supplier-customer interaction and,
    102–106
  sustaining, 110, 114n1, 182–184
Innovation Lab, 155–156
instinct, importance of, 63
Intel, 61
intellectual property rights, 75–76
intelligence. *See* network intelligence
interaction costs
  e-commerce and, 12–14
  organizational structure and, 3–4
  as term, 18n1
interactive TV, 124, 128
intermediaries. *See* hypermediation;
    infomediaries; mobilemediary;
    MySimon; network
    intelligence
internal capital markets, xviii
Internet. *See also* B2B commerce; e-
    commerce; new economy
  clicks as transactions and, 115–116
  culture of, and affiliation, 90–91
  organizational structure and, 12–
    16
  storage and, 205–206
  suitability of syndication for, 22–23
  syndication roles on, 24–27
  ubiquity of, 120–122, 125–129
Internet strategy
  at Avon, 44–45
  contextual marketing and, 119–
    129
  product suppliers and, 87–90
  Semco and, 196–198
Intuit, 15, 169–170

Japan, 123
jargon, viii–x
Johnson & Johnson, 123–124
Johnson Controls, 196
joint ventures. *See also* affiliation;
    alliances
  e-commerce and, 88
  Semco and, 195–198, 201
Juniper Networks, 60–61
Jurvetson, Steve, 167

Kellogg, Scott, 75
Kenny, David, 119–129
Khosla, Vinod, vii, xiv, 51–64
Kleiner Perkins Caufield & Byers, 51
  basis for success of, 59–60
  development process at, 58–59
Knight Trading Group, 137–138
Krauer, Alex, 74
Kriens, Scott, 61

"lead users," 208
life-science industry, xiv–xv, 65–80
  challenges facing, 73–77
  convergence of industries and, xiv–
    xv, 69–70, 71–73
  human genome project and, 66,
    67–68
  patents and, 75–76
  prospects for, 79–80
  public opinion and, xv, 74, 77–79
  R&D costs in, 76–77
  ripple effects of, 71–73
  speed of breakthroughs in, 67–68
  strategic challenges for, xiv–xv, 66–
    67
LinkShare, 26
Lipper, 91
Los Angeles Times, 11
Loudcloud, 46–47
Lyman, Peter, 211–213

Macy, R. H., 108
Malone, Tom, ix–x
Malthus, Thomas Robert, 213
management consulting firms, 57–58

manufacturing industry, and e-commerce, 95–96, 98–99, 127–128
market changes, xv–xvii. *See also* B2B commerce; contextual marketing; customer role, in markets; e-commerce; retailing industry
marketing, "four Ps" of, 123
Marshall, John F., 119–129
mass media. *See* entertainment industry
Mattel, 97
McCallum, Gordon, 164
McKinsey & Company, 180
measurement, and the "ubiquitous Internet," 129
media business, syndication in, 24
Medlin, Milo, 60
mega-exchanges, 141–142, 145
Mendel, Gregor, 67
mergers and acquisitions
capacity for change and, 179, 184, 189–191
creation of capabilities through, 189–191
life-science industry and, 76–77
unbundling process and, 17–18
Merrill Lynch, 183, 188
Microsoft CarPoint, 91
middle management, shrinking of, 42–43
Milacron, 139, 143
Milpro.com, 139
mining companies, 72
mobilemediary, 122, 125–126. *See also* contextual marketing
mobility
of employees, 169–172
of intelligence, 37–38, 39–40
Mobil Speedpass, 122–123
modularity
network intelligence and, xiii–xiv, 39, 43
syndication and, 22
Monsanto, 69, 73, 76, 79, 159, 171
Moore, Geoffrey, 206
Morrison, David, 131–147
Motley Fool, The, 28, 91

music industry, 95–96
MySimon, 136–137

Naidu, N. Chandrababu, 43
National Institutes of Health, 66, 68
navigation
affiliation and, 85, 86, 87, 91–92, 95
brands and, 96–99
dimensions of advantage for, 85–86
as e-commerce business, 84–86
e-commerce doomsday scenario and, 88–89
pure navigators and, 84, 98
reach and, 85, 86–90, 91, 95
richness and, 85–86, 93–99
Netscape, 116
network intelligence
back-end versus front-end, 36–39
business opportunities and, 45–48
common forms of intelligence and, 49
decoupling of intelligences in, xiii, 36–39
definitions and, 36
evolution in, 35–36
fluidity of, xiii–xiv
industry organization, 41–42
location of, 37
managerial challenges and, 48–50
mobility of, 37–38, 39–40
modularity of, xiii–xiv, 39, 43
public sector and, 43–44
reshaping of companies and, 42–45
value and, 38–39
new economy
econometric models and, 54
economies of scale and, xiv
greed and fear cycles and, 56
importance of entrepreneurship in, ix
profitability in, x–xi
stewardship vs. entrepreneurship and, 151
strategy and, ix, xi
syndication and, 21–23
unbundling and, 12–16
value trends in, 38–39

newspaper industry, 9, 11
NexGen, 61
Nike, 47
Novartis, 74, 76
NTT DoCoMo, 123

1–800-FLOWERS, 93–94
optical networking, 59, 60
organizational structure. *See also* core
    businesses; unbundling
  capacity for change and, 184–191
  core businesses and, 5–7
  interaction costs and, 3–4
  network intelligence and, 42–45
originators
  of content, xiii, 24–25
  of transactions, 135, 141, 142–143,
    145
outsourcing
  Internet and, 53–54
  syndication and, 27–28
Overdorf, Michael, xviii, 151–174

Parikh, Deval (Dave), xiii–xiv, 35–
    50
patenting, and life sciences, 75–76
PC industry. *See* computer industry
PeopleSupport, 45–46
personal Web sites, and
    microtransactions, 116, 117
pharmaceutical industry
  biotechnology and, 69–70, 71, 76
  unbundling in, 11–12
Pharmacia & Upjohn, 73
Pioneer HyBred, 69
Platt, Lew, 216
plug-and-play organizations. *See* vir-
    tual enterprises
Point.com, 105–106
portal companies, 18n2, 197
Porter, Michael, ix
Priceline.com, 89
pricing
  B2B models and, 133
  contextual marketing and, 125,
    127
privacy, 94, 212
Procter & Gamble, 29

product development, concurrent,
    207, 218
product information, and e-commerce
    strategies, 95–96
product innovation. *See* innovation
product introductions, simultaneous,
    xix, 206
profitability
  disruptive technologies and, 107,
    178–179
  early days of e-commerce and, 83–
    84
  gross margins and, 178–179
  in Industrial versus Internet era,
    ix–xi
Proflowers.com, 32–33
public opinion, and genetic engineer-
    ing, xv, 74, 77–79
public sector, and network intelli-
    gence, 43–44

RBOCs. *See* Regional Bell Operating
    Companies
reach, 85, 86–90, 95
  competition based on, 86–90
  trade-off between richness and, 91,
    95
Regional Bell Operating Companies
    (RBOCs), 8–9
resource allocation
  coping with disruptive change and,
    188–189
  information technology and, 54–55
  versus resource attraction, xvii–
    xviii, 157–160, 172–174
resources, and capacity for change,
    176
restructuring. *See* mergers and
    acquisitions
retailing industry, xvi. *See also* distrib-
    utors; e-commerce
  patterns of disruptive change in,
    106–114
  Web strategy and, 89–90, 93–95,
    96–99
RGIS (company), 197
richness of information, 85–86
  competition based on, 93–99
  customer information and, 93–95

product information and, 95–96
trade-off between reach and, 91, 95
risk
    adaptability and, 63
    genetic engineering and, 77–79
    internal entrepreneurship and, 161,
        165–166
Rockefeller Group, Cushman &
    Wakefield division, 195
Roddick, Anita, 162
Royal Dutch/Shell, 154–157, 159,
    161–162, 169, 171
Ruettgers, Michael, xix, 203–219

SABRE (company), 89, 92
Sandman, Peter, 78
Sawhney, Mohanbir, xiii–xiv, 35–50
scale, economies of, xii
    assumptions about strategy and, 62
    as diseconomies, xiv, 62
    hypermediation and, 118
    infrastructure management and, 8,
        17
    unbundling and, xii
Schwab, Charles (company), 140,
    144, 147, 183
scope, economies of, xii, 7, 17
Screaming Media, 25–26
search engines, 86–87, 93, 112. *See
    also* navigation
sell-side asset exchanges, 139–140,
    141, 144, 146
Semco, xviii–xix, 193–202
    Internet ventures at, 196–198
    lessons from, 198–201
    management philosophy at, 193–
        194, 198
    open-ended transformation at,
        194–196
Semler, Ricardo, xviii–xix, 193–202
SETI@home, 39–40
Shapiro, Robert, 79
Shell. *See* Royal Dutch/Shell
shopping malls, 109, 113, 127
Silicon Valley, xvii–xviii
    ethos of, 152
    internal market for ideas and, 160–
        165
    payoff of bringing inside, 152–154

resource attraction and, 172–174
Royal Dutch/Shell example and,
    154–157, 159, 161–162
talent retention and, 169–172
venture capital and, 165–169
Simon Properties, 127
Sindhu, Pradeep, 60–61
Singer, Marc, xii, 3–19
skill development, 129, 144–147,
    215–216
Slywotzky, Adrian J., xvi, 101–106
Sony, 96
specialization
    customer-interface intelligence and,
        xiii
    EMC and, 210–211
    hypermediation and, 118
speculation, 137–138
speed
    decision making and, 201
    e-commerce changes and, 113–114,
        129
    economics of innovation and, xii,
        7–8
    EMC and, xix, 206, 207
    entrepreneurship and, 52, 62
    life-sciences industry and, 67–68,
        76
    product development and, 207,
        218
    responsiveness to change and, 216–
        217
    strategy life cycles and, 151
spin outs, 168–169, 184, 185–189
spin ups, 168–169
Springer, Jerry, 21
standards
    collective approach and, 142
    complex transactions and, 134–
        136
    corporate values and, 177–179
    financial industry and, 134–136
    language of genetic code and, 73
    universal information-exchange
        protocols, 40
Stern, Howard, 22
Strategos, 155, 156
strategy. *See also* Internet strategy
    affiliation and, 90–93
    versus business model, viii–x

strategy (*continued*)
  customer information and, 93–95,
    104–105
  profiting from intelligence migra-
    tion and, 45–48
  reach and, 86–90
  richness and, 93–99
  technology as driver of, 61–62
  Web syndication and, 28–30
Strauss, Levi (company), 115
Sun Microsystems, 51, 158–159
supplier relationships, 102–106
sustaining technologies, 110, 114n1,
    182–184
Sweden, 127
syndication, xii–xiii, 21–34
  challenges of, 27–30
  core capabilities and, 31–33
  nature of business and, 33–34
  nature of the Internet and, 22
  versus outsourcing, 27–28
  roles in, xiii, 23–27
syndicators, xiii, 24, 25–26

talent retention. *See also* employee
    empowerment; human
    resources
  incubator initiatives and, 57
  internal markets and, xviii, 169–
    172
  in Silicon Valley, 169–172
teams, creation of capabilities by, 185
technology. *See also* genetic code;
    innovation
  disruptive technologies and, 107
  relationship with business, xiii, 61–
    62
Tedlow, Richard S., 101, 106–114
telecommunications industry, 41
top management
  complacency and, 218–219
  coping with disruptive change and,
    188–189
  role of CIO and, 62
Toyota, 178–179
Toys R Us, 97
traditional companies. *See also* disrup-
    tive change
  collective industry efforts and, 142

deterrents to innovation in, 63–64,
    160–165
  entrepreneurship within, 151–174
  fragmentation of roles and, 135
  Internet challenges for, 61–63
  Internet navigation strategies and,
    85, 89–90, 98–100
  spin outs and, 185–189
  start-up challenges to, 151
  unbundling in, 16–18
transaction costs, 18n1. *See also* inter-
    action costs
Transportal Network, 140

unbundling, xii
  as business strategy, 3–19
  fault lines and, 9–12, 16–17
  Internet companies and, 12–16
  traditional companies and, 16–18
  types of core businesses and, 4–9
Unilever, 124–125
United States Department of Energy,
    66
United Technologies, 53

values, and capacity for change, 177–
    179, 184, 187
vaporware, 207
Varian, Hal R., 211–213
Venter, Craig, 66
venture capital. *See also* Khosla, Vinod
  business models and, 167–169
  company-internal efforts and, 57,
    165–166
  development process and, 58–59,
    60–61
  dot-com bubble and, vii–viii
  incubator initiatives and, 57
  influence of, 205
  Internet investment and, 55–57
  Silicon Valley and, 165–169
Virgin Airlines, 163–165
virtual enterprises, 44
Virtual Vineyards, 87

Wal-Mart, 111
Warren, Tim, 154–155, 157

Watson, James, 67
Web sites. *See* destination site model;
     personal Web sites
Werbach, Kevin, xii–xiii, 21–34
Wheelwright, Steven, 185
Whitehorn, Will, 164
wireless access, 120–122
     Japan and, 123
     ubiquity and, 128–129
Wise, Richard, 131–147
World Wide Web. *See* Internet; new
     economy

Women.com, 26–27
Wurster, Thomas S., xv, 83–100

Yahoo!, 12, 18n2, 41–42
Yodlee platform, 48

Zaplets, 58–59
ZDNet, 124